HAMMER OR ANVIL

THE STORY OF THE GERMAN
WORKING-CLASS MOVEMENT

HAMMER OR ANVIL

THE STORY OF THE GERMAN
WORKING-CLASS MOVEMENT

by

EVELYN ANDERSON

You must rise or fall,
You must rule and win,
Or serve and forfeit,
Suffer or triumph,
Be anvil or be hammer.

Goethe

Oriole Editions : New York

First Published in 1945
by Victor Gollancz Ltd., London
Re-issued 1973 by Oriole Editions Inc.
L. C. Catalog Card Number: 72-92773
I S B N   0-88211-043-8

PRINTED IN THE UNITED STATES OF AMERICA
by SENTRY PRESS, NEW YORK, N. Y. 10013

CONTENTS

5

PART ONE

LABOUR IN THE ASCENDANT
1875–1918

CHAPTER ONE

THE KAISER'S OPPOSITION

For several decades German Labour was the pride and model of the international working-class movement. It led the nation out of the first World War and into the post-war period; it was the founder and backbone of the first German Republic. Yet, the world remembers and judges this movement by one thing only: its failure to stem the rise of German Fascism and its inglorious capitulation before Hitler. As a statement of fact this is true; in 1933 the German Labour movement capitulated without so much as a token of resistance. As a political judgment it is meaningless, because it explains nothing. The collapse of German Labour in 1933 cannot be explained by the circumstances in which it occurred, nor can one gauge the chances of a possible rebirth in the future without an understanding of the deeper and more distant causes which paralysed so powerful a force and led to its eventual surrender.

What, then, was this movement which, in its youth, was a model to the Socialist and Labour movements all over the world, yet which failed in every crisis, once it had reached maturity? Its birth coincided with the birth of the German Reich; its rise to great political strength ran parallel with the rise of Germany to great economic and military power; it grew to challenge autocracy while the imperial rulers of Germany were preparing to challenge the might of Britain.

The German Labour movement had hardly passed beyond its embryonic stage when it was called upon to stand its first political and moral test. Bismarck's Anti-Socialist Law of 1878 suppressed a Free (Socialist) Trade Union Movement [1] that had existed for

---

[1] The ban on the right to combine had been removed in 1869 by the North German Federation, but only for the industrial workers, excluding agricultural workers, seamen, State employees and domestic servants.

barely a decade, and a Social Democratic Party that had just celebrated its third anniversary.[1]

Social Democracy began its history with a tremendous initial success. This success was due, above all, to the incongruity between the political and the economic development of the country. On the one hand, Germany had undergone an unprecedented economic development; there already existed huge industrial and financial combines which, by their ingenious exploitation of the newest inventions and the most modern types of equipment, and by the efficiency of their organisation, were threatening to overtake and even to outstrip Britain, which was then the very embodiment of modern industrialism. Politically, on the other hand, Germany was among the most backward and reactionary of the Great Powers, a circumstance which made her peculiarly unfit to deal with a labour problem of growing urgency such as was bound to accompany this rapid growth of modern capitalism.

The right of combination was still denied to large sections of the working class; and even such Trade Unions as existed were severely handicapped by a discriminatory Criminal Law. In Prussia, the heart of the German Empire, equal suffrage was still unknown, and throughout the Reich political conditions were morally degrading for the worker, who was regarded and treated as a third-rate citizen. The Reichstag—dubbed by the veteran German Labour leader Wilhelm Liebknecht "the fig-leaf of absolutism"—provided Socialists with a useful propaganda platform, but it did not help the workers to gain a share in the control of public affairs.

The replacement of absolutism by democracy became therefore the chief, indeed almost the sole aim of the Labour movement, and it was this aim, as much as its social origin, which separated this movement from most of the rest of the nation. Organised Labour was the only force in Germany that had a practical and vital interest in the attainment of democracy, whereas the middle classes were able to rise to great prosperity, and some armaments industrialists even to a position of great power, under a system of political absolutism.

German industrialists, bankers and merchants benefited as much from Bismarck's and Kaiser Wilhelm's imperialist policy as did the Prussian Junkers who were the political masters of the country. It is not surprising, therefore, that the middle class in Germany had not the same impelling interest in democracy as

---

[1] The Social Democratic Party was founded in 1875 at the so-called "Unification Congress" of Gotha, when various independent Socialist groups amalgamated. Outstanding among them were the so-called *Eisenacher* (under Marxist influence) and the *Lassalleaner*.

the middle classes of other countries where the development of modern capitalism was thwarted by feudal privileges. The German working class, on the other hand, was severely handicapped by the prevailing system of absolutism, not only in its attempt to gain some influence on public affairs, but also in its struggle for daily bread.

This had its effect on the relationship between the industrial and political wings of the movement, which, in its early stages, was just the opposite of what it was in Britain, where the political influence of Labour grew only in proportion to, and as a result of, the growing power of the Trade Unions. In Germany, on the contrary, the power of the Trade Unions grew at first only in proportion to the political influence gained by Social Democracy. This reversed relationship simply reflects the different conditions in which the two movements developed.

The British Labour movement, after the period of Chartism, never had to fight for political democracy; it grew up with it. The German Labour movement had to concentrate all its energies on the attainment of democracy in a bitter struggle against the combined forces of the Emperor, the landed aristocracy (with its offspring, the Prussian Army), and the privileged and leading sections of the middle class. When British Labour began to stake its political claim, political democracy had long become an unquestioned *national inheritance*. When German Labour entered the political arena, the fight for democracy meant fighting against an existing Constitution and, what is more, against the accepted way of life of the rest of the nation. Of necessity, therefore, the fight for democracy in Germany assumed the character of a class struggle. This was to have a far-reaching significance both for the political development of Germany as a whole and, more particularly, for the character of the Labour movement. It also explains many otherwise incomprehensible features of the November Revolution of 1918 and much of the inherent weakness of the Weimar Republic which emerged from that Revolution.

This peculiar development of Germany, which left the working class to fight a lone struggle for democracy against a united front of feudal and capitalist interests—united in an aggressive imperialism which satisfied both of them—was the main cause of that spirit of deep hostility against the existing State order which characterised the Labour movement in the years before the first World War and gave it its revolutionary appearance; it was this same spirit that gave the movement the inner strength to withstand in proud defiance twelve years of Bismarckian oppression and persecution and to emerge after that period stronger and more self-confident than ever before.

Our generation may be inclined to smile indulgently, and perhaps a little contemptuously, at the "persecutions" which German Socialists suffered under Bismarck, and it is true that they hardly deserve that name when compared with the methodical and scientific mass terror introduced by Hitler. But there is little point in applying present standards to past history. Measured by the standards of its own time, Bismarck's oppression of German Labour was real and serious enough. He certainly did his best. The dissolution of all political and cultural working-class organisations and the suppression of the Labour press were very much of a reality. So was the great personal sacrifice of countless Socialists who were imprisoned or exiled. In fact, for twelve long years the Socialists lived the lives of outlaws. Yet, when Bismarck's Anti-Socialist Law was at last repealed in 1890, the Labour movement not only came out unscathed, but emerged from this period of trial stronger in prestige and influence—far stronger, indeed, than any of its leaders had ever dared to hope.

One month after the repeal the Social Democratic Party celebrated its first political triumph in the Reichstag elections of 1890. Twelve years of persecution had increased the number of Socialist voters from half a million to one and a half million and the number of Socialist Members of Parliament from twelve to thirty-five. From that time onwards until the outbreak of the Great War Social Democracy emerged stronger from almost every election. By 1903 it had again doubled the number of its followers. Of a total of nine and a half million voters, three million had voted Socialist. In 1912 the figure rose to 4·3 out of a total of 12·2 million votes, and the membership figure of the Party had reached the million mark.

The Free Trade Unions, at the same time, enjoyed a similar success. After the repeal of the Anti-Socialist Law they formed a central organisation, the so-called *Generalkommission der Gewerkschaften*, later re-named *Allgemeiner Deutscher Gewerkschaftsbund* (*A.D.G.B.*)—roughly the counterpart of the British Trade Union Congress. The 50,000-odd Free Trade Union members of 1877 had increased to 278,000 by 1891, and to 680,000 by 1900. In 1914 the membership figure had risen to 2·5 million.

Labour's successful struggle was aided a great deal by an excellent and lively Labour press, which served the Unions and the Party equally well. At the outbreak of the War, the Party alone owned ninety daily newspapers published in all the important towns and industrial centres of Germany, a number of weekly and monthly periodicals and even its own press service.

This growth in strength and influence was the result chiefly of substantial successes in improving social conditions for a large section of the working class. It is true the actual improvements in the living and working conditions of German workers can in no way be compared with the unparalleled expansion of German capitalism at the same time. Still, there were great improvements. The wages of large sections of German workers were rising and, with rising wages, mass consumption was growing. This success was all the more notable as prices were also rising and as indirect taxation was being increased—the former as a result of Germany's protectionist policy, and the latter in order to allow the Kaiser and Messrs. Krupp and Mannesmann to build more battleships and submarines. Nevertheless, the lot of the working man was definitely improving and, as everyone knew, this improvement was due almost solely to vigorous Trade Union action and to the support which the Unions received from the Social Democratic Party.

A great improvement had also been brought about by the far-reaching social legislation which Bismarck had inaugurated and which the Kaiser continued in order to take the wind out of the sails of Socialist propaganda. This end they never achieved. Bismarck's and the Kaiser's attempts to destroy Social Democracy by means of "bribes for the workers" (as German Socialists called Bismarck's social legislation) failed as completely as did Bismarck's policy of oppression. Far from being impressed by the social benevolence of their rulers, most workers felt that they owed these benefits at least indirectly to the Social Democratic Party and its political pressure. Although designed to make Social Democracy "superfluous" in the eyes of the workers, this State legislation only further increased their loyalty to their Party.

While all these successes—direct and indirect—strengthened the prestige of the Labour movement, they also affected its political outlook. Gradually workers began to realise that they had very much more to lose than their chains. Even most of those who had received a thorough Socialist and Marxist training at the Party schools and Trade Union colleges were impressed by the success of the industrial struggle, which gave them the feeling that there was no limit to perpetual progress, provided Germany could rid herself of the remnants of an obsolete feudalism.

In the realm of Socialist thought this feeling found expression in Eduard Bernstein's "Revisionism". Revisionism became the accepted term for Bernstein's attempt to revise Marxism and to purge it of its "utopian" and "Blanquist" traits. In particular, he opposed the notion that the lot of the working class under capitalism was steadily deteriorating and that the capitalist order of society was heading for a catastrophic collapse. The Social Democratic Party, he demanded, should rid itself of obsolete theories which had been proved wrong by history and which only handicapped it in its active struggle for practical progress. In order to make progress and gain real influence, the Party "should have the courage to appear as what it really is—a democratic, socialist party of reform".

Bernstein, who spent many years in London as an exile, had originally developed these views under the influence of the British Labour movement, but it was in Germany that his ideas caused real excitement and much discussion in the Socialist press and at several Party conferences. There can be little doubt that Bernstein's "revisionism" was in far greater harmony with the real mood of the pre-war German Labour movement than the intransigeance of Karl Marx and the revolutionary fervour of the Communist Manifesto. Nevertheless Bernstein found comparatively few supporters and many powerful opponents.

Opposed to his ideas were not only the small Left-wing and radical groups of the Party who had gathered around Rosa Luxemburg, Franz Mehring, Leo Jogiches, Julian Karski, Klara Zetkin, Karl Radek and others, but also the so-called Party Centre, led by Karl Kautsky, which was backed by the overwhelming majority of the membership and which upheld the banner of "orthodox Marxism".

Among Bernstein's early supporters were a number of prominent Trade Union leaders and certain parliamentary deputies from the Southern German States. The social structure of the Southern German States—Baden, Württemberg, Bavaria and Hesse—differed greatly from that of Prussia. In power there were not the strutting officers, the insolent Junkers and the insatiable armaments kings, but a more or less liberal middle class and more or less conservative landowners and peasants who suffered little interference from their ruling dynasties. In these Southern German States, therefore, the Social Democratic deputies had the chance, if they decided to seize it, not only to use Parliament as a propaganda platform, but to do active parliamentary work for definite limited political ends. In fact, that was done in several cases, particularly in Baden, where the Social Democrats combined with the Liberals against the conservative Catholic Centre, and where they successfully fought for a number of progressive reforms. In order to achieve this they even renounced the symbolic gesture of parliamentary opposition—voting against the budget.

A party bent on the revolutionary overthrow of the existing régime, and actively agitating and preparing for this goal, could not, of course, go this way. But only a very small radical wing of the Social Democratic Party around Rosa Luxemburg and her

12

circle of political friends were so minded. The Party Centre under the official leadership could certainly not be accused of actively preparing a revolution. Nevertheless it was as firmly opposed as the radical Left to the Southern German parliamentarians, to their voting for the Budget and their policy of practical reform. While lacking the courage to go the way of revolution, the Centre was equally afraid of dropping the revolutionary theories of Marx and Engels, and of substituting for the goal of violent revolution the aim of reforms and piecemeal improvements. The Centre thus condemned itself to a completely passive attitude of purely abstract and sterile opposition which got the worst of both worlds.

In some ways, there was more common ground between the extreme Right and the extreme Left of the Party than between either of them and the Party Centre. Both the Right and the Left had a clear conception of what they wanted and an idea of how to get it, while the Centre, each time a concrete issue arose, decided to do nothing rather than risk the immaculate purity of its theories in a practical contest. That this was, in fact, the case did not become clear until much later. For a long time the issue remained confused by the united front which the Left and the Centre offered to Bernstein's revisionist zeal. But, as Rosa Luxemburg wrote in an article after the Party Conference at Jena in 1913, the Party Centre was hostile to Revisionism chiefly because it was incurably conservative. As Marxism happened to be the long-standing accepted body of theories with which the Party had grown up, it had to be defended against all innovations, "revisionist" or otherwise.

The division of the Party into "Marxists" and "Revisionists" was entirely deceptive. Nothing illustrates that better than the varying attitude of the Party and its different wings to the question of the general strike, probably the most controversial single issue before the pre-war Social Democratic Party.

The controversy about the general strike as a political weapon of the working class is as old as the international labour movement. Already the Chartists had proposed their "Sacred Month" as a means of enforcing the aims of the Charter. In the 'sixties of the last century the First International demanded a general strike of the people against the war. The great syndicalist movement in France and elsewhere regarded the general strike as the one effective and universal means of overthrowing the existing order of things which would render superfluous all other forms of struggle, violent rebellions as well as parliamentary work.

The Marxist wing of the international Labour movement had been firmly opposed to these views. In Germany, in particular, syndicalism never found more than a handful of adherents among

13

the working class. But some members of the Left made repeated attempts to raise the issue of the general strike, not as an alternative to the revolution, but as a means of helping and preparing for the revolution. In 1904, at the annual Conference of the Social Democratic Party, Karl Liebknecht and Klara Zetkin moved a resolution demanding that the Party should examine afresh the potentialities of the general strike as a political weapon of the working class. The resolution was turned down by a large majority. A few months later, early in 1905, a similar resolution was almost unanimously rejected by the Cologne Trade Union Congress, which went so far as to condemn even the mere discussion of the issue as a "dangerous playing with fire". Yet, in the autumn of 1905, at the Party Conference at Jena, a resolution was adopted, again by a large majority, which approved of the principle of the general strike as a political weapon which the German working class should use in certain circumstances.

This sudden change of attitude was brought about by the Russian Revolution of 1905 and the deep impression it made on German Social Democracy. However, the 1905 Revolution ended in defeat, and defeated with it was the—mainly emotional—approval which the German Social Democratic Party had given to the concept of the political mass strike. Only Rosa Luxemburg and her immediate collaborators stuck to their earlier opinions. The rest of the Party was swayed by the Trade Union leaders, who had always been convinced that "general strike is general nonsense". The Trade Unions were afraid for their own existence if the strike weapon were used for other than purely industrial purposes. It was they who would be called on to organise a strike, to finance and support it and to risk the legality of their organisations. They were determined not to do so except for purposes of which they wholeheartedly approved and for matters in which they, and not the political wing of the movement, had the initiative and the final decision.

After the defeat of the Russian Revolution they were at last in a position to persuade the official leaders of the Party that they had been right and the Party wrong. In February 1906 a secret meeting took place between Party and Trade Union leaders, at which it was agreed that the Party would never appeal to the working class to strike without the previous consent of the Trade Unions. The Mannheim Party Conference which met later in the same year confirmed this decision.

From that time onwards the Trade Unions won an ever-increasing influence on the Party and more and more shaped its policy, although nominally the two organisations remained separate. From that time onwards also date the increasing conflicts and bitter feuds which more and more separated the Left of the Party from its Centre.

The issue of the political strike, however, was by no means settled. It came up again as a practical question after the elections for the Prussian Diet in 1908, which for the first time won six seats for the Social Democratic Party. It was this very election victory which demonstrated, more than previous defeats, the monstrous injustice of the Prussian electoral system. The six Social Democratic deputies had been elected with 600,000 votes, while 418,000 votes had been sufficient to gain the Conservatives 212 seats. For the first time, in spite of police prohibitions, there were big street demonstrations all over Prussia for equal suffrage. After the Kaiser had promised certain electoral reforms the movement quieted down only to flare up again two years later, when the intended "reforms" were announced. The intended reforms, indeed, mocked the very word reform. Nothing essential was to be changed. Once again the workers went into the streets, demonstrating more determinedly than ever their intentions to see real electoral reforms carried out. In a number of places bloody clashes with the police occurred. In others, particularly in the capital, the Social Democratic organisers of these demonstrations skilfully managed to evade and fool the police. The workers were in an aggressive mood.

In that situation Rosa Luxemburg once again brought up the question of the general strike, as a means this time of intensifying and rendering more effective the agitations and demonstrations for equal suffrage. In this she was supported not only by the Left, but also by a number of prominent members of the extreme Revisionist Right, among them Eduard Bernstein, who were in favour of any active move that seemed to promise practical success, whether it was co-operation with the Liberals in Baden or a political general strike in Prussia. The Party Centre, however, under the leadership of Karl Kautsky and, by that time, strongly under the influence of the Trade Unions, turned against the proposal of a general strike, which was then defeated by the Party Conference.

In the period immediately preceding the outbreak of the Great War, the division of the Social Democratic Party into three mutually hostile wings had thus proceeded very far, although outwardly the deceptive appearance of unity was maintained. At the one end were those who, like Bernstein and his followers, were so impressed by the progress of capitalism and the practical chances of economic and political reform that they began to believe, as firmly as any nineteenth-century Liberal, that the golden age of uninterrupted progress had dawned at last and that, if one but

15

fought for it with sufficient energy and determination, the trans-formation of the Western world into a democratic and socialist commonwealth would gradually but inevitably take place. Hypnotised by the great successes the Labour movement had already achieved, and could still achieve in the future, these men failed to see those tendencies which, in Germany and the world at large, made for crises, disruption and violent conflicts.

Their radical opponents in the movement, such as Rosa Luxemburg and her political circle, understood only too well what was going on in the world. They recognised the signs point-ing to war and revolution, but they, too, had their blind spots. They were unable sufficiently to appreciate the tremendous im-portance, in the lives of the workers, of the successes that had been won by the patient day-to-day work of the Trade Unions and the Party. Because of this lack of understanding they never reached the ordinary worker; they failed to impress him and they never gained his support.

The Party Centre, in contrast to both these groups, had no political line of its own. While clinging to the theoretical acknow-ledgment of orthodox Marxism, it remained undecided and pas-sive in every situation that demanded political decision and action, with the exception only of fulfilling the limited task of fighting election campaigns and supporting the aspirations of the Trade Union movement.

The majority of the rank and file had no part in the more or less theoretical discussions between Right, Left and Centre. These discussions took place almost exclusively among the leading intellectuals of the movement. What mattered to the ordinary workers were more tangible things—working conditions, wages and hours, freedom of organisation and the right to strike, uni-versal and equal suffrage in Prussia and some influence on municipal affairs, less power for the police, and justice in the Courts of Law. Men who helped and organised the workers for this kind of struggle won and retained their allegiance and loyalty, no matter how wrong their own theoretical views or how fatal their political decisions. These men, therefore, chiefly the representatives of the industrial movement, became increasingly powerful in the Labour movement as a whole and, as time went on, Trade Union leaders in Germany began to shape the policy of Social Democracy just as much as British Trade Union leaders determine the character and policy of the Labour Party. In-creasingly, German Social Democracy became the political instrument of the Unions.

The Left Wing of the Party had vainly opposed this develop-ment which, in their eyes, impeded the chances of a successful revolution. With apparent—although not with real—contempt, Rosa Luxemburg had likened the work of the Trade Unions to the "labour of Sisyphus". This, very naturally, earned her the scorn of the Union leaders and, equally naturally, it was little appreciated by the ordinary worker who enjoyed the fruits of the "labour of Sisyphus". That was one of the chief reasons why Rosa Luxemburg and the entire Left remained strangers to the mass of the workers, no matter how firm their loyalty to the cause of Socialism, how profound their political judgment and how unflinching their courage and devotion.

The deep fissure which gradually developed in the Labour movement and which eventually was to break it into two bitterly hostile camps did not become clearly visible to the movement at large until after the outbreak of the War. But when at last the crisis came, the controversy over social revolution and social reform, over Marxism and Revisionism seemed to count for little, and the movement split over the attitude to the War itself.

CHAPTER TWO

AUGUST 1914

On the 4th of August, 1914, the chairman of the Social Democratic Party read this declaration of his Party in the German Reichstag:

"We are faced now with the iron fact of war. We are threatened with the horrors of hostile invasions. We do not decide to-day for or against war; we have merely to decide on the necessary means for the defence of the country. Much, if not everything, is at stake for our people and their freedom, in view of the possibility of a victory of Russian despotism which has soiled itself with the blood of the best of its own people.

"It is for us to ward off this danger and to safeguard the culture and independence of our country. Thus we honour what we have always pledged: in the hour of danger we shall not desert our fatherland. We feel ourselves in agreement with the International which has always recognised the right of every nation to national independence and self-defence, just as we condemn, also in agreement with the International, any war of conquest. We demand that, as soon as the aim of security has been achieved and the opponents show themselves ready for

17

peace, this war should be ended by a peace which makes it possible to live in friendship with neighbouring countries.

"Guided by these principles, we shall vote for the war credits."

There was not a single voice of dissent in the Reichstag on that fatal Fourth of August.

No action of German Social Democracy—not even its silent capitulation before the onslaught of Hitlerism—has been so passionately condemned all over the world as this capitulation before German imperialism.

Criticism came from two entirely different sources and was based on two entirely different points of view. There were, first of all, the Labour movements of the Western Democracies, which had rallied behind their Governments in a war that was "to make the world safe for democracy". They, or at least the majority of their members, felt it their right, and indeed their duty, to defend democracy against the onslaught of Prussian militarism and absolutism. In their eyes the guilt of German Social Democracy lay in the fact that it was making common cause with this enemy of human progress and liberty.

The soundness of this argument was violently disputed by that group of international Socialists who later became the founders of the Third International. They were themselves no less critical of the attitude of German Social Democracy to the War; but they denied that, in 1914, a legitimate distinction could be made between aggressor and defender nations, or between a more progressive and a more reactionary camp. They did not think in terms of national guilt, but attributed the responsibility for the war to the supra-national causes of capitalism and the imperialist rivalry of the ruling classes of all countries involved. British, French and Belgian Socialists who supported the War were as guilty and as treacherous in their eyes as the German Socialists. To them it was not the German Party, but the International that had failed. Yet, in a sense, they, too, put the chief blame on German Social Democracy. They did so not because they believed the Germans to be worse than others, but because, in the past, they had believed them to be much better. They had felt an almost boundless admiration for the great German Labour movement, which they took to be the truly Marxist model organisation, the revolutionary workers' party *par excellence*. Their disillusionment was correspondingly greater when they found that even the Germans had failed them.

Right from the beginning of the war there was a minority in the German Socialist movement which shared these views. On the other hand, there was practically no one in Germany who agreed with the criticism which came from the Labour movements of Western Europe. The chief and obvious reason for this was the alliance of the Western Democracies with Tsarist Russia.

"German fear of Russia is as deep and hereditary as the French fear of Germany. . . . The Empire of the Tsar, mysteriously remote, incalculably powerful, a hinterland of barbarism and the matrix throughout history of devastating migrations, this was Germany's real enemy."[1]

Something like this was undoubtedly felt by the vast majority of the German people. It was felt in particular by the working class, which for decades had been swamped with anti-Russian propaganda. True, German absolutism was bad, and the worker had fought it honestly and bravely. But compared to the barbarism of Russian Tsardom, it was decidedly the lesser evil. This the overwhelming majority thought or, at least, felt. And they were as honestly convinced that they were defending civilisation against a barbarous enemy as any French or British worker who took up arms against the Kaiser.

The German Government did not fail to make use of this deep anti-Russian feeling for the purpose of its war propaganda. The Social Democratic Party spoke of nothing else. Here are some extracts from Social Democratic newspapers of 1914:

> *Bielefelder Volkswacht, August 4th:* "The slogan is the same everywhere: against Russian despotism and treachery!"
> *Braunschweiger Volksfreund, August 5th:* "The irresistible pressure of military power affects everyone. However, the class-conscious workers are not merely driven by force. In defending the soil on which they live against the invasion from the East, they follow their own conviction."
> *Hamburger Echo, August 11th:* "We have to wage war above all against Tsarism, and this war we shall be waging enthusiastically. For it is a war for culture."

There cannot be the slightest doubt that words like these truthfully expressed what the majority of the German nation and, in particular, the majority of the working class felt in the days of August 1914. This has been confirmed by every historical testimony and by the great number of personal memoirs that have since been published.[2] The Social Democratic leaders certainly

---

[1] F. P. Chambers: *The War behind the War* p. 6, 16 (London 1939).
[2] Konrad Haenisch, for instance, writes in his book *Die deutsche Sozialdemokratie in und nach dem Weltkrieg*:

"All the hatred, all the disgust which for decades we had been feeling against Russia and her accursed despotism—a hatred which, time and again,

did not "betray" the German working class when they spoke and acted as they did. On the contrary, they behaved simply as the faithful mouthpiece of the masses, and avoided thereby the extreme unpopularity which a more independent attitude would have involved. Some who had hesitated at first were easily convinced of the correctness of the Party attitude because they were afraid of this unpopularity.

They were afraid, too, of being driven into illegality. In that situation, revolutionary opposition to the war would have meant to accept in advance the inevitable suppression of the Party and the Unions. It would have meant causing indirectly the destruction of organisations which had been built up in years of struggle and sacrifice, and which had become the greatest pride, the very life of their members. Deliberately to sacrifice these proud organisations and the successful work of decades, voluntarily to go underground, to face prison and perhaps the firing squad for the sake of a "mere gesture", when it was too late to stop the war— that was something for which the mass party of the German working class and its leadership were as little prepared as any democratic mass party of the workers in any other country.

It is no mere chance that the chief revolutionary opposition to the war came from the Russian Socialists. On the one hand, they could not possibly claim to be fighting against a more reactionary régime than that of their own country; and, on the other hand, they had no mass organisation to sacrifice, had never known "legality", and, even in peace-time, had been forced to work underground.

Yet, while Social Democracy certainly did not "betray" the German working class by the policy it adopted on August the Fourth, it did betray the revolutionary principles it had so frequently professed in the past. This accusation is irrefutable, although some German Social Democrats made a serious effort to explain their attitude at the outbreak of the war as "the only Marxist attitude". Suitable quotations from Marx, Engels and others were sought and found. The following sentence, written by Karl Marx in 1848 (in an article in the *Neue Rheinische Zeitung*), was quoted again and again:

---

was given fresh food by the horrible descriptions which reached us from the dungeons of the Peter-Paul Fortress, the *Schlüsselburg*, the Warsaw Citadel and the ice deserts of Siberia—all the wild rage which, again and again, had been whipped up by news of the white terror in the Tsarist Empire which could defend itself against its 'dear' subjects only with the aid of martial law and gallows, murder and the treachery of its *agents provocateurs*—all these feelings suddenly burst out when, in the first days of August 1914, many millions of voices joined in the mighty chorus that sounded throughout the German lands: 'Against Russia!!!—Down with Tsarism!!!' "

"Only the war against Russia is the war of a revolutionary Germany. In such a war Germany can clean herself of the sins of her past and can become manly; in such a war she can defeat her own autocrats and promote the cause of civilisation by the sacrifice of her sons; she can liberate herself at home by liberating herself abroad, as befits a nation which shakes off the fetters of a long and patient slavery."

An even more suitable testimony was provided by Friedrich Engels, who, in 1859, had expressed his hatred of Napoleon III by exclaiming:

"Long live the war when Frenchmen and Russians attack us at the same time!"

The revolutionary Left, represented by Lenin in Russia and by Rosa Luxemburg in Germany, scorned as pure sophistry the attempt to justify an indefensible political attitude with the aid of quotations from the "masters" that referred to an entirely different situation in an entirely different period of history. No such quotations could alter the fact that the attitude adopted in practice by German Social Democracy in 1914 was in flagrant contradiction to its former declarations.

However, the crime of having betrayed its own professed principles was one that the German Party shared with practically all other Socialist and Labour parties whose countries had become involved in the War. It was not only the German Party, but the International which, as late as 1912, at the International Conference at Basle, had denounced the coming World War as "an imperialist war" against which "the workers of all countries should set the force of the international solidarity of the proletariat". Lenin was therefore only logical when, in his criticism of the Labour attitude to the war, he spoke, not of the collapse of German Social Democracy, but of the collapse of the Second International.

If nevertheless the German Labour movement came in for more blame than others, the reason was that there had been more illusions about that Party than about any other. No one described these illusions better than Rosa Luxemburg:

"German Social Democracy was regarded as the embodiment of Marxist Socialism. It claimed and possessed a special position as the teacher and leader of the Second International. . . . As the Vienna *Arbeiterzeitung* wrote on August 5th, 1914: 'German Social Democracy had been the jewel in the organisation of the class-conscious proletariat'. It served as a model for French, Italian and Belgian Social Democracy and for the working-class movements of Holland, Scandinavia, Switzerland and the United States; and the Slav countries, the Russians and the Balkan Social Democrats looked up to it with a boundless admiration which hardly admitted any criticism. . . . With a blind confidence did the International accept the leadership of the admired and powerful German Party which had become the pride of all Socialists and the terror of the ruling classes in all countries."[1]

This description of what German Social Democracy was believed to be is in no way exaggerated. Yet, it is equally true when Friedrich Stampfer writes that, in actual fact:

"The character of German Social Democracy did not change on August 4th, it merely revealed itself to everyone. What did break down was the wish-dream of a revolutionary mass party which, in reality, had never existed."[2]

CHAPTER THREE

PATRIOTISM AND NATIONALISM

THE EXPERIENCE of the rise of National Socialism in Germany and the outbreak of the second World War convinced many that the German people's attitude to the first World War— and more especially that of the German workers—could only be understood as symptoms of a particularly violent and aggressive nationalism peculiar to the German nation. This nationalism, it is now said, revealed itself in 1914 just as in 1933 and in 1939.

What are the facts? Germany hailed the outbreak of the first World War. It was greeted enthusiastically by practically all the people. Exactly the same happened in other countries.[3] It was patriotism, however misguided and exploited, that asserted itself in Germany as in other nations, a patriotism that proved to be a

---

[1] Junius (Rosa Luxemburg): *Die Krise der Sozialdemokratie*, pp. 6, 7.
[2] Friedrich Stampfer: *Die vierzehn Jahre der ersten deutschen Republik* (Karlsbad, 1936), pp. 22, 23.
[3] Twenty-five years later, the outbreak of the second World War was received with equal uniformity in all countries, although the mood was a very different one. In spite of the school of Hitlerism, the German people showed as little enthusiasm as the British or the French. In 1939, fear and horror of war were as universal as the naïve jubilations in August 1914 (cf. pp. 181–183).

deeper and more spontaneous emotion than all other feelings and considerations. Let no one mistake this for an apologia. But nothing is more necessary, for the purpose of practical politics as well as for the sake of historical truth, than to recognise exactly where in the case of Germany ordinary patriotism ends and aggressive imperialism begins.

In times of peace there had been no practical conflict between this patriotism, on the one hand, and international solidarity and the struggle against imperialism and militarism on the other. The two had been perfectly consistent with each other. They ceased to be consistent when war came—in practice if not in theory. In theory it could of course be argued that, under capitalism, the workers had no fatherland and that there was a more genuine community of interest between them and their fellow workers on the other side of the trenches than between them and their imperialist rulers. In practice, however, nation faced nation, separated by barriers of language and tradition; French guns against German guns; British warships against German warships; Russian soldiers against German soldiers. The plain reality of war, and not the resolutions of the International, determined the attitude of the common people of all nations.

Modern patriotism has taken hold of the masses throughout the world. Time and again its elemental force has proved more powerful than rational considerations and strongly held political views. From the point of view of international Socialism it may be argued that patriotism is a virtue in a democracy on the defensive, but becomes a vice in an aggressive autocracy; but mass patriotism is not a feeling that can be turned on and off like a tap, according to the circumstances. Just because of its elemental power it can so easily be abused and exploited by the unscrupulous.

It was one of the greatest tragedies of the German Labour movement that, ever since 1914, it had been faced by the dilemma that it must either be anti-patriotic or else acquiesce in the aggressive imperialism of Germany's rulers. There was only one way out of this dilemma—namely, to break, once and for all, the power of those whose traditions and interests were indissolubly bound up with the power of aggressive imperialism. But for so drastic a solution the movement never grew mature and strong enough.

If the average German worker was not a revolutionary in Lenin's or Rosa Luxemburg's sense, neither was he the jingo he appeared to be to the outside world. At least during the initial phase of the War, he was honestly convinced that he was called upon to "defend his fatherland".

The Imperial Government fully appreciated that the difference between ordinary patriotism and aggressive imperialism was a

23

very real one, and took good care, right up to the Treaty of Brest-Litovsk, to conceal their plans of conquest. The Chancellor Bethmann-Hollweg excelled in those ambiguities which let it appear as though Germany wanted nothing but a just peace without annexations. He could hardly have hoped to deceive Allied or neutral Powers with his pious declarations, but he did hope to impress the German workers, who, in their vast majority, were firmly opposed to the idea of annexations.

Obviously, the definition of the attitude of the German workers as patriotic but not nationalistic has the same limitation as any such general description. It was true for the average, for the majority; it was not true for every individual. Workers, even organised workers, do not live in water-tight compartments separated from the rest of the nation. They are not immune from outside influence. There were individual jingoes among the workers as among all other classes. There certainly were jingoes—"social patriots" or "social chauvinists", as they were then called—within the ranks of the Social Democratic leadership, men like Scheidemann, Haenisch, Cunow, Winnig, Heine, Lensch. As men in leading Party positions they were much in the limelight and exercised considerable influence. But in the movement as a whole they remained a small minority, and were as little typical of German Labour in general as were, at the other extreme, Karl Liebknecht and Rosa Luxemburg.

At the beginning of the War the majority of the Social Democratic and Trade Union leadership faithfully reflected the attitude of the average German worker. They, too, behaved as naïve and unquestioning patriots, not as aggressive imperialists. But they were in a vastly different position. The ordinary worker perhaps could not be expected to withstand the surge of national emotion which swept the country, confusing heart and brain. But men who had accepted the task of leadership could be expected to keep a cool head and to be able to see through a lying propaganda. They at least should have known that this was not a war of defence, and they should have had the courage to act accordingly, to enlighten the workers and lead them into opposition.

If they did not do so, they behaved, in their own opinion, no differently from the Labour war supporters in Britain or France. Yet, in contrast to Britain and France, Germany was not a democracy, and German Social Democratic support for the War meant appeasement of a régime which the working class had considered its mortal enemy. The revolutionary critics of the Social Democratic Party, quite logically, therefore, condemned the Party even more for the political truce to which it had consented than for its support of the War as such.

For some of the Party and Trade Union leaders the truce was, no doubt, not only a political handicap, but, as they saw it, a great political opportunity. Both as individuals and as the representatives of their organisations, they had been social outcasts and third-class citizens in the pre-war Empire. A revolutionary may proudly suffer this situation, which for him may even prove a source of moral strength. But the average Social Democratic and Trade Union leader had neither the character nor the temperament of a revolutionary. He had opposed the existing order of society precisely because it prevented him from living a "normal" peaceful and secure life, as an equal among equals, and not because revolt was in his blood and rebellion in his nature. There is very little doubt that the much-ridiculed words which the Kaiser spoke at the beginning of the War, "I know no more parties, I know only Germans", made a deep impression on some Social Democratic and Trade Union leaders. Here at last was the chance for which they had been vainly hoping and battling all their lives—to be recognised as full citizens and to take an active part in shaping the affairs of the country, if not by political direction, at least through bureaucratic influence.

Only in rare cases was it consideration of a personal career that drove these men to adopt this attitude. They were concerned rather with getting at last a place in the sun for the organisation and movement and class they represented. They were greatly helped, of course, by the patriotic fever which seized the whole country in the early days of the War. In fact, all the Party leadership had to do on August 4, 1914, was what they had done on most other occasions—to follow the mass of their followers instead of leading them.

With secret qualms, as many have testified, but in practice only too readily, they adapted themselves to the mood of the moment. They acted as the willing instrument of the masses rather than as their guides. While some of them lacked the necessary insight, others were perfectly conscious of what they were doing, and all lacked the courage to strive against the current and to give an independent lead in a situation in which independence would have meant, at least temporarily, extreme isolation and unpopularity, and the sacrifice of legality.

A small number of individuals apart, they let themselves be guided and pushed forward (or backward) rather than give a lead. They were at the tail end of the movement instead of at its head. And when critics suggested that this attitude was unworthy of men entrusted with the leadership of a movement,[1] they argued

[1] Lenin, for instance, wrote:
"The masses . . . could no nothing. The leaders, however, had the possi-

that such was the only possible attitude of a democrat whose rôle it was to represent the people and to express their will, but not to impose his own will upon them.

Already before the War, the task of leadership seemed to increase in difficulty as the movement grew in numbers. Numerical growth inevitably implied the growth of a bureaucratic apparatus with its inherent, and essentially undemocratic, tendency to become rigidly conservative and self-perpetuating. The danger was therefore not only that democratic leaders ceased to be leaders, but also that the Party ceased to be democratic except in name. This danger was particularly great in periods of instability when the attitude and mood of the people underwent sudden and rapid changes. In such periods the Party leadership, because of its bureaucratic inflexibility, tended to represent the members' attitude of yesterday rather than of today.

This is, of course, a phenomenon of modern politics generally and not peculiar to German history. But it was conspicuous in the history of the German Labour movement and had very much to do with the split that occurred during the War.

In August 1914 the Social Democratic Party had expressed more or less adequately what the mass of the German workers then felt and thought. As the War dragged on, however, as its sacrifices and misery grew and as it became increasingly difficult to camouflage as a "defensive war", the working class grew more and more hostile to it. The Social Democratic Party was slow to notice this change and even slower to adapt its attitude to it. Eventually, the gap between its official policy and the increasingly bitter opposition to this policy among large sections of the movement became so wide that a split was the inevitable result.

CHAPTER FOUR

AGAINST THE WAR

From the beginning a minority within the Social Democratic Party had opposed the official Party attitude to the War. How large this minority then was is not known exactly. Local and

---

bility and the duty to vote against the war credits, to make a stand against the political truce, to declare themselves in favour of the defeat of their *own* Governments, to organise an international machine for the purpose of propagating fraternisation in the trenches and of publishing underground literature, preaching the necessity of revolutionary action, etc., etc." (Lenin: *Der Zusammenbruch der Zweiten Internationale. Ausgewählte Werke*, Vol. V, p. 199. Wien, 1933.)

provincial Party organisations, editors of certain Party newspapers and a number of other well-known individuals immediately protested against the War and against the political truce, the officially proclaimed *Burgfrieden*. Few of these protests reached the public because of the strict censorship which, as part of the state of siege, had been introduced on the first day of the War.

On August 4th, 1914, fourteen out of ninety-two members of the Parliamentary Party had been in favour of voting against the war credits. This opposition, however, submitted to Party discipline and voted with the majority. In December 1914 the Government demanded new war credits. Liebknecht was then the only member of the German Reichstag who voted against the credits.

While Liebknecht was alone in his demonstration, he was not alone in his opposition. For tactical reasons, even some of his closest collaborators had advised Liebknecht against this demonstration which, they thought, might do their cause more harm than good. The voting in the Reichstag was certainly not a true mirror of the attitude of the people—at least not before 1917. Nor was there any other way by which public opinion could easily be gauged. The Press was muzzled. Open-air demonstrations were suppressed by the police and the military. Party meetings could only be held under police supervision.

Nevertheless, opposition to the War grew. It expressed itself in a flood of pamphlets, tracts and papers, which were illegally printed and distributed, in secret meetings of small opposition groups all over the country, and, above all, in the general mood of the people which, although inarticulate, could be sensed by all who had eyes to see and ears to hear. The Social Democratic leadership had neither very sharp eyes nor very good hearing. It continued to represent the workers' "attitude of yesterday", and failed to keep in step with a rapidly changing mood. That was the chief reason for the success of the organised opposition in the latter part of the war.

Rosa Luxemburg and her small circle of political friends had begun the struggle against the War and the truce on the very day on which War was declared. With her, from the beginning, were Julian Karski, Klara Zetkin and the seventy-year-old Franz Mehring, the great historian who, through his books, had done more than anyone else to destroy the historical legends with which the imperialist rulers and their obedient hirelings among the intelligentsia had sought to confuse and mislead the German people. Karl Liebknecht very soon joined them, and gradually others followed. By the beginning of 1915 their number had grown considerably, but they were still a circle of like-minded

27

political friends rather than a political organisation. At that time they decided to try to broaden their influence by the publication of a periodical. In April 1915 the first number of *Die Internationale* (The International) appeared, with articles by Rosa Luxemburg, Franz Mehring, Johannes Kaempfer (Julian Karski), Paul Lange, Kaethe Duncker, Klara Zetkin, Heinrich Stroebel and August Thalheimer. Most of the articles were on a very high intellectual level, and they scathingly criticised the attitude of the Party to the War and the truce. The first number of this review was also its last. The editors, publishers and printers were indicted for high treason.

Rosa Luxemburg had already been for two months in prison (serving a pre-war sentence for anti-militarist propaganda) when *Die Internationale* appeared. She was released in February 1916, but re-arrested in July of the same year. From then on she remained in "protective custody" until the Revolution of 1918 at last secured her the few weeks of freedom she was allowed to enjoy before her assassination in January 1919.

From the name of the periodical the group around Rosa Luxemburg later adopted the name *Gruppe Internationale*. The public, however, renamed it Spartakus League after it had begun to issue its series of political "Letters" signed "Spartakus". That name stuck not only throughout the War years, but even for a long time after the Spartakus League had amalgamated with other groups in the newly founded Communist Party.

The first important direct appeal to the people against the War appeared in May 1915, in the form of a leaflet written by Karl Liebknecht which bore the caption "The Main Enemy Stands At Home" (a number of other leaflets had been written before, but they were not very widely circulated, nor did they seem to make any noticeable impression). One month later there appeared the so-called "Appeal Of The Thousand"—a letter addressed to the Executive of the Social Democratic Party and signed by about a thousand Party members and officials, many of them in important and responsible positions, declaring that the War had by now clearly revealed its character as an imperialist war of conquest, and demanding that, as a consequence, the Party ought to break the truce and fight for immediate peace. This "Appeal Of The Thousand" was also distributed in form of a leaflet.

The "Appeal" caused a great stir in the Party, but an even greater impression was created by another public appeal on similar lines which appeared soon afterwards in the *Leipziger Volkszeitung* (one of the most important dailies of the Party) under the heading "The Demand Of The Hour", and which was signed by three of the best-known and most respected leaders of the Party, Karl Kautsky, Eduard Bernstein and Hugo Haase. Hugo Haase was, at that time, the President of both the Party and the Parliamentary Party.

In the meantime, unofficial attempts had been made in several countries to revive international Socialist contacts, a task which the Labour and Socialist International was no longer able or willing to perform. As soon as the War broke out the Second International split into two hostile groups along the division lines of the War. Each of the two groups held separate meetings early in 1915; the Parties belonging to the Allied countries met in London in February 1915, while the Parties belonging to the Central Powers met two months later in Vienna. Between the two meetings, in March 1915, the first genuine international conference of the War took place in Berne—the International Socialist Women Conference. Seven members of the German Party, led by Klara Zetkin, were among the twenty-five delegates assembled for this conference; they had not, however, come as the official representatives of their Party, for the German in common with the French Party had refused to send an official delegation. The Conference issued an appeal to the working women of the warring countries asking them to get together and fight for immediate peace without annexations and indemnities.

Far greater than the effect of this meeting was that of the international Socialist conference which had been called to Zimmerwald for September 1915. The German movement was represented by three different groups at the Zimmerwald Conference: Rosa Luxemburg's *Gruppe Internationale* (Spartakus League) represented by Ernst Meyer and Bertha Thalheimer, a more moderate group headed by Georg Ledebour and Adolf Hoffmann, and a third radical group represented by Julian Borchardt, editor of a Left-wing monthly called *Lichtstrahlen* (Rays of Light), who cooperated closely with the Russian · Bolsheviks. It had been Lenin's intention to use the Zimmerwald Conference as the starting point for the definite and final break away of the anti-war and anti-imperialist Left from the Social Democratic Parties supporting the War in their respective countries, and as the nucleus of a new revolutionary International. But the majority of the Conference, under the leadership of Ledebour, rejected this proposal. Of the German delegation, only Borchardt was in favour of Lenin's policy; the Spartakus delegates, while agreeing with Lenin's criticism of the Second International, and of German Social Democracy in particular, were yet unwilling to take the step of cutting loose from the Party, and thereby from the chance of ever winning the rank and file for their views.

The Zimmerwald message to the workers of the world appealing for international class solidarity and for action against the War made a strong impression on Socialists in Germany; so did the even more strongly worded message issued by the second international Socialist conference which met in Kienthal in the following year. But international conferences and resolutions were not able to do what the national opposition movements in the various countries had left undone.

Inside the German Social Democratic Party, meanwhile, conflicts between the steadily growing opposition and the War supporters became more and more frequent. In the autumn of 1915 Kautsky demanded publicly that the minority of the Parliamentary Party, which had been in favour of voting against the war credits, should break the Party discipline and record their opposition in the Reichstag. The fifth war budget came before Parliament on December 29, 1915. In the meeting before the Reichstag session forty-five members of the Social Democratic Party had been in favour of voting against the war credits. Twenty actually did so against the Party decision; another twenty-odd abstained from voting.

After this, Karl Legien, the President of the *Generalkommision der Gewerkschaften* (the German equivalent of the T.U.C.), demanded the expulsion of the members who had broken the Party discipline. This was turned down, but shortly afterwards Karl Liebknecht was expelled. It was at that time that the first national conference of the *Gruppe Internationale* was called which transformed this group from a loose circle of friends into a proper political organisation, which adopted a provisional programme drafted by Rosa Luxemburg. On January 27, 1916, the organisation published the first of its famous series of "Spartakus Letters" which gave it the name by which it became known all over the world. Most of the Spartakus Letters were written by Rosa Luxemburg, some during her short months of freedom, the majority while she was in prison. Other authors of Spartakus Letters were Franz Mehring, Karl Liebknecht, Ernst Meyer, Paul Levy and Julian Karski. Their editor, Leo Jogiches, who was, above all, a highly efficient organiser, was responsible not only for ordinary editorial work, but also for the highly complicated task of getting the manuscripts from the authors—many of whom had to smuggle them out of prison—and having the Letters illegally printed and distributed.

The most famous publication of the German opposition during the War appeared in April 1916 under the title "The Crisis of Social Democracy", better known as the "Junius Pamphlet", Junius being the pseudonym chosen by its author, Rosa Luxemburg. The pamphlet, which was written in prison a whole year before its publication, has become one of the great classics of socialist writing, equally remarkable for the profoundness and clarity of its analysis, its passionate human protest against the slaughter of the war and the brilliance and scathing irony of its style.

But the Spartakus League—although it counted among its leaders many of the most highly idealistic, the most passionately sincere and also the most intelligent Socialists of the German Labour movement—some of whom, notably Rosa Luxemburg herself, towered high above their contemporaries—remained a comparatively small and uninfluential group as long as the War lasted, even at a period when opposition to the War had become almost universal within the German working class. They had no organisation of their own when the War broke out, and under the double handicap of being persecuted by the police and denounced and defamed by their own Party Executive and the Trade Unions, they had no chance of building up an organisation throughout the Reich. They had groups in Berlin, Brunswick, Württemberg and Chemnitz, and they won a few new groups in the course of the War, but not enough to give them a real influence on the working class. They were for the most part intellectuals whose level of discussion was above the heads of most ordinary workers. Those workers whose adherence they won were, on the whole, the most desperately poor unskilled labourers, who were more attracted by the violence of the Spartakists' language than by the soundness of their arguments.

Apart from the Spartakists there were several other small left-wing groups, best known among them Julian Borchardt's "International Socialists" and the so-called "Bremen Left" (grouped around the *Bremer Bürgerzeitung*, one of Germany's oldest Social Democratic papers), led by Jan Knief and Karl Radek. These groups closely co-operated with the Bolsheviks, whereas the Spartakus League, in particular Rosa Luxemburg herself, always maintained a critical attitude *vis-à-vis* Lenin and his party.

The mass opposition to the War which developed from 1916 onwards was not led by any of these organisations, but by the group of oppositional Members of Parliament who later founded the Independent Socialist Party. In March 1916, after the parliamentary opposition group had once again refused to submit to Party discipline and voted against the Emergency Budget, the Party majority passed a resolution declaring that the opposition had forfeited the right of belonging to the Parliamentary Party. The opposition thereupon formed its own parliamentary group, called the *Sozialdemokratische Arbeitsgemeinschaft*. When it was

31

founded the *Arbeitsgemeinschaft* consisted of eighteen Social Democratic Members of Parliament, among them the ex-President of the Party and Parliamentary Party, Hugo Haase, and the champion of "Revisionism", Eduard Bernstein.

For Mayday 1916 the Spartakists had issued an appeal by Karl Liebknecht asking the working class to demonstrate everywhere against the continuation of the War.

"Workers, Party Comrades and women of the people", this leaflet said, "Do not let the second Mayday of the War pass without making it into a demonstration of international Socialism and a protest against the imperialist slaughter. On the First of May we stretch out a fraternal hand, beyond all frontiers and battlefields, to the people of France, Belgium, Russia, England, Serbia and the whole world. On the First of May we call in a thousand voices:

" 'Make an end to the vile crime of nation murdering nation! Down with all who organise it, incite to it and profit from it! Our enemies are not the French or the Russian people—our enemies are German Junkers, German capitalists and their executive committee—the German Government.

" 'Into battle against these mortal enemies of freedom, into battle for everything that constitutes the well-being and the future of the workers' cause, of humanity and civilisation!

" 'End the War! We want peace.

" 'Long live Socialism! Long live the workers' International! Workers of the world unite!' "

In Berlin about ten thousand workers responded to this appeal, gathering in the Potsdamer Platz in the early morning hours of the First of May. A large force of mounted police was in attendance, who immediately seized Liebknecht when he shouted to the crowd: "Down with the War! Down with the Government!"

On June 28th Liebknecht was sentenced to two and a half years' hard labour, despite his immunity as a Member of Parliament. On the same day a strike broke out in protest against this sentence. In Berlin alone over fifty thousand workers downed tools. This was the first great political strike that occurred in Germany after the outbreak of the War. The majority of the workers who took part in the strike did not do so because they identified themselves with Liebknecht's social-revolutionary programme, of which most of them anyhow knew little. They struck because Liebknecht had become the symbol of their hatred of the War and their hatred of the Imperial Government, which they held increasingly responsible for the unending slaughter and mounting misery.

The growing opposition caused the Government to intervene, more ruthlessly against its actual or potential leaders. One after another of the prominent Spartakists was sentenced to prison or taken into "protective custody" or—sent to the front; among the better known, apart from Luxemberg and Liebknecht, were Mehring, Crispin, Hoernle, Niebuhr, Ernst Meyer and Klara Zetkin. Even in prison most of them continued their anti-war writing, and successfully managed to smuggle out their manuscripts which were then published by their friends still at liberty.

The Executives of the Social Democratic Party and of the Trade Unions helped, in their own way, in the fight against the opposition. They did so chiefly with the aid of administrative measures designed to deprive the opposition of their means of propaganda. When War broke out many of the numerous Party papers were edited by men and women opposed to the official line of the Party. Wherever it was possible (*i.e.*, in all those cases where a local paper depended on subsidies from the Party's central funds) the Executive replaced the unruly editors by their own obedient nominees, whether the local Party organisation concerned agreed or not. The first case of this kind was that of the *Schwäbische Tagwacht*, whose editors, Crispin, Walcher and Hoernle, were replaced by nationalistic nominees of the Executive Committee without previous consultation with either the editors or the local Party membership. Many similar "purges" followed. The most notorious case was that of the *Vorwärts*, which filled the double rôle of being the central organ of the Party as well as the paper of the Berlin organisation.

From the beginning of the War the *Vorwärts* had supported the moderate opposition. The editors had protested to the Executive against the Party vote for the war budget on August 4th, 1914, although that protest was not published until after the War. As the War went on, the *Vorwärts* more and more identified itself with the policy of the parliamentary opposition, which, in March 1916, had formed the *Sozialdemokratische Arbeitsgemeinschaft*. For this policy the paper had the support of the majority of the Berlin Party organisation.

In October 1916 the military authorities suspended the *Vorwärts*, for the fourth time since the outbreak of the War, because of an alleged violation of censorship regulations. The Party Executive seized this golden opportunity for what became known later as "The Rape of the *Vorwärts*". In negotiations with the military authorities about permission to republish the paper the Executive offered to appoint a new editor who was to take political responsibility. This offer went farther than the demand of the military authority, who would have been satisfied with the appointment of an Executive nominee responsible only for censorship matters. In spite of the protest of the editorial staff, as well as of the Berlin Party organisation, which owned the paper, the Executive appointed Herman Müller as chief of the *Vorwärts*, with sole responsibility. The editors were not even allowed to print the story of what had happened. They did so, however, in form of a leaflet. From that time onwards the *Vorwärts* became the symbol of the Executive's dictatorial interference against the Left—a fact which largely explains why the first act of the people who, in January 1919, took part in the Spartakus rebellion was to occupy the building of the *Vorwärts*.

As the War dragged on, as the number of losses steadily mounted, and as hunger and privation visited more and more working-class and even middle-class homes, war-weariness and opposition to the truce quickly increased. In November 1916 the notorious *Hilfsdienstgesetz*[1] was passed. In the same month of November a huge political demonstration took place in Frankfurt-am-Main, where some thirty thousand workers demanded immediate peace without annexations and indemnities.

Even the imperial Government was compelled to react somehow to the growing hostility to the War. In December 1916 Bethmann-Hollweg announced in the Reichstag that the German Government was ready to make peace and that a Note to that effect had been dispatched to the Allied Powers. The Social Democratic *Arbeitsgemeinschaft* rightly pointed out that a "peace offer" without peace conditions was a mere farce. It is doubtful whether the members of the official Parliamentary Party were really naïve enough to believe that the Kaiser's peace offer had been meant seriously; some of them probably were. But a growing number of Socialist workers in the country most definitely were not.

A glimmer of hope came into this winter of misery, hunger and cold with the publication of Wilson's peace message in January 1917. But it quickly died down again when the Imperial Government retorted with the extension of the U-boat war and when America entered the War.

All the deeper was the effect of the news of the Russian

[1] The *Hilfsdienstgesetz*—the Auxiliary National Service Act—conscripted all Germans between the ages of seventeen and sixty for National Service of any kind and in any district. This Act particularly embittered the workers, who felt that their last freedom was taken away from them while there was no corresponding restriction on the power of capital and while, for all practical purposes, the middle and upper classes remained exempt from any such service.

February Revolution, which went like wildfire through the factories and tenement houses of Germany's big industrial centres. The opposition took fresh courage. In March 1917 the *Sozialdemokratische Arbeitsgemeinschaft* convened a conference at Gotha, where it reconstituted itself as a political party of its own, the *Unabhängige Sozialdemokratische Partei Deutschlands*, generally known by its initials *U.S.P.*, the Independent Social Democratic Party of Germany. From that time onwards the original Social Democratic Party was generally referred to as the "Majority Socialists".

The new Independent Socialist Party was composed of very heterogeneous elements. The dividing line between the War-supporters and the opponents of War and political truce ran right across the familiar division into a Right and a Left wing. "Marxists" and "Revisionists", social reformers and social revolutionaries suddenly found themselves united in their common opposition to the War and the political truce. On the one hand, the radical *Spartakusbund* affiliated *en bloc* with the Independent Party; on the other, men like Eduard Bernstein—Rosa Luxemburg's greatest opponent within the Labour movement—joined it. That is not to say that old conflicts had died. They remained as strong as ever and, at a later period, caused the Independent Party to disintegrate and to split again. But during the War these conflicts remained in the background because they concerned matters which were not then topical and practical. For the moment, all opposition was opposition to the Kaiser's War, and, on this basis, there existed sufficient unity among the various opposition wings of the Social Democratic Party to establish a common platform.

The Independents very soon dominated many of the local and constituency Social Democratic parties, including those of important industrial centres such as Greater Berlin, Halle, Leipzig, Bremen, Brunswick and others. By July 1917 the Independents had won the adherence of sixty-two Social Democratic constituency parties and had founded nineteen new ones.

Shortly after the foundation of the new Party, in April 1917, the second mass strike occurred in Germany. Two hundred thousand workers struck in Berlin and Leipzig. The Leipzig strikers formulated seven demands, of which the second urged the Government to declare its readiness for immediate peace and to renounce all plans of conquest. The remaining six demands dealt with internal questions, such as the immediate democratisation of the country and the guarantee of sufficient food and coal supplies.

Three months later, in July 1917, the German Reichstag

adopted the famous "peace resolution" in favour of a negotiated peace without annexations. Thus the majority of the Reichstag, including the middle-class parties, had officially adopted the programme of the opposition. This remains true although the German Chancellor added his notorious "as I interpret it", and although action did not follow. The Reichstag was completely impotent. It had remained the "fig leaf of absolutism". Stronger forces were needed to overthrow absolutism than parliamentary speeches and resolutions.[1]

Not even the workers were strong enough to enforce, by their own action, the peace they desired, before the armies in the field were decisively beaten. This was shown by the outcome of the great munition workers' strike of January 1918. It was by far the greatest strike which occurred in Germany during the War. According to reliable accounts more than one million armament workers were involved. The strike was mainly political in character. It was called in protest against the Treaty of Brest-Litovsk, which Germany was about to enforce upon the revolutionary Government of Russia.

Historians called this strike the "dress rehearsal of the Revolution". But it was not by accident that the strike remained a "rehearsal" and failed to develop into a revolution. The German Government and the military machine based on a still undefeated Army were too strong to be overthrown by a strike movement. Even the much weaker Austro-Hungarian Empire, where an equally big, if not bigger strike movement had broken out earlier in January, was able to withstand and outlast this popular eruption.

At that time working-class opposition to the War had become practically universal. But this mood was hardly reflected in the relative strength of the two Labour parties. In the ranks of the Majority Socialists there were as many opponents of the War as there were among the Independent Socialists. Nevertheless, the leaders of the Majority Party continued to support the Government[2] to the very end of the War. They did so, more and more, against the will of the rank and file; and yet, out of sheer loyalty, hundreds of thousands of workers stuck to their old Party which they had helped to build, no matter how violently they dis-

---

[1] Yet, even this pious "peace resolution" caused great apprehension among the Pan-German Right. They immediately proceeded to counter it by the foundation of a centre for annexationist propaganda—chiefly among the troops—the so-called Fatherland Party, led by Tirpitz and Kapp (the same Kapp who in 1920 attempted the notorious *putsch*).

[2] They even failed to vote against the Treaties of Brest-Litovsk and Bucharest with the idiotic excuse that this demonstrated their true love of peace—a bad peace being better than no peace at all!

agreed with its policy. This continued support, incidentally, was one of the causes of the failure of the Social Democratic leaders to adapt their policy to the changing mood of the masses. They mistook loyalty and Party discipline for political consent.

Loyalty to his organisation has become a matter of instinct for the worker. All organised workers feel that their strength and the progress they have made are much more due to their organised coherence than to principles or programmes. Party discipline induced even a man like Liebknecht on August 4, 1914, to vote for the war credits, in spite of his passionate opposition to the War.

There were, on the other hand, hundreds of thousands who felt that their loyalty had been strained too much. It was upon them that the Independents could rely when they formed their own party.

The Trade Unions remained officially aloof from the quarrels among the various political groups, but in practice their official policy was the same as that of the Majority Socialists. The Trade Union rank and file, on the other hand, was at least partly identical with the membership of the Socialist parties and, as a consequence, their ranks were torn by much the same political differences as split the political movement.

The opposition within the industrial movement was led by a group which became known under the name of *Revolutionäre Obleute* (Revolutionary Delegates). The *Revolutionäre Obleute* developed out of a small circle of Berlin metal workers. All their members were highly skilled craftsmen and active trade unionists of long standing. They had come together because of their opposition to the War and to the political truce. Later on they joined the Independent Party, but maintained a separate existence within that Party, just as the *Spartakusbund* did. On occasions they co-operated with the Spartakists, but they would not accept Spartakist leadership. Their field of activity lay in the workshops and in the Trade Unions. Their main attack was directed against the Trade Union leadership, first of all because it had accepted the political truce and outlawed strikes for the duration of the War, and, secondly, because it refused officially to concern itself with politics. The chief aim of the *Revolutionäre Obleute* was to transform the Unions from purely industrial into political and revolutionary organisations.

They themselves were neither a political party with a definite programme, nor a Trade Union with specific industrial aims, nor even a shop-steward organisation in the present sense of the word—*i.e.*, an organisation representing the particular local interests of the workers employed in a particular factory. They were in a class by themselves; a fairly exclusive body of highly skilled men—politically-minded, class-conscious and revolutionary.

It was the *Revolutionäre Obleute* who, in Berlin, organised the great political strike of January 1918,[1] and who later played an equally important part in the November Revolution. They were one more living proof of the falseness of the Communist theory which alleged that the most highly paid (*i.e.*, the most skilled) workers had been "corrupted by the *bourgeoisie*" and become the mainstay of working-class reformism. On the contrary, as Richard Müller, their leader, rightly remarked:

"During the War, the driving force of the political mass movement did not come from the lowest strata of the working class, which were suffering most from the effects of the War; it came from the upper strata, from highly skilled and specialised workers, from that section of the working class which has been called 'working class aristocracy' and which, later on, was wrongly accused of having paralysed the German Revolution."[2]

The *Revolutionäre Obleute* became the leading organisation of this "working-class aristocracy". The Government sought to eliminate their influence by sending the leaders to the front. It was a well-tried practice. However, in this case it was much more difficult to carry out than in that of the Spartakists and other Left-wing groups, composed mainly of intellectuals and un-skilled labourers. Skilled workers were precious. In many cases employers found themselves compelled—much against their inclination—to protect the most troublesome workers in their factories from the Police and the Army simply because they were indispensable. Thus the *Revolutionäre Obleute* enjoyed a compara-tive immunity which the Spartakists, for instance, never enjoyed. For all these reasons, the *Revolutionäre Obleute* were an organisation of great potential importance. As it turned out, they did not live up to their own expectations. They had two great weaknesses. One was that their influence in the provinces was not nearly as great as in Berlin. The other—and this was decisive—was the total absence of a practical programme for the Revolution which was approaching. In this they resembled all the other sections of the working-class movement. No one in the German Labour movement knew how to use the power which suddenly, on November 9th, 1918, fell into their hands.

[1] Representatives of the two Socialist Parties (Majority and Independent Socialists) joined the strike committee; but they had had nothing to do with the original preparation for the strike.

[2] Richard Müller: *Vom Kaiserreich zur Republik* (Wien 1924), Vol. 1, p. 131.

PART TWO

AN EXPERIMENT IN DEMOCRACY
1918-1919

CHAPTER FIVE

THE PARTIES OF THE REVOLUTION

THE GERMAN Revolution of 1918 broke the political domination of the Junker class and swept away the monarchy which based its power on this class. Germany became a Republic and gave herself "the most democratic Constitution in the world". That was the achievement of the Revolution which, in its early stages, was erroneously called a "Socialist revolution". In fact the social structure of the country remained untouched. The German working class thus brought about a transformation which, in the Western democracies, had been the work of the rising middle classes, and which Arthur Rosenberg once described as "a middle-class revolution won by the working class in a struggle with feudalism".

There are certain features which the German November Revolution has in common with the Russian Revolution of February 1917. But the Russian February was followed by the "Red October". The German Revolution just fizzled out.

The February Revolution in Russia brought men to the head of the nation who were either unable or unwilling to meet the two demands of the moment for which the masses had been clamouring most urgently: immediate peace and the distribution of the land among the peasants. In Germany, by contrast, the Revolution brought men to the head who, whatever their faults and shortcomings in other respects, stood for precisely those things which the majority of the German nation then wanted: immediate peace, democratisation of the country and social improvements. The achievements of the Russian February Revolution therefore left the majority of the Russian workers and peasants unsatisfied, but the German Revolution appeared to give the majority of the German workers exactly what they had wanted. That this was only an illusion was not realised until it was too late.

There is another equally decisive difference between the two revolutions. In Russia, a political party emerged, the Bolsheviks, whose leaders knew what the mass of the people wanted and what they wanted themselves, who had the keenest sense of power and the courage to act boldly. In Germany such a political party was totally lacking.

German Social Democracy understood well enough what the workers and soldiers desired most. What the leaders of the Party never learnt was to think in terms of power and to act accordingly.

The Independent Socialist Party was torn by internal differences which came to a head as soon as their one common goal had been reached and peace had come. The Right Wing of the Independents had no fundamental quarrels with the Majority Socialists. The Left Wing came increasingly under the influence of the *Revolutionäre Obleute*, who were revolutionary in spirit and in temperament, but completely undecided as to what practical course they should follow. They had firm principles, but no programme of action, and they wasted precious time on endless arguments over trifles and general theoretical discussions.

The *Spartakusbund* was weak, and it, too, was torn by internal conflicts. In December 1918 it officially severed connections with the Independent Party and, together with some other small Left-wing groups, founded the Communist Party of Germany. Of the new members that it attracted many were simply embittered insurrectionists, more concerned with the act of rebellion than with its success. They were as hostile to the slow and rather pedestrian Trade Unions and to the "bourgeois" idea of parliament as they had been to Ludendorff and to the Kaiser's absolutism. They were brave enough to act upon their convictions and to pay with their lives for their ideals. But they lacked all understanding of the mentality of the ordinary worker, who, defying their theories, was born neither a revolutionary nor a corrupt traitor. He was, had they but seen it, a man who wanted peace and "normality" more than anything else. He wanted regular work with decent working conditions and good wages; a pleasant home and freedom from oppression and arbitrariness. Many of the Spartakists were blind to this simple reality, and because of their complete lack of human understanding they were quite incapable of conceiving a realistic political strategy.

The leaders of Spartakus—at least some of them—had hardly more in common with many of their own followers than with any other political group and party. The programme which Rosa Luxemburg drafted for the newly formed Communist Party was in itself a condemnation of utopian insurrectionism. One of its passages reads:

"The proletarian revolution can reach full maturity and clarity only in stages, step by step, on the Golgatha path of bitter experience and through defeats and victories. The victory of Spartakus cannot be the beginning but only the end of the revolution. . . .

"*The* Spartakusbund *will never take power unless this be the clear and unambiguous will of the great majority of the proletarian masses of Germany, and unless this majority consciously approve of the views, aims and methods of the* Spartakusbund."[1]

This was the spirit of democracy, angrily protesting against the *putsch* tactics of the desperados. The fact that the programme was adopted also by those members of the *Spartakusbund* who thought and acted quite differently only shows how little importance they attached to any programmatic declaration.

Rosa Luxemburg had spent practically the entire War in prison and in "protective custody". Owing to her imprisonment, her influence on the practical development of the *Spartakusbund* was almost non-existent. When the Revolution freed her at last, the time that was left to her was much too short for her to have any decisive influence on the course of events. It is idle to speculate whether or not she could have helped to save the German Revolution, for three months after its outbreak she and Karl Liebknecht were done to death.

Of all the political groups which in 1918–1919 competed for the support of the German workers, only the leaders of the Majority Socialists had a rough idea of the sort of country they wanted and of the practical steps they had to take in order to get it. What they wanted was a parliamentary democracy on the Western pattern, a comprehensive system of progressive social legislation and a friendly understanding with other nations on the basis of equality and self-determination.

This was clearly a liberal democratic, but not a Socialist programme. Nevertheless, they continued to call themselves Socialists. They did not feel that there was any contradiction, because, to them, Socialism was a vague and far-off ideal that had no real bearing on practical politics. Socialism, they thought, might be the eventual result of gradual reforms brought about by parliamentary legislation, if and in so far as they succeeded in educating and winning the nation for this ideal. Their chief concern, therefore, was to re-establish order and lay the foundations for legislation and political education, that is to say, arrange for general elections to be held as quickly as possible.

What they did not want, and had never wanted, was a social

[1] My italics.

41

revolution. They feared that social revolution might lead to civil war and, eventually, to the establishment of a dictatorship. Moreover, they feared that the Allied Powers might intervene and forcibly prevent a social revolution and, as a counter-move, support separatist movements in Bavaria and the Rhineland, thus causing the total disintegration of the German Reich. Thirdly, the Majority Socialists were frightened of what they called "economic and administrative experiments" in view of the country's economic plight, with millions of people near starvation, and in view of the continued blockade. Finally, they feared that the transport of the armies back to Germany and their demobilisation could not be carried out with the speed demanded by the Allies without the co-operation of an experienced General Staff—that is to say, without the very men who directly represented the régime against which the country had just revolted.

None of these fears was in itself quite unfounded. But no one has yet won a war or a revolution without taking risks. The dangers threatening a social revolution in post-war Germany were not greater than the dangers which threatened other revolutions. Moreover, by trying to by-pass these dangers, the Majority Socialists created other and far greater dangers than the ones they were trying to escape. Anxious to avoid a struggle that was inevitable, they gave their enemy the breathing space which he needed to recover his strength until such time when he could rise again and strike.

The Right Wing of the Independents disliked the practical consequences to which this policy led. But they did not quarrel with its general principles and were, in fact, more in agreement with the leadership of the Majority Social Democrats than with their own Left Wing.

The real opposition to this policy came from the Left-wing Independents, led by the *Revolutionäre Obleute*, and from the Spartakists. They were not satisfied with the overthrow of the autocratic Monarchy and the introduction of political democracy. They wanted more. They wanted a *social* revolution which would break the power not only of the Kaiser, but also of the generals; not only of the Prussian nobility, but also of all vested interests.

CHAPTER SIX

RATE OR PARLIAMENT?

A LONG and embittered struggle ensued between the Right and the Left of the movement which, in the end, led to bloody street fights. Yet, to all intents and purposes, this struggle had nothing to do with the one real issue then facing Germany, the transformation of the political into a social revolution. The struggle was fought over a constitutional issue—the question whether Germany was to be a parliamentary democracy or a *Räterepublik* (Government by Workers' and Soldiers' Councils).

The Left was in favour of the Council system, a form of representative government in which the representatives were elected not in geographical constituencies, but in factories, offices, farms and other places of work and only by those who lived on earned income.

The Majority Socialists were in favour of a parliamentary system based on proportional representation. They were violently opposed to the *Räte* system. They argued that the *Räte* were something foreign to German tradition and a mere imitation of the Russian Soviets. A *Räterepublik*, moreover, was in conflict with the principles of their old Party programme—which demanded parliamentary democracy—and would, so they thought, inevitably lead to civil war and to the establishment of dictatorship ruling by terror.

The Left were as attracted by the Russian example as the Right were horrified by it. But the *Räte* were not simply an imitation of the Russian Soviets. The German *Arbeiter und Soldatenräte* (the Workers' and Soldiers' Councils) were a spontaneous creation of the German Revolution, just as the Soviets had been a spontaneous creation of the Russian Revolution. They had not come into existence in response to foreign or sectarian propaganda, but as the natural *ad hoc* organisations of masses in revolt.

During the first days of the November Revolution, Workers' and Soldiers' Councils were elected in all workshops, mines, docks and barracks. The people were in motion. Wherever crowds assembled, they nominated spokesmen and elected delegates, who were to speak and act on their behalf as their direct representatives. This happened all over the country.

Indeed, the Revolution was not the work of any of the traditional organisations of the German working class, neither that of the Socialist parties and groups not that of the Trade Unions.

Even the *Revolutionäre Obleute*, who, in their own organisation, had anticipated something rather similar to the Workers' Councils (and who were, later on, to play a leading part in the Berlin Executive Committee of the Workers' and Soldiers' Councils), became active in the Revolution only after it had started elsewhere.[1]

This Revolution was supremely an *action directe*. Spontaneously, the masses formed Workers' and Soldiers' Councils as the instruments of their revolutionary will. During the earlier stages these Councils held all the power in their hands. The Berlin Workers' and Soldiers' Councils elected a Central Executive Committee, which, in turn, nominated the first Government of the German Republic, the so-called Government of the People's Commissars. This Government consisted of three Majority Socialists, Ebert, Scheidemann and Landsberg, and three Independent Socialists, Haase, Dittmann and Barth. The Executive Committee of the Berlin Workers' and Soldiers' Councils reserved for itself the right of control of the Government.

One important feature of the *Räte* system is the direct and permanent control of elector over deputy. The deputy can be deprived of his mandate at a moment's notice if and when he does not exercise it in accordance with the will of his electors. The *Räte* system is therefore an even more extreme and direct form of democracy than a parliamentary system. It is the very opposite of a dictatorship. It does not become a dictatorship, even if those living on unearned incomes are deprived of their right to vote, because this section of the population is numerically negligible. In every democracy certain sections of the populations are excluded from the franchise—the very young, for instance, or, until not so very long ago, women. If democracy means the rule of the majority it can, on principle, be exercised by *Räte* (or Soviets) just as well as by Parliament.

It is perhaps not unnatural that the *Räte* system and dictator-

[1] Many weeks before the Revolution broke out, the *Revolutionäre Obleute* had held secret meetings, discussing technical plans for an eventual rising down to the minutest detail. On November 2nd, 1918, after a heated debate, they decided that the Revolution was to begin on November 11th. However, history disregarded the plans they had so carefully prepared. The Revolution began, in fact, on November 3rd, with the Naval Mutiny in Kiel. Sailors', Soldiers' and Workers' Councils took control of the town. On November 6th, Sailors', Soldiers' and Workers' Councils were in power in Hamburg, Bremen and Lübeck. On November 7th and 8th, Dresden, Leipzig, Chemnitz, Magdeburg, Brunswick, Frankfurt, Cologne, Stuttgart, Nuremberg and Munich followed suit. In Berlin, however, which had been the centre of revolutionary propaganda and the place where the most careful preparations had been made, the Revolution did not begin before November 9th. According to the timetable of the *Revolutionäre Obleute*, even that was two days too early.

ship should have been so often confused. Such confusion arose, of course, from the common, if mistaken, comparison with Russia, where the Bolsheviks were, in fact, using the Soviets as a means to establish their Party dictatorship. However, without a centralist party, determined to take full control, a *Räte* or Soviet system might conceivably lead to anarchy, but certainly not to a dictatorship.

A political party willing or able to perform a rôle corresponding to that of the Bolsheviks in Russia did not exist in Germany. The *Spartakusbund*, which had the greatest sympathies for Lenin's achievement, was itself definitely not an organisation of this type. In fact so democratic was this organisation that on several important occasions the will of the rank and file triumphed over that of its leaders. Most of the leaders were firmly opposed to the idea of a dictatorship. Rosa Luxemburg, for instance, in spite of her boundless sympathy for the Russian October Revolution and for the aims of the Bolshevik Party, violently criticised the first symptoms of the Bolshevik dictatorship:

> "Freedom only for the followers of the Government, only for the members of a party—however numerous they may be—is not freedom. Freedom is always the freedom of those who think differently. . . .
>
> "With the suppression of political life in the country as a whole, life in the Soviets, too, will be suffocated. Without general elections, without unrestricted freedom of the Press and freedom of association, without the free battle of opinions, life in every public institution must wither away; it becomes a sham life in which bureaucracy remains the only active element. No one can escape this law. Public life gradually falls asleep. A dozen party leaders with an inexhaustible energy and boundless idealism direct and rule. . . . Not the dictatorship of the proletariat, but the dictatorship of a handful of politicians . . ."[1]

It is quite untrue, therefore, that the conflict over *Räte* or Parliament, which split the German working-class movement into two increasingly hostile camps, was identical with the struggle between the democrats and the advocates of dictatorship. Even those who clamoured for the "dictatorship of the proletariat" meant by this term nothing more or less than the "dictatorship of the working people over the idlers and exploiters"—*i.e.*, the substitution of the dictatorship of the overwhelming majority for the dictatorship of the privileged few, which makes the very word

[1] Rosa Luxemburg: *Die russische Revolution*; edited by Paul Levy (Paris 1939), pp. 46, 47.

"dictatorship" nonsensical and which is only another—and perhaps very unfortunate—expression for a democracy unhampered by privilege.

Nor had this conflict about *Räte* or Parliament anything to do with the social revolution which the Left wanted and which the Right feared. The Government, which the Berlin Workers' and Soldiers' Councils had put into power, did not wait for a parliamentary majority to govern and to make laws. Such decrees as the Government issued were exclusively concerned with questions of political liberty and certain social reforms, such as the introduction of the Eight-hour Day. This self-restraint had its reasons. But the reasons were certainly not constitutional ones. It was no more "constitutional" to issue these decrees than any others. The Government might just as well have decreed the expropriation of the large feudal estates in eastern Prussia (with or without compensation) and the distribution of the land among agricultural workers and small peasants; it might have decreed the nationalisation of the coal mines and of the big industrial and financial monopoly trusts; it might have taken all power from the hands of the old officer caste and the imperial generals and formed a reliable militia under the supervision of the Soldiers' Councils, whose task it would have been to demobilise the army and to protect the young Republic from its internal enemies.

Whether or not any of these things were done had nothing whatsoever to do with the constitutional issue *Räte* or Parliament. Yet, strangely enough, it was on this issue that all political discussion focused. The Majority Socialists insisted that general elections for a National Assembly should be held as quickly as possible and that no decisive steps must be taken in the meantime. The Left concentrated almost all its fire against this demand for general elections. Richard Müller, the leader of the *Revolutionäre Obleute* and Chairman of the Executive Committee of the Berlin Workers' and Soldiers' Councils, became generally known under the name of *"Leichen-Müller"* ("Corpse-Müller"), after he had exclaimed in the heat of a debate: "The way to the National Assembly leads over my dead body!"

There was a good reason, of course, why the Left agitated so furiously against the plan of immediately holding general elections. They felt instinctively that the Revolution and its positive results could only be safeguarded by those who had brought it about—the Workers' and Soldiers' Councils. They also felt that unless decisive steps were taken immediately to reduce and, if possible to liquidate, the material power of the old ruling classes, and to break up the anti-democratic State machine of the *ancien régime* they might never be taken at all, once the slow-moving machinery of parliamentary government had begun to operate. What the Left failed to understand was the fact that they could not hope to save the Revolution by the extremely unpopular and merely negative attack on the National Assembly. All they achieved was unholy confusion.

The majority of the German people who took an active part in the Revolution had revolted first and foremost against the continuation of the War. They had revolted against those responsible for the War; and they had revolted against feudal privileges and arbitrariness, against excessive exploitation and blatant social injustice. Instinctively, they chose as their symbol the Red Flag of Socialism. They did not do so because they were all convinced Socialists, but because here was the flag of a Party which, in the past, had stood for democracy and freedom, for peace and international co-operation, for social progress and justice for all.

Even the most militant sections of the working-class movement, which had led the great strikes during the War, were chiefly concerned with the political aims of the revolution, and very little with its social content. The slogans they had formulated on several occasions during the War were peace without annexation and indemnities and the immediate democratisation of the country.

"Democratisation" had always implied full parliamentary democracy. Parliamentary democracy had been the first demand of the Erfurt Programme of the Social Democratic Party of 1891. Even Friedrich Engels, in his critique of this Programme, did not suggest that this demand was wrong, but merely that it did not go far enough. For many decades, parliamentary democracy had been the unquestioned aim of the entire German Labour movement, from the extreme Right to the extreme Left.

It was, therefore, more than confusing for the workers when, after the Revolution, the Left Wing suddenly came out against this traditional ideal of German Labour. The workers might have understood and supported a policy which declared: "We have won our political revolution; we have ended the War and we have chased the Kaiser away. At last, we have established political liberty. But we can safeguard our victory only if, once and for all, we break the power of those who have been and will be the enemies of democracy, who have had and will continue to have a vested interest in war, who have been and will be the sworn enemies of social progress." Propaganda on these lines might have gripped the workers. It would have expressed what millions of them vaguely felt to be the truth. It was the truth.

The peculiar historical development of Germany had brought

about an alliance between the feudal landed aristocracy and its offspring, the Prussian Army, on the one hand, and the great industrial and financial magnates, on the other. This alliance was essentially anti-democratic, reactionary and aggressively imperialist. These numerically small groups, and their good servants among the German intelligentsia, held in their hands all the instruments of real power. They controlled the Army, the Police, the higher ranks of the Civil Service and the Judiciary. They controlled an essential part of agriculture and all important positions in industry, finance and commerce.

To leave all this concentrated power in the hands of a fundamentally anti-democratic and imperialist minority was tantamount to condemning the young democracy to utter impotence. In Germany, political democracy could not and never can function without a substantial minimum of social democracy. This point is most important. In fact, radical changes of her social structure were a necessity not only if full-fledged Socialism was the aim, but as a safeguard for political democracy.

What, then, were the most urgent social changes? First of all, the remaining power of Prussian feudalism had to be broken. To break it, its economic basis (the huge estates of the Prussian gentry) would have to be liquidated and the land distributed among the peasants. At the same time industrial feudalism would have to be attacked by nationalising the banks, the mines and the big industrial combines. The Civil Service would have to be "purged" so that trustworthy democrats could take the place of Monarchists and men of the *ancien régime*. Prussian officers and anti-republican judges would have to eliminated from positions of influence in the young democratic Republic.

This is not a complete list of the most urgent social changes. It is not intended to be one. But the crucial point is that the men of the Left, who demanded social changes of this sort, believed them to be incompatible with parliamentary democracy, and therefore opposed the parliamentary system with their demand for a *Räte* system. In point of fact, none of these social changes would have been incompatible with political democracy. On the contrary, they were the very prerequisites of a genuine democratisation of Germany. But this interdependence of political revolution and social change was never recognised.

The insistence of the Left on a *Räte* system and their hostility to parliamentary democracy were greatly influenced by the Russian experience. In Russia the Bolsheviks had fought the Duma and had become victorious under the slogan: "All power to the Soviets!" This slogan seemed to be the key to victory. The difference was that the Bolsheviks, in contrast to their German

48

would-be imitators, managed to conquer the majority of at least
the more important urban Soviets with a clear and simple policy
which expressed precisely what the mass of the Russian workers
and peasants then most urgently wanted—peace and land.
Without such a popular policy the Bolsheviks could never
have gained the support in the Soviets which they eventually
gained; and without a reasonable chance of gaining support in
the Soviets, their slogan "All power to the Soviets" would have
been quite senseless from their own point of view.

The reason for the Bolshevik success in this field was plain.
The Kerenski Government was determined to continue the War,
and it delayed the distribution of the land. The Russian Parliament backed Kerenski, if only half-heartedly. In Russia, therefore, the issue "Soviets versus Parliament" was not a semi-
academic squabble, but a political and social issue of the first
order.

In Germany, on the other hand, the whole passionate dispute
about the respective merits of *Räte* and Parliament had no reality.
It merely helped to confuse people's minds and to draw a veil over
all really important social and political issues of the moment.
The vast majority of workers and common soldiers who had
revolted against war and absolutism were convinced democrats
in the ordinary sense of the word. So were their representatives
in the Workers' and Soldiers' Councils.

The Left was therefore isolated as soon as it began agitating
against the National Assembly. The Majority Socialists, on the
other hand, calling for immediate general elections, won overwhelming support in the Workers' and Soldiers' Councils, particularly among the soldiers, who, after four years in the trenches,
desired nothing more urgently than to return to ordered and
peaceful conditions.

To the stupefaction of the Left, the Workers' and Soldiers'
Councils supported the plea for parliamentary elections, surrendered their own power and destroyed their *raison d'être*.

This happened at the first *Räte* Congress, which was held in
Berlin in December 1918, and to which the Workers' and Soldiers'
Councils from all over the country had sent delegates. Out of the
400 delegates present, only ninety-eight were in favour of a *Räte*
government. Four-fifths of the delegates favoured a parliamentary democracy. But that is not to say that the Congress
identified itself in other questions with the conservative policy of
the Majority Social Democrats.

CHAPTER SEVEN

WHOSE ARMY?

HAVING SUPPORTED the Majority Socialists with a clear vote in favour of the National Assembly, the *Räte* Congress showed its radical mood when the position of the German Army came up for debate. Almost unanimously, the Congress adopted a resolution on this question which the Hamburg delegate Lampl had moved. The resolution consisted of seven demands of which these four were the most important:

(1) As a symbol of the destruction of militarism and the principle of blind obedience (*Kadavergehorsam*), all badges of rank are to be removed, and no arms are to be carried by soldiers off duty.

(2) The Soldiers' Councils (*Soldatenräte*) are responsible for the reliability of the troops and for the maintenance of discipline. Superior ranks are not recognised outside the Service.

(3) The soldiers *elect* their leaders. Former officers who enjoy the confidence of their men may be re-elected.

(4) Speedy measures are to be taken for the abolition of the standing army and the constitution of a people's militia.

This resolution was passed practically unanimously; it was also made the occasion of a powerful demonstration by the Berlin workers and soldiers, who sent a special delegation to the Congress in support of these demands.

The passing of this resolution as well as of others demanding the immediate socialisation of a number of key industries clearly shows that the majority of the delegates wanted a great deal more than parliamentary elections, and there can be no doubt that their attitude represented the feeling in the country. But who was there to lead the country and to translate the radical mood of the people into a policy which was both radical and practical? There was no one. None of the existing organisations of the Left was able to give this lead. None could proclaim and carry out a programme of action responding to the mass longing for peace and to the universal readiness to accept even the most drastic social changes.

Those groups and individuals who were eager for radical changes isolated themselves from the majority of the people by their intransigeant hostility to parliamentary democracy. The others, who had won the adherence of the people, thanks to their propaganda for the National Assembly, were incapable of understanding that, in order to safeguard democracy, radical measures against its inherent enemies were inevitable. They would not see that the risk of temporary "chaos" and social unrest was much smaller than the danger threatening the young Republic from its foes within.

The resolution on militarism, adopted by the Reich Congress of the Workers' and Soldiers' Councils, was the first test case for democracy in Germany. The High Command, still undissolved and cautiously operating from Kassel, made its first stand. It refused to recognise the decision taken by the *Räte* Congress. General Gröner informed Ebert that he and the entire High Command would immediately resign if the Government insisted on carrying out these measures. Their attempt to kill the resolution was understandable. For, carried into practice, it would have meant the definite end of their power. A compromise between their wishes and those of the *Räte* Congress was impossible. It was up to the Government to lend its authority to the one or to the other.

The Congress of the Workers' and Soldiers' Councils, it should be remembered, was the highest political authority in Germany in the absence of a functioning Parliament. The Government had been nominated by the Workers' and Soldiers' Councils, and it was bound to abide by their decisions. Nevertheless, Ebert yielded to Gröner's blackmail. The resolution was never put into operation, and the German High Command was allowed, therefore, to win the day.

Whether Ebert and his supporters among the Majority Socialists gave in because they were scared of the "chaos" which might follow the resignation of the High Command, or whether they merely pretended approval of the Congress resolution from the beginning and never intended to carry it out, is an academic question. The Left have branded Ebert as an "arch-traitor", and if that term means that Ebert actively helped to prevent and stop the social revolution, which, in his own words, he "hated like sin", it is, no doubt, correct. But Ebert was not a traitor in the sense that he betrayed his own principles. His principles were moderately liberal-democratic. His instincts were ultra-conservative. His highest ideal in life was "order". He was convinced that order could be kept only by those accustomed to wield authority. He was the very opposite of a revolutionary, and he was naïve enough to believe that the High Command of the Imperial Army and the Prussian *Junker* caste might yet be converted into peaceful democrats, naïve enough to believe that, at any rate, they were "honourable gentlemen".

The co-operation between Ebert and the German High Command in the early days of the Revolution is an undisputed fact. But it should be remembered that it was not the Social Democratic Party, but Ebert and a few of his personal collaborators (most notorious among them Gustav Noske) who were solely responsible for this co-operation. The Party as a whole, even many of the Executive members, had no idea of the game that was being played. The resolution on militarism, adopted by the Congress of Workers' and Soldiers' Councils, clearly shows how differently the overwhelming majority of organised Labour thought about this question. Four-fifths of the delegates to the Congress were either organised Social Democrats or Social Democratic voters. Moreover, even as far as Ebert and Noske were concerned, it had presumably been their intention simply to use the militarists by co-operating with them. They had not meant to strengthen the High Command although that precisely was the result. They chose this way because they were blinded by their fear of civil war and what they called "Russian conditions".

CHAPTER EIGHT

FORCES OF COUNTER-REVOLUTION

THE FEAR of civil war was not completely unfounded, but it was vastly exaggerated. So overwhelming was the unity of the common people against war-mongers and war-profiteers, against the old ruling cliques and the militarists, that an attempt to organise counter-revolution would have been utterly hopeless, and without counter-revolutionary intervention there would be no civil war. Even so staunch a supporter of Ebert's conservative policy as Hermann Müller writes of the November days:

"Where were the forces of counter-revolution? The bourgeoisie stood to lose everything in a civil war; the Monarchists did not even dream of counter-revolution. They were glad that the Revolution had spared their lives."[1]

The Generals had lost effective control over the Army. It was not they who demobilised the soldiers; the soldiers demobilised themselves and simply went home. Only a very small number remained in the barracks, those who had no homes and those who could not get used to the idea of returning to a civilian life for which they had been spoiled by four years of war. The Generals fully realised that they had no army with which to organise counter-revolution. They knew they could do nothing but wait

[1] Hermann Müller-Franken: *Die Novemberrevolution* (Berlin 1928), p. 120.

and hope for "better times". In the meantime, they proclaimed their loyalty to the Republic and to the cause of democracy.

When, eighteen months later, Kapp made the first serious attempt at counter-revolution, it was broken without a civil war, by means of a general strike. In the winter of 1918–1919 the working class and its allies among other classes were hardly weaker than in the spring of 1920. The spectre of civil war was very largely a bogey.

Of course, there were forces on the Right who might have opposed, by armed intervention, any attempt to interfere with the privileges of their class. They were the sons of the Aristocracy, and of the upper middle class, of the officials in the higher Civil Service and of university professors; young men who had received their education in the *Kadettenanstalten*[1] or in the exclusive feudal student corps of the German universities.[2] They became the leaders of the notorious Free Corps formed after the war. They began their post-war career by fighting Bolshevism in the Baltic countries, supported, for a time at least, by the Allied Powers; they continued by fighting radical workers all over Germany and were responsible for an endless series of murders of men and women known for their Left-wing or anti-militarist views.[3] They became the nucleus of the Black Reichswehr of 1923, and after 1939 they were to be found among the leading men in Germany's war organisation. The thought of compromise was to them as unbearable as the thought of defeat, the idea of democracy as intolerable as the idea of peace.

They drew into their orbit some of the uprooted rabble that every war produces—men whom four years in the trenches had made unfit for peace, men who had neither a home nor a job to which to return, men who had learnt but three things in their lives: to kill, to obey and to observe the rules of a rough comradeship.

In a sense the German Free Corps were comparable to organised

[1] The *Kadettenanstalten* were special schools for future professional officers. Boys were accepted immediately after preparatory school, at the age of nine or ten, and educated in the spirit of Prussian militarism. School-leaving certificates of the *Kadettenanstalt* qualified the seventeen-year-olds for immediate entry into the army as officer-cadets.

[2] The German universities—in contrast to those of Britain and France—have always been conspicuous for the absence of any liberal or socialist radicalism. Insignificant minorities apart, teachers and students alike belonged either to the ultra-nationalistic Right or else to the completely non- and even anti-political type of ivory tower philosophers and unworldly scientists.

[3] Between January 1919 and July 1922 more than 350 political murders were registered. Among the better-known victims were Karl Liebknecht, Rosa Luxemburg, Kurt Eisner, Leo Jogiches, Mathias Erzberger and Walter Rathenau.

gangsterism in America, except that they were much more dangerous than the Al Capones of the new world because they were fanatical fighters for "ideals" which happened to be as great a menace to German democracy as to world peace.

In 1918–1919 these "gangsters with ideology" might possibly have offered armed resistance to any revolutionary steps. Undoubtedly they would have had the support of many individuals in high places, and would certainly not have lacked funds or arms. Yet, they could easily have been disarmed and suppressed by an energetic Government because, in such a case, the Government could have relied on the sympathy of practically the entire nation and on the active support of organised Labour.

Such a policy, however, could have been carried out only by a Government that was not afraid of invoking the initiative of the masses. It could have been carried out only by men who were not afraid of arming their own supporters, the working class. It could have been carried out only by men who felt themselves essentially at one with the desires of the mass of the people and who had sufficient confidence in themselves to know that they could guide a spontaneous movement from below and give it a clear purpose.

The Ebert Government was not of this type.

CHAPTER NINE

CIVIL WAR FOR LAW AND ORDER

THE EBERT Government consisted of men who were haunted by the fear of taking risks because they had never learnt to lead or to govern. There was no spark of imagination in any of their actions, no vision in any of their words. They were deeply afraid of not being able to fulfil their great task, and in their anxiety, they made a fetish of "law and order" at any price.[1] They forgot —or perhaps never understood—that revolution is a process in which the old "order" is replaced by a new one, and that to call for "law and order" in a revolutionary period before any of the essential changes have taken place is simply to call for the maintenance of the old order.

In Germany of 1918–1919 the problem was, therefore, not to establish an abstract order against an equally abstract chaos.

[1] Ebert's first "revolutionary" proclamation to the German people, dated November 9th, 1918, culminated in the appeal: "Fellow-citizens! I beg of you urgently: Stay away from the streets; see to it that there is law and order!"

54

The problem was whether a *new* order would be established or the old one re-established. In the first case, need it be said, the Government would have had to rely on the forces that made the Revolution, on the common people, who had elected the Workers' and Soldiers' Councils. It would have had to select reliable recruits for a people's militia and entrust them with the task of disarming the counter-revolutionary remnants of the *ancien régime* and of protecting the young Republic against all attacks from within.

The Ebert Government did not choose this course. Instead, it relied for the task of enforcing "order" on the worst enemy of German democracy, on reactionary officers and the Free Corps. What could have been more paradoxical and tragic than a situation in which a Social Democratic Workers' Government sanctioned the civil war of counter-revolution in order to avoid a civil war which might possibly break out as a result of radical social changes?

Formally, the officers and Free Corps were in the service of the Republican Government. In charge of these troops, since the end of December, was the Social Democratic Defence Minister Gustav Noske, who was soon to become one of the best hated men in Germany. It was Noske who ordered the officers to suppress, by main force, the so-called Spartakus Rebellion of January 1919.

This was not the first instance of an armed clash between Left-wing radicals and regular troops commanded by the old officers and called in by the Government. On December 23rd and 24th a regular battle took place between a group of mutinous sailors stationed in Berlin (the so-called *Volksmarinedivision*) and troops under the command of General Lequis whom the Government had called to its aid against the sailors. The immediate cause of the clash was entirely unpolitical, but the effect was highly political.

The radical workers of Berlin were embittered about the use of regular troops under the command of a notoriously reactionary General against the revolutionary sailors—whatever the original merits of the case. After this occurrence, the three Ministers of the Independent Socialist Party left the Government in protest. Right-wing Majority Socialists took their places, among them Noske. The gulf between the Right Wing and the Left Wing of the German Labour movement widened.

In January 1919 a civil war began in Germany, which was to make this gulf so deep that it could never again be bridged. It was a perverted civil war in which the Social Democratic Government summoned reactionary and anti-democratic officers to suppress radical workers—with the aim of making Germany safe for Democracy. It was in those days that Germany was made safe for the eventual victory of Adolf Hitler.

Throughout the month of December the country was flooded with a furious atrocity propaganda against the Spartakists in which the press of the Majority Socialists, particularly *der Vorwärts*, took an active part. Rosa Luxemburg, whose nobility of mind and deep humanity were no less outstanding than her brilliant intellectual gifts, was pictured as a wild bloodthirsty beast, and her comrades as a band of unscrupulous ruffians who specialised in murder, rape and arson. Huge posters appeared in the towns and villages of the country informing the people that the Spartakists wanted "to socialise women"; others demanded the assassination of the Spartakist leaders in so many words. One of these posters read:

Workers, Citizens!

The Fatherland is approaching ruin.

Save it!

It is not threatened from without, but from within:
By the Spartakus Group.

Kill their leaders!

Kill Liebknecht!

Then you will have peace, work and bread!

The Front Soldiers

Many, particularly soldiers returning from the front who had never heard of Liebknecht or the Spartakists and knew nothing of their views and records, were not unaffected by this propaganda. Nor were they surprised when, early in January, they learned that "Spartakus had started a bloody rebellion which aimed at throwing the country into chaos and anarchy".

The immediate occasion for the Spartakus Rebellion was the sudden and unprovoked dismissal of the Berlin Police President Emil Eichhorn, who was a member of the Independent Socialist Party. On January 4th the Prussian Minister of the Interior announced his dismissal and his replacement by the Right-wing Majority Socialist Eugen Ernst. Eichhorn refused to go. In this he had the support of the Executive of the Independent Party, of the *Revolutionäre Obleute* and of the newly founded Communist Party, the former Spartakus League. The three organisations combined in an appeal to the Berlin workers to demonstrate on

January 5th in protest against Eichhorn's dismissal. Hundreds of thousands responded to this appeal. In the course of the demonstration someone in the crowd suggested occupying the *Vorwärts* building. The suggestion was immediately acted upon. The occupation of other newspaper buildings followed. Years later, the official Investigation Committee of the Prussian Diet found that most of these newspaper buildings had been occupied on the suggestion of *agents provocateurs* or at least highly doubtful elements who had no connection whatever with the Spartakists. The column, for instance, which occupied the *Vorwärts* was led by the waiter Alfred Roland who was later unmasked as an *agent provocateur*.

No doubt these acts accorded well with the anger of the people, who had the memory of General Lequis' attack on the sailors still fresh in their minds, and were now newly infuriated by the dismissal of Eichhorn. And no doubt, among the people who stormed the *Vorwärts* building there was a large contingent of Spartakists who felt they had to square old accounts. But the action was neither planned nor prepared nor directed by the Spartakus League.

While the demonstrations took place and the newspaper buildings were occupied the Executive of the Independents, the *Revolutionäre Obleute* and the Communists met once again. Pressure for further and more energetic action came chiefly from some of the Independents and *Obleute* who belonged to Eichhorn's closest circle. After endless discussion it was eventually decided to make an attempt to overthrow the Ebert Government. Liebknecht and Pieck, the two Communist representatives, agreed, although such had not been the previous decision of their Party. A "Revolutionary Committee" was formed, headed by Georg Ledebour, Karl Liebknecht and Paul Scholze, which was to take over the new Government.

This Revolutionary Committee called the workers into the streets for another demonstration on January 6th. Once again huge masses followed the appeal, crowding the streets and waiting for a lead and direction. No such direction was given; because, in spite of the formation of the Revolutionary Committee, a rising had been planned by no one—except perhaps by those intent on crushing it. The men who had occupied the newspapers offices refused to accept the Government ultimatum to evacuate. It was their only tangible success; which they were determined to defend, if necessary with their lives.

On January 10th the attack against them was opened by the Regiment Potsdam led by Major von Stephani, later one of the leaders of the notorious *Stahlhelm* organisation. On January 11th

57

Noske came to his aid with a further contingent of troops collected from outside Berlin. On January 12th the battle was over. The surviving defenders evacuated the buildings they had occupied and surrendered.

There can be very little doubt that the Spartakus Rebellion was the work of the forces of counter-revolution as much as, if not more than it was the work of the Spartakists. In his testimony under oath (in the course of the so-called Munich *Dolchstoss* Trial of 1925) General Gröner gave this account of the preliminaries of the January battle: "On December 29th (*sic*) Ebert called Noske in order to lead the troops against Spartakus. On the 29th the voluntary formations assembled and now the battle could start."[1] And another German General, General Maercker, reported in his memoirs:

> "Already during the first days of January, a Conference had taken place in the building of the General Staff in Berlin between the leaders of the Free Corps about the details of the entry (*i.e.*, of the troops into Berlin) in which also Noske participated who had just returned from Kiel."[1]

The action, which was lost before it had begun, had not even the approval of the Spartakus leaders, although, out of sheer loyalty and solidarity, the leaders supported it once it had started.

The majority of organised Labour, even the radical sailors, remained neutral. However, after Noske had brought in the old officers and Free Corps men to fire on the rebels, ordinary men and women were outraged and ashamed, bitter and bewildered, and genuine sympathy went out to the Spartakus victims. Were not the Kaiser's officers and the Free Corps men the enemies of all workers? Three days after the end of the Berlin street fights the officer clique that had been called to protect German democracy carried out the well-planned double murder of Rosa Luxemburg and Karl Liebknecht.

During the following months one "punitive" expedition after the other was carried out. It began in Bremen, in February 1919, where Government troops occupied the town and by armed force removed the Workers' and Soldiers' Council. Similar actions followed in Bremerhaven and Cuxhaven. Then came the turn of Central Germany, where Government troops occupied one town after another, in many cases after heavy fighting. Many thousands were killed during street battles.

In Berlin fighting broke out again during March. The Communists and Independents had called a general strike for the

[1] Both these quotations are taken from Paul Froelich's *Rosa Luxemburg*, Paris 1939.

purpose of disarming the counter-revolutionary officers and in order to form a Workers' Militia. Troops were sent to the Capital. Noske, as Commander-in-Chief, issued his famous *"Schiessbefehl"* (the order to shoot at sight any person opposing or obstructing Government troops). In this one "expedition" alone over 1200 persons were killed, among them a group of twenty-nine sailors who had taken no part in the fighting. They were arbitrarily arrested and machine-gunned to a man by order of one Lieutenant Marloh.

It was during those days that Kammerherr Elard von Oldenburg-Januschau, one of the wealthiest landowners of Eastern Germany and a close friend of Field-Marshal von Hindenburg, made this comment in the conservative *Deutsche Tageszeitung*:

> "Well, and who is now protecting the Government and the Fatherland against Spartakus? The very same people whom the *Vorwärts* is accustomed to denounce as Junkers and the friends of the Junkers."[1]

Particularly violent actions were fought in the Ruhr district and in Brunswick. Finally, on May 1st, Munich was "liberated" by Government troops.

Since the beginning of the Revolution, Munich had been the centre of political drama. Bavaria had been the first German State to overthrow the monarchy. On November 7th Kurt Eisner proclaimed the Bavarian Republic in Munich. Eisner was a member of the Independent Socialist Party which commanded the allegiance of only a small minority among the people of Bavaria.[2] But Eisner's popularity went far beyond the members and supporters of his Party. Friends and foes recognised him as a man of rare idealism, utterly honest and unselfish. His energy was untiring, and he was a great orator who could kindle the flame of enthusiasm even in an indifferent audience. He became the unchallenged leader of Bavaria and, in contrast to the Berlin Government, he did not seek to suppress the Workers', Soldiers' and Peasants' Councils, which trusted him, but to govern with them and through them.

Bavaria was the only German State in which a section of the peasants made common cause with the workers and elected *Räte* to represent their interests in the new Republic.

The success of the Bavarian Government looked like becoming too dangerous to the forces of counter-revolution. On February

---

[1] Quoted from Freidrich Stampfer: *Die Vierzehn Jahre der ersten deutschen Republik*, p. 101.
[2] In the elections of January 12th, 1919, for the Bavarian Diet, the Independents gained only three out of 180 seats.

21st, 1919, Eisner was assassinated. His murderer was Count Arco, a fanatical nationalist student. The anger over this deed was deep and lasting among the Bavarian workers. Spontaneously they got together, armed themselves and decided once more to take the destiny of Bavaria into their own hands. But after the death of Eisner, they were without leadership. Men came to the head of the Bavarian *Räte* who were poets, artists, writers,[1] but not political leaders. They represented the small and noisy circle of Munich's artistic intelligentsia, but not the industrial workers, the peasants or any other important section of the common people.

On April 7th, under the impact of the newly formed Hungarian Soviet Government, they proclaimed Munich a *Räte* Republic. They proceeded to issue a number of fantastic and utopian decrees, with the result that they made the peasants their embittered enemies. After one single week this political adventure broke down.

The Communists had taken no part in this Munich *Räte* Republic, which they severely criticised as a childish game. But when it collapsed they, in turn, proclaimed their own *Räte* Republic in order to save the Revolution in Munich. After two weeks the Communist Government was overthrown by a majority decision of the *Räte* Congress. Ernst Toller became the leader of the third *Räte* government of Munich. It lasted a few days only.

On May 1st Government troops occupied Munich. Workers offered resistance. About 1000 people were killed during the battle. Between 100 and 200 revolutionaries were murdered, among them Gustav Landauer. The Communist leader, Eugen Leviné, was court-martialled and executed after a passionate speech of defiance which ended with these words, which became famous throughout the German working-class movement:

> "I have known for a long time that we Communists are but dead men on leave. It is up to you, gentlemen, to decide whether my ticket of leave will once more be extended or whether I must join Karl Liebknecht and Rosa Luxemburg. You may kill me—my ideas will live on."

What was the net result of it all?

Many thousands of German workers were killed, among them a great many who had never taken part in any rising. The working class was finally disarmed. The Workers' and Soldiers' Councils were reduced to impotence. On the other hand, there had come into being a powerful nucleus of a new German army, composed of the most ruthless and the most reactionary elements

[1] Outstanding among them were Gustav Landauer and Ernst Toller.

of the old Imperial Army. Tragic and paradoxical indeed, for it was all allowed to happen by men who, in their blind obsession with "law and order", had surrendered real power to their own mortal enemies, betraying their followers without intention to betray, and drifting along, while every outrage committed by the Free Corps soldiery so compromised the name of Social Democracy that the revolutionary minority of the working class could never again be reconciled.

One year later the Kapp *putsch* showed in a flash where this policy ended. Then Noske was swept from office by the anger of the working class. But much of the damage had already been done and no one could undo it. Yet, all along, for the ordinary rank-and-file member of the Social Democratic Party Noske was an exception, a sort of tumour that had to be cut out. The Party—that was something different. The Party—that was he himself and his colleague who worked on the same bench, his friend from the same tenement house who thought and felt like himself, who had built up this Party in the past and fought in its ranks and watched it growing stronger and stronger until, at last, it was at the head of the nation. To this Party, as they saw and knew it, most German workers, in particular most Trade Unionists, remained loyal, no matter how much they disliked this policy or that individual leader, no matter how acute their occasional disgust, no matter how deep and permanent their sense of frustration.

CHAPTER TEN

THE FIRST CONSTITUTIONAL GOVERNMENT

SHORTLY AFTER the Spartakus rising had been quelled and while the young Republic was having its first taste of armed suppression of revolutionary movements, the first democratic Parliament of Germany was elected revealing the extraordinary solidity of the Social Democratic vote. Elections for the National Assembly (which later resumed the name of "Reichstag") took place on January 19th, 1919.

The Majority Socialists polled eleven and a half million votes, the Independent Socialists slightly less than two and a half million. The Communists had decided to boycott the elections (against the advice of Rosa Luxemburg). Together the two Socialist Parties polled about 45 per cent. of all votes. Many

Catholic workers, voted for the Centre Party, which received almost six million votes. The newly formed Democratic Party (Left-wing Liberal) attracted almost as many. But the two nationalistic Right-wing parties, the (agrarian) German Nationalists and the (industrial) German People's Party polled together hardly 15 per cent. of the total vote.

The election result was an overwhelming victory for democracy.[1] But the Socialists did not gain that absolute majority which they had so confidently expected and which they might have got but for the deep fissure within their own ranks. The Independent Socialists declined an invitation of the Majority Socialists to enter the Government.

The Majority Social Democrats then approached the Democrats and the Centre with proposals for a coalition Government on condition that the two parties agreed (1) to give unreserved support to the Republic; (2) to co-operate in a policy of financial reform based, above all, on taxation of property and capital; and (3) to work out a programme of far-reaching social reforms, including the socialisation of "industries ripe for socialisation".

The two non-Socialist Parties accepted these conditions, including the programme of socialisation, although, at that time, they could hardly have realised that even this partial socialisation was to remain as pious and ineffective a wish as the often proposed democratisation of the Army or the agrarian reform in East Prussia.

All these measures could have been carried out even by the coalition Government which was formed with the Social Democrat, Philipp Scheidemann, as Premier.[2] It would not have been Socialism, but these measures would have provided some elementary safeguards for German democracy. Moreover, they would have had an immensely popular appeal not only to Socialists but equally to the vast number of people who had voted for the Democratic and Catholic Parties.

However, nothing of the sort was done. Once again, lack of self-confidence and fear of taking risks proved stronger than the reforming urge. The new Government feared "that precipitated experiments might destroy the last chance of saving the people from starvation".[3] They were afraid of economic sabotage by the

[1] Not only the votes for the two Socialist Parties, but also those for the Democratic Party and most of the votes for the Centre Party (which included the Christian Trade Unions) were, at that time, a clear and unmistakable demonstration in favour of democracy.

[2] Four months later Scheidemann resigned in order to escape the responsibility for signing the Peace Treaty. His successor was his Party colleague Gustav Bauer.

[3] Friedrich Stampfer: *op. cit.*, p. 74.

big capitalists and the feudal landowners; they doubted that they could find a sufficient number of "experts" for a democratic administration and sufficiently energetic Republicans for a democratic defence force. On the other hand, they appeared to have a rather exaggerated confidence in the perfect Constitution and in the automatic effectiveness of a well-paragraphed charter of democratic rights and duties. Naïvely, they hoped that somehow everything would turn out well once "order" had been established and the Weimar Constitution had become the law of the land.

CHAPTER ELEVEN

THE PEACE TREATY

GERMAN SOCIAL Democracy can rightly claim that its difficult task was made considerably more difficult by the political and economic effects of the Treaty of Versailles. It is, of course, very important to distinguish between the actual repercussion of the Treaty and the legends which National Socialist propaganda has since created.

There was probably not a single person in Germany, at that time, who did not feel that the Treaty of Versailles was a great injustice. I cannot do better than quote R. T. Clark's description of German reactions to the Peace Treaty:

". . . Nations, even minor nations, do not take kindly to a confession of transgression against someone else's conception of a non-existent international morality. . . . Out of the bloody welter and chaos of the war the righteous judges proposed to create now the new moral order by whose non-existent laws Germany was judged. . . . Germany was to remain pilloried to eternity as the one great and horrible example and from that new order the new revolutionary Germany was to be barred as a moral leper. . . .

"It was, therefore, natural that Germany should be stunned not merely by the terms of the Treaty, but also by the manner of their presentation and the method of their justification. It was not surprising that the Germans should be indignant at the failure to realise that there had already been conversion. Dismiss the German urge to democracy as one will, the fact remains that the German nation had got rid of the autocracy—it was the fact not the manner that weighed with the German—that it had repented of war madness, that it had established a demo-

63

cratic régime. To the best minds of Germany the establishment of democracy was much more than a mere change of régime . . . to them it meant that Germany had abandoned her historic position of an Imperial power in Europe; she had severed age-long ties and had come voluntarily to join the Western democracies. They felt that in some peculiar way the revolution, such as it was, was a demonstration of the solidarity of the West and its civilisation, and instead it had afforded a reason for something which . . . was quite rationally described as making permanent a long schism on the ground that there was no reason to believe that it had been healed. That was a verdict that no thinking German could accept. . . .

"What worse terms could have been submitted to Wilhelm? It was the new order which had bade the nation put its trust in the Fourteen Points and the Allied profession of devotion to democracy and the right of self-determination. What worse terms could an old-fashioned autocratic imperialism have dictated? . . . (The Germans) were now asked to admit that Germany, the new Germany, the democratic Germany and every individual German in it, including the unborn, was bloodguilty of an outrage on humanity and was not worthy to associate with civilised men. In all its exaggeration of bitterness, in all its outraged romanticism, the indignation was natural and it provoked a graver crisis, moral and material, than even the days of November had done."[1]

Yet, in spite of this universal indignation, there was only a very small minority in favour of refusing signature to the Treaty. So great was the desire for peace that it overshadowed all other feelings and considerations. Strange though it may sound, the decision to sign the Treaty was one of the most democratic decisions ever taken by a German Government and was based on the consent of the overwhelming majority of the nation. This consent was quite genuine, but it was no more than the unavoidable acceptance of a *fait accompli*. Consent was given because it could not be refused without once more going to war. Faced by this alternative Germany decided to sign. But she signed grudgingly.

It was this grudge or rather the memory of it which later on made it so easy for Hitler to convince millions of Germans that the "November Traitors" (the Labour leaders and those who sided with them in the November Revolution) had actually "betrayed" the German nation and had acted against its will when they signed the Treaty of Versailles.

It was the same grudge which, after the outbreak of the second

[1] *The Fall of the German Republic* (London 1935), pp. 60 ff.

World War, led a number of observers in Allied countries to the equally wrong conclusion that German Social Democracy had played a dishonest double game and that, while paying lip-service to the idea of international co-operation, it was, in its feelings and its actions, as nationalistic and "latently aggressive" as the Nazis. To suggest this is a sign either of complete ignorance or of deliberate misrepresentation. No German with an iota of natural patriotic feelings could possibly have welcomed the Treaty of Versailles. No Social Democrat, no Trade Unionist did. But never for one moment had German Social Democracy intended anything but a peaceful revision of the Treaty. In that it found itself in complete agreement with the entire Labour and Socialist International,[1] while the Communist International was agreed that the Versailles Treaty was at least as unjust—if not more so—as the Treaty of Brest-Litovsk.[2]

In nothing was German Social Democracy more in earnest than in its desire to come to a lasting understanding with the Western democracies. To make Germany a democracy on the Western pattern—only more perfectly so—had been the one great aim of the internal struggle which the Social Democratic Party had carried on against its opponents on the Right and on the Left. To achieve an alliance with the Western democracies had been the one aim of its foreign policy.

The "policy of fulfilment" which internationally became associated with the name of Stresemann was, in reality, the policy of Social Democracy. To this "policy of fulfilment" and the co-operation with Stresemann in foreign affairs the Social Democratic Party sacrificed much of its independence and freedom of action in home affairs and hence, indirectly, a great deal of its popularity. Social Democracy has richly deserved much of the criticism directed against it; the Party may rightly be accused of its childish faith in the good-will of German reaction, of lack of boldness and foresight. But it cannot be accused, with justification, of having failed to attempt peaceful international co-operation.

[1] At Whitsun 1923 the Hamburg Congress of the Labour and Socialist International adopted a resolution to that effect.

[2] In the course of a speech on the Russo-Polish War of 1920, Lenin, for instance, said: "You know that the Allied imperialists—France, England, America and Japan—concluded the Versailles Treaty after the destruction of Germany, which, at any rate, is incomparably more brutal than the notorious Treaty of Brest which caused such an uproar." (Lenin: *Reden und Aufsätze über den Krieg*, II. Berlin, 1926.)

CHAPTER TWELVE

INDUSTRIAL DEMOCRACY

THE DEMOCRATIC concept of peaceful international co-operation on a basis of equality had its exact parallel in internal politics where Social Democracy, at least for some time, favoured a policy of class collaboration—also on a basis of "equality". The Party leaders realised, of course, that no such thing as social equality existed in Germany. They hoped to achieve it by strengthening the collective power of the workers, *i.e.*, the power of the Trade Unions whose weight and influence they sought to increase. This had been the traditional and hitherto successful method of Labour policy, hampered only by the restrictive legislation of the Kaiser-Reich. As the Revolution removed these restrictions, the road to unlimited progress seemed open at last.

One of the first actions taken after the Revolution was, therefore, the establishment of the so-called *Arbeitsgemeinschaft* following an agreement which the Trade Unions and the Employers' Associations concluded on November 15th, 1918. This November Agreement—as it came to be known—was based on the unconditional recognition of the Trade Unions as "the official representative of the working class". The employers agreed to withdraw their support from company unions. Furthermore, the Agreement laid down that:

(1) all demobilised workers are entitled to return to their former working places;

(2) all working conditions are to be regulated by means of collective bargaining;

(3) all collective agreements must contain provisions for arbitration in case of conflict;

(4) in every enterprise employing 50 or more workers, a shop steward committee is to be set up to represent the employees;

(5) the maximum working day in all factories is to be eight hours;

(6) a National Committee consisting of an equal number of workers' and employers' representatives is to be set up for the purpose of "jointly solving all economic and social questions in trade and industry".

The Trade Union leadership celebrated this November Agreement as a great triumph of trade unionism. As they saw it, they had at last achieved what they had been struggling for in the past.

Suddenly the employers seemed only too eager to give whole-hearted support to principles which, in the old days, they had fought with utmost vigour; harmony between capital and labour seemed at last established on the basis of Labour's demand.

The November Agreement was backed up by State legislation. By Government decree the Eight Hour Day became law on November 23rd, 1918. Another decree, of the same date, established that written wage agreements should be legally binding and, in certain cases, universally binding for whole industries. Yet another decree of the same date dealt with the functions of the Arbitration Boards. It authorised the Arbitration Boards to declare their awards binding even after they had been rejected by both parties concerned. Apart from that, this decree drastically curtailed the employers' "power of the sack", limiting their rights to dismiss workers to cases in which full employment could not be maintained even by the introduction of shorter hours.

The Social Democratic Ministers who issued these decrees must have been convinced that the task of fixing working conditions was best left to negotiations between employers and workers. No doubt they expected the newly won freedom of the Trade Unions to create a sufficiently strong counterweight to the established power of capital which would enable employers and workers to arrive at a working compromise. State intervention was reserved for emergency cases; the Trade Union leaders felt confident that such State intervention would, on the whole, only be needed in exceptional cases of obstruction by particularly unreasonable employers.

It did not occur to them then that State intervention might be used to compel the workers to comply with the wishes of employers. For, to them, the State that had emerged in November 1918 was *their* State. In the past only the workers had stood against autocracy. Did it not follow that democracy, once it had come, was bound to be *their* democracy? Democracy had been the workers' goal. The victory of democracy therefore was the workers' victory. Almost by definition, the democratic State could not conceivably go against the workers' interests. At the very worst, the State would be a neutral power representing the national as against sectional interests. But since the working class formed by far the largest section of the nation, its own interests and the interests of the country as a whole could not possibly clash in any serious question.

Such was the reasoning on the Labour side that led to the "November Agreement", and to the Government decrees.

The more radical sections of the working-class movement sharply opposed this policy and the ideas on which it was based.

67

They attacked the November Agreement between Trade Unions and Employers' Associations as bitterly as they had attacked the co-operation of Ebert and Noske with the officers of the old Imperial Army. This attack on the policy of class collaboration was again linked with attacks on the principles of parliamentary democracy. On this issue too the Left regarded the *Räte* system as the one cure against all evil.

The Trade Unions opposed the *Räte* idea for the same reasons as the Majority Socialists. They were convinced democrats and, in their opinion, a *Räte* system was the surest way to a dictatorship. But opposition on general grounds quite apart, the Unions had reasons of their own for their hostility to the *Räte* idea. During the November days the Trade Unions had somehow been pushed into the background. Completely new organisations had sprung up—the Workers' and Soldiers' Councils—which almost seemed to make the Unions superfluous. Moreover, Workers' Councils had even been founded in areas where the Unions had hitherto been quite unable to set up or expand their own branches. That was particularly so in the Halle and the Ruhr area, and some of these new bodies were extremely radical. In fact, there seemed to be a danger that the Workers' Councils might eventually take the place of the Unions.[1] Faced with this danger, the Union leaders decided not to fight the Workers' and Soldiers' Councils outright (this policy would have been too unpopular), but to reduce them to shop steward committees with strictly limited functions. The idea was that the shop steward committees should closely co-operate with and be guided and controlled by the Unions.

With this policy the Unions had complete success. Gradually the Workers' and Soldiers' Councils made room for Works' Councils, *i.e.*, shop steward committees. Their tasks were indeed strictly limited and their aspirations very much more modest than those of the original Workers' Councils. Nevertheless the shop steward committees were to exercise some important functions.

An Act of Parliament of February 11th, 1920, the *Betriebsräte-*

[1] Only an insignificant syndicalist minority within the German Labour Movement actually propagated the replacement of both the Unions and the Socialist Parties by Workers' Councils. One of the few German syndicalists, Fritz Wolffheim, wrote in a pamphlet entitled *Factory Organisation or Trade Union?*:

"The Trade Unions are interested in the daily economic struggle. The old Social Democratic Party is interested in parliamentary politics. A struggle, however, which is revolutionary and both economic and political can be led only by the masses themselves; and they can lead it only with the aid of organisations which they create for the purpose of this struggle." (Quoted from Richard Seidel: *Die Gewerkschaften in der Revolution*, pp. 28–29.)

gesetz—defined the rights and duties of the Works Councils. They were to be elected in all factories with more than fifty employees. One of their tasks was to work out the factory rules jointly with the employers. Furthermore, they were to supervise the observance of all collective agreements, of the factory rules and of precautionary measures against accidents, etc. The Works Councils had a limited right of veto against the dismissal of individual workers and could sue the employer for reinstatement or damage if the dismissal was not withdrawn. Members of the Works Councils themselves could not be dismissed.

The Unions considered the Works Councils an important link in the machinery which they hoped to set up for the introduction of industrial democracy. They thought of industrial democracy chiefly in terms of institutions closely parallel to the parliamentary system of political democracy. Indeed, in the early debates on the functions of the Works Councils, the phrase "factory parliamentarism" was frequently used. Industrial democracy was to be achieved by democratic compromises in all stages. All that was needed, in the opinion of the Unions, was a suitable machinery of which the Works Councils were to be the beginning. Apart from them, there were to be regional organisations and, at the top, a National Economic Council. At the insistence of the Unions, Article 165 which made provisions for such a machinery was incorporated into the Weimar Constitution.

Industrial democracy based on parity between employers and workers remained a wishdream—to the great disappointment of the Trade Union leaders and others who thought like them. There was not and there could not be parity—except in numbers. Of course, the power of the Trade Unions had tremendously increased. But the power of capital had increased equally.

As a counterweight against Trade Union organisations the employers had set up their own employers' associations. At the same time competitive capitalism developed rapidly into monopoly capitalism. After a transitory period of increased Trade Union power, the unequal nineteenth-century struggle between the individual worker and the individual employer was reproduced, on a higher level, in the twentieth-century struggle, no less unequal, between organised labour and organised capital.

The German Trade Union leaders acted like a general who develops his plan of campaign on the basis of obsolete facts about the enemies' strength and strategy. Neither the Unions nor the Social Democrats dared to interfere with the power of monopoly capital for fear of causing economic chaos, and since the tremendous material power of German monopoly capital had in no way been curtailed, it remained as superior to organised labour as the individual factory owner had been *vis-à-vis* the unorganised labourer. In these circumstances industrial democracy became a hollow phrase and the machinery set up for it was condemned to rot.

It is true, a provisional National Economic Council was created in accordance with the Constitution. But the regional organisations were never formed and the National Council remained an advisory body whose advice no one ever heeded.

Of the whole machinery of "industrial democracy" only the Works Councils had some measure of importance. This importance, however, was a strictly limited one. The Works Councils could make themselves heard regarding questions of working conditions in individual factories, but they never had the least influence on production policy or on any important question connected with the general economic development of the country.

Many German workers felt that the Works Councils were but a poor substitute for the Workers' Councils they had formed during the first days of the Revolution. There was strong rank-and-file support for the attack which the Independent Socialists and the Communists made on this replacement of Workers' Councils by Works Councils. The two Parties organised demonstrations in protest against the Works Councils Bill (*Betriebsrätegesetz*) that was about to be passed by the National Assembly. Many tens of thousands Berlin workers followed their call and marched to the Reichstag Building. The police became nervous and opened fire on the unarmed demonstrators. Forty-two of them were killed. Once again workers' blood was shed for the sake of preserving "law and order" This happened on January 13th, 1920.

PART THREE

YEARS OF CRISIS
1920–1923

CHAPTER THIRTEEN

THE KAPP *PUTSCH*

KAPP'S ATTEMPT of March 1920 to overthrow the democratic Republic by a *coup d'état* ended in a fiasco. His defeat was a greater victory for the German working class than the November Revolution itself had been.

On March 13th, 1920, the Ehrhardt Brigade [1] staged a march on Berlin in order to establish a military dictatorship. The leader of this rebel force was Wolfgang Kapp, one of the war-time founders of the "Fatherland Party". The Government fled from Berlin, first to Dresden and then to Stuttgart. In this first case of real emergency the Republican Government discovered to its dismay that there were no troops on which it could rely. The *Reichswehr* officers on whom Noske had been able to rely against radical workers were not prepared to move a finger against a rebellion from the Right.

The Trade Unions and the Social Democratic Party appealed to the nation to defend the democratic Republic, and called a general strike. This appeal was signed, among others, by the Social Democratic members of the Government.

A Government call for a general strike is in itself something unique. The issue of such an appeal was particularly strange for a Government which had incessantly warned against strikes and which had constantly intervened, by main force, against direct action by the working people. The main initiative for the general strike did not, however, come from the Government, but from the Trade Unions. Its direction lay chiefly in the hands of the aged Trade Union leader Carl Legien, who organised the action from a hide-out in a cellar of Berlin. The Majority Socialists co-operated with Legien. The Independent Socialists and the Democratic Party immediately joined the movement. The Communist

---

[1] The Ehrhardt Brigade consisted of a detachment of marines stationed in Doberitz. Most of the officers and men had taken an active part in the anti-Bolshevik campaign in the Baltic countries.

Party joined in with one day's delay, after an initial show of "neutrality".

On the first day of the *putsch* the Communist Party had issued a leaflet in which it prophesied that the workers "will not move a finger for the democratic Republic", but that they would fight against militarism when they considered the moment favourable and, so the leaflet concluded, "this moment has not yet come".[1]

The Communists were mistaken. While their leaflet was being distributed the general strike was already paralysing the country. On the following day the Communists adapted their policy to the accomplished fact and officially joined the strike movement. The German working class had risen as one man. A considerable number of civil servants, even many of the higher ranks, took part in the strike. Against such resistance the Kapp *putsch* was bound to fail. It collapsed after four days. On March 17th the Ehrhardt Brigade evacuated Berlin.

Never before and never after was the solidarity of the common people of Germany as great as it was during the Kapp days. Never before and never after had they so great a chance to rid themselves, once and for all, of the powers of reaction and aggression and to lay the foundations for a living democracy. This chance they forfeited.

In a sense, the Communists had been right when they doubted that the German workers would rise to defend the Bauer–Noske Government. Indeed, the workers did not rise in defence of this Government. They rose to ward off the danger of a military dictatorship. Their first demand, after their victory, was for the immediate removal from office of Noske and of two other Ministers, Heine and Schiffer, who had become notorious for their cooperation with the militarists. This demand came not only from the Left, but from the entire working-class movement, whose spokesmen sat on the Central Strike Committee under the leadership of the Right-wing Trade Unionist Carl Legien.

After the defeat of Kapp, the Strike Committee called a meeting with representatives of the Government parties. A number of demands were formulated and accepted by the Government parties. The most important of these demands were: (1) the formation of a new Government in which the Unions were to have a decisive influence; (2) severe punishment for the instigators of the rebellion and the participants in it; (3) a thorough purge of the Army; (4) a thorough purge of the Civil Service and (5) the socialisation of all "industries ripe for socialisation". After the acceptance of these and some other demands the strike was officially called off.

[1] M. J. Braun: *Die Lehren des Kapp Putsches* (Leipzig, 1920), p. 8.

The sort of Government which the Strike Committee wanted was very different from the Coalition Government then in office. It was to be a real Workers' Government, composed exclusively of representatives of organised Labour—the Majority Social Democrats, the Independent Socialists, the Free and the Christian Trade Unions. Nothing came of this plan because the Independents, under the pressure of their Left Wing led by Däumig, refused to co-operate with the Majority Socialists. They even refused to do so after the enforced resignation of the Prime Minister, Bauer, the Defence Minister, Noske, and the Prussian Minister for Home Affairs, Wolfgang Heine. Following this refusal, the Majority Socialists formed another Coalition Government of the old type, with Hermann Müller as the new Premier.

The nation was deeply disappointed. It had not struck against Kapp for a mere return to the *status quo ante*. After the first successes of the Revolution the political situation had steadily degenerated. Already in June 1919, at the Weimar Conference of the Social Democratic Party, Rudolf Wissel (then Minister of Trade) had described the frustration and the disappointment of the masses.

"In spite of the Revolution"—he said—"the hopes of the people have been disappointed. The Government has not lived up to the expectations of the people. We have constructed a formal political democracy. . . . The masses are angry and we did not satisfy them because we had no proper programme. . . . Essentially, we have governed in the old ways and we have not been very successful in creating a new spirit. . . . The people believe that the achievements of the Revolution are of a merely negative character; they believe, that only the persons who exercise military and bureaucratic power have been exchanged and that the present principles of government do not fundamentally differ from those of the old régime. . . ." [1]

These warning words had been spoken in June 1919—nine months before the Kapp *putsch*. In those nine months anger grew more intense and frustration more deadly. Much was happening: the lower middle classes were hit hard by the beginning of inflation; the workers struggled to adapt their wages to the rising prices. Strike movements flared up everywhere.

At the same time, Stinnes and other industrial magnates prospered as never before. At the stock exchanges the little jobbers and the big investors were running amok. Giant enterprises were bought, sold, re-sold and amalgamated. The Socialisation Com-

[1] Quoted from Arthur Rosenberg: *Geschichte der deutschen Republik* (Karlsbad, 1935), p. 105.

mittee, created to work out plans for the nationalisation of the mining and other industries, had died an inglorious death and dissolved itself. The politics of 1919–1920, right up to the Kapp *putsch*, had been equally squalid and depressing. The punitive expeditions of the Free Corps and the *Reichswehr* against radical workers had created a bitter and lasting hatred between the workers and the armed forces.

The professional character of the German Army and its isolation from the rest of the nation enabled the *Reichswehr* to preserve its militarist tradition and to develop into a small but highly efficient State within the State, led by men whose single-mindedness made them fanatics, but whose intelligence bade them wait their time. In 1920 they sympathised with Kapp as later, in 1923, they sympathised with Hitler. But their sense of realism was too highly developed to be easily tempted. They were careful not to gamble away their chances. They waited patiently, and they proclaimed their political "neutrality" while maintaining secret contacts with the Free Corps and, later, with the "Black" *Reichswehr* and with all the numerous conspiratorial organisations which organised the *Fehme* murders and prepared the way for Hitler.

These contacts remained well camouflaged. The German public heard occasional rumours, but had no real knowledge of what was going on. This, however, did not lessen working-class suspicion of the Army, and nothing created greater dismay among workers than the co-operation of "their" Government with the Generals.

Then suddenly things appeared to change. The call to strike against Kapp and his mercenaries at last ended the deadly frustration. Four days of action—four days of new hope; until it was stifled in a grievous anti-climax: another coalition Government of the old type.

Worse still, in one part of Germany, in Bavaria, counter-revolution had actually been victorious. While the Ehrhardt Brigade was occupying Berlin, a number of officers, led by General von Möhl, enforced the resignation of Johannes Hoffmann, the Social Democratic Premier of Bavaria. In Bavaria the rebel officers succeeded in gaining the support of all non-socialist parties. Herr von Kahr became their new Prime Minister, and from that time until Hitler's victory Bavaria remained the refuge and breeding-ground of all counter-revolutionary elements.

The opposite development had taken place in the Ruhr and Rhine areas and in some of the industrial districts of Central Germany. There, particularly in the Ruhr, the workers succeeded in arming themselves, and their Red Brigades drove the Free Corps and *Reichswehr* troops out of the district. A united front of all socialist parties and Free Trade Unions was formed. Encouraged by their military success and by unity so suddenly achieved, the men felt that the time had come for that second revolution which would make Germany socialist.

Meanwhile Kapp had been defeated. The Government had returned to Berlin on March 20th, and two days later Noske resigned. The general strike had officially been called off on the 23rd. Many of the Ruhr workers, however, were determined not to lay down their arms without having achieved more than the formation of yet another Coalition Government of essentially the same type as the previous one.

The Government decided to send the Socialist leader and former leader of the Berlin metal workers, Karl Severing, to negotiate with the representatives of the Ruhr workers. Severing's negotiations ended with an armistice, the so-called Bielefeld Agreement of March 24th. The main points of this Armistice Agreement were: (1) the immediate release of all prisoners, and (2) the disarmament and dissolution of the Red Brigades. For the rest, the Bielefeld Agreement was virtually a replica of the demands which earlier on had been put forward by the Central Strike Committee as a condition for calling off the anti-Kapp strike.[1] However, the Bielefeld Agreement remained a scrap of paper. Fighting went on in the Ruhr area while the Agreement was being negotiated and continued after its conclusion.

Two days later, on March 26th, the Bauer Government resigned, to be replaced on the following day by a new Coalition Government under the Social Democrat Chancellor, Hermann Müller. The Hermann Müller Cabinet decided to send *Reichswehr* troops against the Ruhr rebels. The troops which three weeks earlier had refused to protect the Republican Government against Kapp now went into action without hesitation. The Ruhr rebellion was suppressed with much brutality. Hundreds of workers were killed in action while hundreds more were stood against the wall and shot.

Once again "order" had been re-established in Germany. But the prestige of the Government and of the Parties that supported it had sunk very low indeed. Against Kapp and his soldiery the Government could rely only on the working class, because the Army would not defend it. Against the radical workers, however, the Government relied on this very Army while, at the same time, Kapp's opposite number in Bavaria was allowed to establish a dictatorial régime that refused to recognise the authority of the Reich Government.

In these circumstances it was not surprising that the Govern-

[1] Cf., p. 72.

ment parties suffered a crushing defeat in the General Election held three months after the Kapp *putsch*. The Social Democratic vote dropped from 11·5 million (in January 1919) to 5·6 million. The Democratic Party lost proportionally even more. Its vote dropped from 5·6 million to 2·2 million. The Centre Party vote decreased from 5·9 to 3·5 million.[1]

The Independent Socialists, on the other hand, more than doubled their vote, which went up from 2·3 million (in 1919) to 4·9 million. The Communists, who took part in the elections for the first time, polled less than half a million votes. Altogether the working-class vote had dropped from 13·4 to 11 million, but this drop was less striking than the clear swing to the Left within the Labour movement and an even greater swing to the Right in the *bourgeois* camp. The two Right-wing parties, the German People's Party (the party of big business) and the German National Party (the party of big landowners), together polled 7·3 million votes as against 4·5 million in 1919.

This tremendous shift in public opinion was the direct result of the Kapp *putsch* and of the patent inability of the moderate Government parties to find an adequate solution for any of Germany's problems.

Ever since then Germany has been split into two irreconcilable camps with interests so fundamentally opposed that a genuine democratic compromise between them became impossible. The traditional enemies of democracy on the Right were strengthened by the support of millions of middle-class men and women who in 1918–1919 had been willing to give democracy a trial, but who had been deeply disappointed by its failure to provide solutions for the country's problems in general and the problems of their class in particular.

The disappointment within the working classes was no less acute. Democracy, which had been their one great aim and hope, had freed them neither from the militarists nor from economic insecurity and social injustice. But these were the things that counted most in their daily lives. Gradually, therefore, democracy became something which the mass of the workers regarded with growing indifference, and a minority even with hostility. For, as they experienced it, democracy had failed them.

[1] The Centre Party loss looks bigger than it really was, for, in the meantime, a separate Catholic Party had been founded in Bavaria, the Bavarian People's Party, which refused to take part in the Coalition Government, and closely co-operated with the ultra-right forces that ruled Bavaria.

CHAPTER FOURTEEN

THE COMMUNIST PARTY

D URING THE hectic years that followed the Kapp *putsch* changes of great importance took place within the working-class movement. The general swing towards the Left expressed itself, first of all, in the great increase of votes for the Independent Socialists. During the decisive days of the Kapp *putsch*, and immediately after, the Independents had in fact failed just as dismally as the Majority Socialists. At the time their own failure was less conspicuous because they had no share of Governmental responsibility; but in a sense their responsibility was even greater. Their stubborn and self-righteous refusal to co-operate with the Majority Socialists prevented the formation of the Workers' Government which Legien had proposed and which might yet have changed the course of Germany's development.

As a result, disunity, which had always existed in the ranks of the Independent Socialists, increased further. The Communists sensed the big chance which this disunity gave them and seized it eagerly.

In accordance with a decision of their Leipzig Party Conference of 1919, the Independents had sent a delegation to the Second World Congress of the Comintern in order to discuss affiliation to the Third International. The Comintern wanted to win the rank and file of the Independents, but not their leaders, who were regarded as incurable "opportunists"; nor did the Comintern intend to grant affiliation to a party which insisted on retaining some measure of independence.

To achieve its purpose, the Comintern formulated eighteen conditions for the affiliation of the Independent Socialist Party to the Third International. These conditions were designed to attract the rank and file, but to make acceptance impossible for the leadership of the Party. To the utter consternation of the Communists, the leaders of the Independents, who had come to Moscow to negotiate, were prepared to accept all eighteen conditions. Hastily three more conditions were added which served the purpose. One of these conditions demanded the expulsion of "notorious opportunists" such as Kautsky, Hilferding and other outstanding leaders. Another condition demanded the break with the "Yellow Amsterdam International" (the International Federation of Trade Unions).[1] These conditions were indeed un-

[1] Because of this particular demand, many prominent Trade Unionists within the Independent Party who had been in favour of affiliation to the Comintern changed their minds.

acceptable to the leaders of the Independents. Thus, the immediate purpose of the "Twenty-One Points"—under which name the final version of the Comintern conditions became known in the Communist movement—was achieved—the splitting of the Independent Party. The actual split occurred in October 1920, at the Halle Conference of the Independent Socialists. After a dramatic speech by the Comintern President, Zinoviev, the majority of the Conference decided to accept the "Twenty-One Points" and to leave the Independent Party in order to join the Communists. Rather sadly, the minority tried for some time to maintain a precarious independent existence, until, in 1922, it rejoined the Majority Socialists.

One fact stands out: after the Halle Conference of the Independent Socialists, the Communist Party suddenly emerged as a mass party, and although it still represented only a minority of the organised Labour movement it was, from that moment on, a political factor that had to be taken into account.

Within this young Communist Party there was endless passionate discussion on the right way to victory, the right means to choose, the right moment to strike. There were violent struggles between warring factions within the Party which caused expulsions, resignations and frequent changes of leadership.

After the assassination of Liebknecht and Luxemburg, Paul Levy, one of Rosa Luxemburg's disciples and closest collaborators and, at that time, undoubtedly the ablest man in the Communist Party, had come to its head. At his insistence, the ultra-Left Wing of the Party was expelled. And it was chiefly due to his efforts that the majority of the Independents decided to join the Communists. Shortly afterwards, however, in February 1921, Levy resigned from the leadership of the Party on account of a conflict with the Comintern over questions concerning the Italian Labour movement.

Under its new leadership, the Communist Party decided to do away with "opportunism" once and for all. The German Communists were only too conscious of the fact that they, too, had failed to make political capital of the defeat of the Kapp rebellion. But at that time they had been only a small organisation with very little influence in the country. Now, after the affiliation of the majority of the Independents, they had become a big party, with a membership approaching half a million. They were convinced, moreover, that they had every chance of winning the support of the majority of the Labour movement in view of the fact that the masses of the workers were so obviously disappointed with the policy of the Social Democrats.

This expectation was not at all unjustified. The social catastrophe which inflation and the Ruhr struggle was to bring to the common people—working and middle classes alike—caused not only despair, but a torrent of radicalism. With a realistic policy, based on actual conditions in Germany, the Communists might well have become the strongest, if not *the* working-class party.

Their policy was, however, as little suited to the needs and wishes of the German workers as that of the Social Democrats. The Communists seemed to be possessed by an unhappy genius inducing them to work out theories and stratagems which were in almost every case impracticable when put to the test and invariably in flagrant contrast to the actual conditions and to the prevailing mood of the people.

The Communists understood well enough that Labour's fundamental mistake during the Kapp rebellion had been its failure to follow up its defensive victory with offensive action. But the lesson they drew was not that this mistake had to be avoided in a similar situation in the future; instead they produced a general theory proclaiming that defensive actions as such are futile and that, on principle, "the proletariat must take the offensive". What was worse, they acted in accordance with that theory at a moment most unsuitable for "offensive action".

In March 1921, when the Communists attempted to translate their new theories into practice, the working class had not yet recovered from the depression that followed the Kapp rebellion. The inflation was in its early stages, and, on balance, the forces of reaction were stronger after the Kapp *putsch* than they had been before.

Nevertheless, the Communists decided to "act". A local conflict in Mansfeld provided the desired opportunity. What followed was the famous *Märzaktion* ("March Action"), without doubt one of the most pathetic chapters in the history of the German Labour movement.

Hörsing, the Social Democratic District Governor, dispatched police troops to Mansfeld with orders to occupy the mines so as to prevent thefts of coal by the miners.

In itself, this incident may have been of little importance. But here is a classic example of the gulf between Social Democrats and Communists—an incident that goes a long way to explain the tragic fratricidal hatred that destroyed the German Labour movement long before Hitler delivered the *coup de grâce*.

Whether or not an occasional sack of coal had been stolen by a Mansfeld miner is completely beside the point. Hörsing's decision to reinforce the local police had political motives. The

Mansfeld miners were extremely radical and strongly under Communist influence. What could have been more provocative for a Social Democratic Governor like Horsing than to allege that the radicalised workers were nothing but common thieves? Hörsing was asking for trouble, and trouble he was to get.

The miners were outraged by this act and refused to work as criminal suspects under police supervision. They rose in arms. Their leader was Max Hölz, the only really romantic figure in the German working-class movement. Of politics Max Hölz was utterly innocent. He was a born *condottiere* with a social conscience and the temperament of a rebel fighting for the poor and oppressed. Later he joined the Communist Party, although he fitted into that party of scientific Socialism and Bolshevik discipline about as well as Robin Hood or his German equivalent, the Schinderhannes, would have done.

To the Mansfeld miners and the wretchedly poor inhabitants of that area, Max Hölz became an almost legendary figure. The battles they fought under his leadership remained a local affair, although they were bloody enough. The workers in the rest of the country vaguely sympathised with the Mansfeld miners. They did not feel, though, that this local revolt against the police affected them.

The Communists simply refused to take any notice of this attitude. They went about "acting", and proclaimed a general strike. They called the workers to rise in arms in support of the Mansfeld miners. The workers of the neighbouring Leuna Works followed the call and occupied the plant. They were driven out and defeated after a bitter and bloody battle. In Hamburg, too, Communist workers occupied the docks, but were soon defeated. The non-Communist workers remained unmoved by the Communist appeal. In some parts of the country it even came to fights between unemployed Communists trying to enforce the general strike and employed workers who refused to down tools for a hopeless cause.

Hundreds of faithful Communists were killed in this abortive rebellion. Thousands were thrown into prison for their participation in the fights. And that was the end of the "March Action".

In a foreword to a famous pamphlet in which he bitterly attacked this *putsch*, Paul Levy wrote a few days after its end:

"When I drafted this pamphlet, there existed in Germany a Communist Party of 500,000 members. Eight days later, when I wrote it, this Communist Party was shaken to its foundations. Its very existence was in balance." [1]

[1] Paul Levy: *Unser Weg wider den Putschismus* (Berlin, 1921), p. 3.

Actually the Communists lost almost two-thirds of their members, who turned their backs on a party which so frivolously played with the cause of revolution. Paul Levy was expelled, although Lenin and the Comintern leadership approved in substance of his criticism. What they would neither tolerate nor forgive was the fact that Levy had publicised a Communist family quarrel when he wrote his pamphlet. Many of the ablest party officers thereafter broke with the Communists.

Even those who remained could not very well help understanding that their "offensive strategy" had suffered a crushing defeat. They learnt their lesson, but again in the same abstract fashion which was so characteristic of their way of thinking. "Offensive strategy" was thrown overboard. The Party reversed its policy. But it reversed it so thoroughly and so completely that, in the Summer of 1923, when a chance for decisive action really offered itself—the last chance—the Communists failed for exactly the opposite reason.[1]

CHAPTER FIFTEEN

INFLATION AND RUHR STRUGGLE

AFTER ITS failure to turn the defeat of Kapp into victory for its own cause the Labour movement had lost the greatest opportunity of its history. Its enemies eagerly seized this chance of strengthening their hold on the country. In July 1920 a new Cabinet had been formed, with Fehrenbach of the Catholic Centre Party as Premier, in which none of the working-class parties was represented, although the Majority Socialists (despite their losses) had remained the strongest single party in Parliament and although the working-class parties together had polled more than 42 per cent. of all votes.

The change-over from a governing coalition party to a party in opposition was, of course, not in itself a sign of weakness. On the

[1] A complete change of tactics was decided on at the Third World Congress of the Comintern, which met in 1921 shortly after the catastrophe of the German Communists. For Russia, too, a great turn had come. The civil war and the period of "War Communism" was over. A policy of compromise had been inaugurated with the introduction of the NEP and the attempts to find some mode of living with the Capitalist countries of Europe. Rapallo followed soon afterwards. The Communist Parties of Europe, too, had to attempt a new policy of compromise and collaboration. The new tactics were those of a united front wth Social Democrats and the Trade Unions, and the new slogan was "Towards the masses!"

contrary, with a strong and clear policy the Socialists might have recovered in opposition some of the strength they had lost while in office. During that period, however, the real struggle was fought, not inside, but outside Parliament, and the offensive was taken, not by Labour, but by the Military, on the one hand, and big business, on the other. The instrument of the former was murder, that of the latter inflation; and both of them combined to confuse the country with a flood of nationalistic demagogy which was well timed to coincide with the genuine and universal despair over the exorbitant reparation demands and the subsequent occupation of the Ruhr by the French.

It has been frequently suggested that Germany deliberately staged the inflation in order to escape reparation payments. If the word Germany in this context is to stand for the majority of the German people, or the parties representing this majority, this allegation is absurd. The effect of the inflation on the German people, with the exception of a numerically small group of inflation profiteers, was so devastating that only a lunatic could suggest that they deliberately supported attempts to engineer it; nor is it justified to say that the German Government did so.

The charge against the Government would be true if they had deliberately printed banknotes and increased the currency circulation in order to cause a rise in prices. But this is not what happened, at least not before November 1922, when the inflation had already proceeded very far. One of the most objective surveys of what actually took place is contained in a book written by the American economist, James W. Angell, and published by the U.S. Council of Foreign Relations:

"At the time of the inflation and afterwards, many foreigners asserted that the German Government was deliberately depreciating the currency in order to bring about a crash and thus checkmate the Allied efforts to extract reparation payments. That particular charge which rests on a survival of war-psychology is unproved and untrue, but in other respects the German Government was not free from blame. . . .

". . . In every case the first thing that happened was a renewed depreciation of the foreign exchanges followed closely by an almost equivalent rise in internal prices and more slowly by wages. . . . The increase in the currency circulation and in the floating debt of the Reich followed only more gradually and was primarily a result rather than a cause. In no case did the increase in the volume of the currency *precede* the rise in prices and the exchanges; and to that extent the German Government must be exonerated. The successive waves of exchange depreciation in turn were due in the first instance to adverse political events. . . . In the last analysis, however, these events taken together were themselves the product of the fundamental contradiction between the two great aims of the Allies, security and reparation. Complete security entailed crushing Germany's military and economic power, but a crushed Germany could not and did not pay Reparations. The German foreign exchanges were jammed between these two millstones, and the value of the Mark was ground in dust. . . ." [1]

It should be added that there was not one, but three different Governments in office during the inflation period, and while all three certainly failed to stop the inflation, only the last of the three—the Cuno Government—can be accused with justification of having deliberately and actively aggravated the inflation. It did so, as will be seen further below, as the direct instrument and in the interest of that small circle of Ruhr industrialists who, in contrast to the people and the Governments of the earlier period, had indeed a vested interest in the inflation which they sought to promote for their own ends.

However, the inflation was not the beginning, but rather the climax of a struggle which the representatives of big business had fought against the ascending power of Labour ever since the Revolution. As soon as they saw that the new régime did not dare to interfere seriously with their vested interests, they went over to the attack.

The first contest was fought out in the so-called "Socialisation Commission". In March 1919 the National Assembly had passed an Act empowering the Government to nationalise, by special legislation, "all industries ripe for socialisation", especially the mining industry. On the same day a law was enacted which placed the entire coal industry under the control of the newly created National Coal Council. The National Coal Council was composed of representatives of the Trade Unions, the Employers' Associations, consumers' organisations (Co-operative Societies, etc.), and the State. This was of course not nationalisation. All the same, the employers were afraid of precedents and bitterly objected even to this partial and very ineffective attempt at public control. A "Socialisation Commission" was set up to investigate details. In its composition the Socialisation Commission closely resembled the National Coal Council. One months later the Commission resigned because its members were unable to agree on a single point. The Trade Union conception of "industrial

[1] James W. Angell: *The Recovery of Germany.* Yale University Press, 1929, pp. 26, 28–29.

democracy" based on "parity" had suffered its first severe shock.

After the defeat of the Kapp *putsch* a second Socialisation Commission was appointed at the request of the Unions. This second Commission achieved no more than the first. The conflict between the employers' views and those of the workers was so sharp that it made compromise impossible. In November 1920 the Commission published the so-called "Essen Memorandum on the Socialisation of the Coal Mines". The Memorandum represented, however, the views of only half the Commission—the views of the employers. The workers' delegates [1] had refused to sign it, because it explained in detail why socialisation was both impracticable and inadvisable. And that was the end of the second Socialisation Commission.

Surely this was a remarkable victory which big business had thus achieved over the Trade Unions—exactly two years after the November Revolution. But Stinnes and, indeed, the overwhelming majority of the big industrialists were far from satisfied with merely having warded off the danger of socialisation. The ease with which this victory had been won only encouraged them to continue their offensive against Trade Unionism and against the social achievements of the Revolution.

In December 1921 the railwaymen had asked for an increase of wages. When the Government [2] refused, the railwaymen went on strike. The Unions achieved a compromise which failed to satisfy the men, and so the strike was continued in many districts without Union sanction. At the same time another unauthorised strike broke out among the Berlin gas, water and electricity workers. The Government called in the *TENO* ("Technical Emergency Squads") in order to maintain a skeleton service. [3] In point of fact, the *TENO* was an organisation of strike-breakers, similar to the American Pinkerton group. Most of their members were ultra-Right-wing students, young engineers and former Army officers. Naturally the Unions had always regarded this organisation as a "gang of blacklegs".

The fact that the Government made use of *TENO* services during a strike which the Unions themselves had refused to sanction

[1] The workers' delegates were Werner of the A.D.G.B. (the German T.U.C.), Wagner of the (Socialist) Miners' Union and Imbusch of the Christian Trade Unions. The employers' delegates on the Commission were Stinnes, Vögler and Silverberg.

[2] German railways were State property; as employees of the Government the railwaymen had therefore the status of civil servants.

[3] The *TENO*, which was formed during the Revolution, claimed to be a strictly non-political body of men who were pledged to volunteer in any national emergency in order to maintain transport and essential services.

created for the Unions a most difficult situation. They understood very well that their own position was endangered once such a precedent had been created.

The Eleventh Trade Union Congress, which met in Leipzig in June 1922, therefore unanimously adopted a resolution condemning the use of *TENO* squads.[1] However, the *TENO* was not abolished. In later years it was often used to break the organised resistance of Labour.

The *TENO* resolution was only one of several important decisions taken by the Eleventh Trade Union Congress. Another concerned the form of Trade Union organisation. A resolution moved by the Independent Socialist Dissmann proposed an all-round replacement of craft Unions by industrial Unions. In Germany, as in Britain, industrial Unions had developed side by side with craft Unions. While the concentration of capital was rapidly progressing, leading to the formation of giant trusts, German Trade Unions found themselves at a definite disadvantage when a number of different Unions had to negotiate with a single and single-minded employers' representative. Dissmann's resolution, which called for large and strong Unions, covering entire industries including all related branches, met therefore with general approval. It was adopted by a large majority. An amendment proposing that craft Unions were immediately to be dissolved and amalgamated (with or without the approval of their members) was defeated. But in fact craft Unions soon lost all influence.

A third and equally important resolution demanded the withdrawal of the Unions from the November Agreement with the Employers' Associations. The resolution was adopted by the majority of the delegates present; but, as it turned out, the minority of the delegates represented a slightly greater number of members. Whether or not the resolution had been carried was never settled at the Conference. It was settled soon afterwards by unilateral action on the part of the Employers' Associations.

The Conference debate on the November Agreement was dramatically interrupted when news reached the delegates of the assassination of Germany's Foreign Minister, Dr. Walter Rath-

[1] The resolution read:

"This Congress regards the *TENO* as a danger to the efforts of organised Labour, particularly if it is used to interfere in industrial conflicts. Recent experience has shown that this organisation is developing more and more into an organisation of strike-breakers. This Congress therefore declares its hostility to the *TENO* and protests energetically against the use of public funds for the maintenance of this institution. Moreover, this Congress holds that any connection with the *TENO* is incompatible with Trade Union membership."

enau. Here was a rude reminder that a great deal of political house-cleaning had to be done before Labour could dream of industrial democracy.

Rathenau had been anything but a Socialist. But he was generally respected in the Labour movement for the sincerity of his democratic views and the genuineness of his conversion from a one-time imperialist to a man who earnestly worked for a real and lasting understanding between Germany and her former enemies. The news of his assassination brought once more all the rival factions of the German working class together, just as the Kapp *putsch* had done. Joint protest demonstrations of all working-class parties and Trade Unions were organised. The Unions and the three Socialist parties sent a joint appeal to Parliament, demanding a Bill for the Protection of the Republic which would ensure energetic punishment for this and for similar crimes. They further demanded (a) effective suppression of the military leagues which had organised most of the political murders, (b) a thorough purge of the Civil Service, the Army and the Law Courts of all anti-republican elements and (c) an immediate amnesty for all political prisoners, with the exception of those who would stand guilty under the terms of the new Bill.

A Bill on these lines was in fact passed by Parliament; but its effect was small. The chief reason for its ineffectiveness was the political bias of practically all higher judges, who had been taken over from the old régime. Their undisguised discrimination between Right-wing and Left-wing offenders was a notorious feature of the Weimar Republic. It caused many public scandals and roused bitter comment, but nothing was ever done against it.

To give a few striking examples: of Karl Liebknecht's murderers and their accomplices one was sentenced to three months' imprisonment, another to a small fine. The rest were found "not guilty", although their guilt had been clearly established. Of Rosa Luxemburg's murderers one was allowed to escape, another was sentenced to two years' imprisonment and the rest went scot-free. The murderers of Jogisches and Dorrenbach were never tried, although their identity was known. Lieutenant Marloh, who had twenty-eight innocent sailors shot in cold blood, was sentenced to three months' *Festung* ("honourable confinement"). Most of the Kapp rebels went scot-free. Yet thousands of workers who had been involved in the fights in the Ruhr and in Central Germany were sentenced to extremely long terms of imprisonment and hard labour.

In his book *Vier Jahre politischer Mord*, E. J. Gumbel published the following figures, covering the period between January 1919 and June 1922:

	POLITICAL MURDERS COMMITTED BY PERSONS BELONGING TO THE	
	RIGHT	LEFT
Number of political murders committed	354	22
Number of persons sentenced for these murders	24	38
Death sentences	—	10
Confessed assassins found "Not Guilty"	23	—
Political assassins subsequently promoted in the Army	3	—
Average length of prison term per murder	four months	fifteen years
Average fine per murder	two marks	—

After the Rathenau murder it looked as though the democratic and Republican forces in Germany were once more drawing together and gaining new strength. It was not a Socialist, but the Catholic Premier, Dr. Wirth,[1] who exclaimed in the Reichstag: "The enemy stands on the Right".

The days of Wirth and his democratic coalition were, however, numbered. The dual attack that brought his fall was led by Poincaré, on the one hand, and by Stinnes and his associates, on the other. The latter considered that the moment had come for an open attack on the social achievements of the November Revolution. Their first and chief target was the Eight Hour Day.

In October 1922, when inflation was racing towards its climax, Fritz Thyssen addressed an open letter to Dr. Wirth, in which he stated that "Germany's salvation can only come from a return to the Ten Hour Working Day". A fortnight later Hugo Stinnes made a speech in the National Economic Council, in which he said:

"I do not hesitate to say that I am convinced that the German people will have to work two extra hours per day for the next ten or fifteen years. . . . The preliminary condition for any successful stabilisation is, in my opinion, that wage struggles and strikes be excluded for a long period. . . . We must have the courage to say to the people: 'For the present and for some time to come you will have to work overtime without overtime payment.'"

[1] Dr. Wirth had been in office since May 10th, 1921. He headed a Coalition Government composed of the Centre, the Social Democratic and the Democratic Parties.

This speech was made on the fourth anniversary of the German Revolution. The irony which lay in the choice of the date merely underlined the new self-confidence of Stinnes and the few magnates of heavy industry who were well on the way to regain that absolute mastery which the Revolution had kept in check for some time. Just a word should be said about the ominous Dr. Hugo Stinnes. To gauge the political effect of Stinnes' Ninth of November Speech it is not enough to remember that of Germany's great industrial magnates, Hugo Stinnes was by far the most powerful. More important is the fact that his name had become a German by-word for inflation profiteering. Quite apart from his calculated challenge to the Labour movement, any public statement of Hugo Stinnes' was nothing short of a deliberate provocation in a situation in which practically the entire nation was on the verge of starvation.

The inflation had devoured all small savings and had reduced the real income of all wage- and salary-earners, of pensioners and rentiers to a level far below the red line of the officially recognised minimum of existence. Wage and salary increases were granted only after terrific struggles.[1] But even such increases as were granted still remained far behind the rapid rise in prices. In such a situation to ask for "wage struggles and strikes to be excluded for a long period" was tantamount to asking for a permanent reduction of the standard of living to a starvation level.

The Trade Unions argued that this policy was short-sighted even from a capitalist point of view, because the steady fall in consumption would eventually also lead to an all-round fall in production and profits. In the prevailing circumstances, this argument was a fallacy, because Stinnes and his associates did not depend on the home market. They produced almost entirely for export. The cheap labour they employed, thanks to inflation, enabled them to compete successfully on foreign markets. The export profits were invested in stable foreign currencies which would not depreciate in value. Early in 1923 the flight of capital from Germany was estimated to have surpassed the amount of one milliard gold Mark. The mounting profits from export dumping gave the industrialists vested interest in postponing the stabilisation of the Mark as long as possible. Unscrupulously they pursued the narrowest interests of their class; and they cleverly exploited the national indignation over the Reparation demands by persuading the country that the misery of inflation was solely due to the Reparation payments.

They were quite right in maintaining that Germany was in-

[1] 1922 was the year with the maximum number of strikes ever. 1·6 million workers were involved in 4338 strikes.

88

capable of fulfilling all the economic obligations imposed on her by the Allies and that complete fulfilment would bring permanent economic ruin not only to Germany, but in the end also to Europe and the world at large. They were wrong, or rather, they deliberately misrepresented the situation, in maintaining that Reparations alone were responsible for the inflation.

This type of propaganda, based on half-truth rather than outright lies (which Hitler, later on, was to perfect to a real art), had the success it was intended to have. It utterly confused the people. It confused, in particular, the working class, which became less and less certain as to who was responsible for their growing misery—Stinnes or Poincaré.

The Stinnes clique soon lost all restraint. The National Association of German Industrialists offered a loan to the State, which, owing to the inflation, was unable to find funds for its most urgent expenditure. The offer was made on the condition that the State Railways and all other State-owned enterprises were to be handed over to private owners. The Trade Unions furiously protested against this "attempted blackmail" and successfully prevented the conclusion of the deal. The employers, in the meantime, continued their attack on the Eight Hour Day and stubbornly refused to adapt wages to the rising level of prices. Social tension almost reached breaking point.

Tension was also growing between Germany and the Allies. It seemed that no solution could be found for the problem of Reparations. One fruitless international meeting followed another. The Allies remained adamant in their demands, while the German delegates insisted that, even with the best will in the world, Germany could not fulfil her obligations.

This aggravated conflict gave the German Right a welcome opportunity to deflect to other objects the anger of the masses against inflation profiteers and political assassins. The enemy—that was France, and the cause of all misery was her mercilessness and her greed. Stinnes and other Ruhr industrialists did their best to sharpen the Franco-German dispute while resisting vigorously the popular clamour for the stabilisation of the currency.

Their business prospered as never before while the nation was starving and the State was facing bankruptcy. In the end they achieved what they had set out to obtain—a Government that was a pawn in their game. Wirth was overthrown. A new Cabinet was formed with Wilhelm Cuno, director of the Hamburg-Amerika Line, as Prime Minister.

Not quite two months after the formation of the Cuno Government the French occupied the Ruhr. The German Government called for passive resistance. For a short period it looked as though the deep national anger roused by the occupation had swept all other feelings aside; it looked as though once more an *union sacrée* had emerged in Germany. That was exactly what Stinnes and his clique had wanted. But their triumph was only apparent.

The indignation over the Ruhr occupation was universal; but domestic social and political conflicts had not disappeared. On the contrary, they became sharper during the Ruhr struggle and as a result of it.

The Ruhr industrialists organised a series of demonstrations against the French. But most of the workers soon refused to take part in these demonstrations, although many of them would willingly have responded to a call for a general strike against the French, had this call been issued by the Unions. The Communists agitated for a general strike, but without the support of the Unions they were unable to organise it. The Unions and the Social Democrats opposed the general strike as they had pledged themselves to avoid everything that would further sharpen the conflict with the French.

Very soon it became clear that the nationalistic propaganda of the Ruhr industrialists and their supporters in other parts of the Reich had anything but patriotic motives. The louder they shouted for national resistance against the French the less were they prepared to take even a small share of the sacrifice involved in this resistance. They wanted to rule, but the sacrifice was to be made by the common people. They protested indignantly against demands for increased wages, increased benefits or increased taxes on higher incomes, denouncing such demands as "unpatriotic" and "egotistic"; but they saw to it that the prices of their own products soared and that their own profits increased steadily. They found it quite in order that miners' real wages dropped to one-third of their peace-time wages, whereas the price of coal (calculated in stable currency) was twice as high as the peace-time price.

An ugly mood was growing in the mining and steel towns of the Ruhr. The people had become cynical and debunked about the Thyssen and Krupp brand of patriotism. Of course they wanted to get rid of French occupation and publicly demanded the withdrawal of the foreign troops. But with equal urgency huge workers' meetings were clamouring for immediate stabilisation of the currency by means of a compulsory gold loan. Private property should be mortgaged for the purpose of Reparation payments. And, finally, they demanded the overthrow of the Cuno Government.

The struggle which had begun as national resistance against the French ended in a period of the fiercest class war that Germany had ever experienced. In May 1923 great spontaneous strike movements took place, in the course of which the workers again called for the replacement of Cuno's Cabinet by a Government that would take energetic measures against economic chaos. By then inflation had caused such misery and turmoil that, by comparison, the French occupation appeared as a minor problem.

Already in April, a conference of the Miners' Union had asked for the end of passive resistance. The Social Democratic Party [1] supported this demand. In those days, however, the influence of the Social Democrats and the Trade Unions was waning. Although membership of the Unions was larger than ever before, the inflation had robbed them of all funds with which to support their members, to finance strikes or even to pay their officials. Moreover, normal Trade Union activity had become quite impossible in a situation in which nominal wages and salaries had lost all meaning.

The Social Democrats approached the Cuno Government and entered into negotiations, suggesting a number of financial reforms. Above all, they asked for measures by which wages and salaries could be brought up to and kept level with the soaring prices of all commodities. Most of these demands were perfectly sensible, though not nearly far-reaching enough to put an end to the inflation. At that moment, however, the relative merit of this or that proposal was a matter of no interest to the man in the street. What did matter was the fact that the Social Democrats negotiated with the Cuno Government instead of fighting it unconditionally, for the people were in a fighting mood. The situation had driven them to despair. They were no longer in the mood for parliamentary niceties or negotiations with a Government which allowed these frightful conditions to develop unchecked.

In those days masses of German workers turned their backs on the Social Democratic Party and followed the Communists. There are no figures available to show the extent of this shift. But many who took an active part in the working-class movement of that time have testified to the fact. That was the heyday of the German Communist Party. Masses of radicalised Social Democrats and Trade Unionists flocked to that Party in the hope of being led out of economic and political chaos. The Communist failure of March 1921 was forgotten. Then, the Communist rising

[1] By then the Social Democratic Party also included the remnants of the former Independent Socialist Party which, after the assassination of Rathenau, had amalgamated with the Social Democrats.

had been an irresponsible action of isolated groups of insurrectionists. In 1923 a situation had developed in Germany in which "anything was possible". In 1923 the people—and by no means only the industrial working class—had become insurrectionist and the time had really come for that "offensive strategy" which two years previously had failed so miserably. The situation had changed decidedly.

But the Communist Party, too, had changed. Unluckily its change had worked in exactly the opposite direction. For fear of repeating the "ultra-left" mistakes of 1921, the Communists had reversed their policy so thoroughly that they were quite incapable of taking action when the time for action came at last.

Many individual Communists, of course, played a prominent part in countless strikes and hunger revolts which broke out all over Germany during the summer months. But so did many Social Democrats and Trade Unionists. In no way did the Communists lead or organise the movement. Like others, they merely took part in it. As a Party, they, no less than the Social Democrats, were left behind by the spontaneous initiative and violent intensity of that mass movement, and, as a consequence, that movement remained without direction and leadership, and therefore purely negative.

On August 11th, 1923, the spontaneous popular movement culminated in a general strike which began in Berlin, and from there spread over the country like wild fire. The aim of the strike was simple: the overthrow of the Cuno Government, which had become the symbol of everything that was hateful to German workers. It was held responsible for the devastating inflation, which it did not even attempt to check. It was regarded as the agency of big business, which prospered as never before as a result of that inflation. It had tolerated the terror, the violence and the political assassinations by members of the military leagues and the Black *Reichswehr*. It had bungled all chances of coming to an understanding with the French. On August 12th the Cuno Government was overthrown as a result of the general strike. The strike became known as the "Cuno strike".

Next to the strike against the Kapp rebellion the Cuno strike was far the biggest and most successful mass action ever undertaken by the German working class. There were important differences, however, between the two strikes. In March 1920 German workers had responded to the joint appeal of their Unions and parties. In August 1923 no such appeal had been issued, either by the Unions or by any of the working-class parties. The Cuno strike was entirely spontaneous, and as such it was a unique action in the history of the German Labour movement. Shop stewards and local workers' representatives took the initiative and led the movement. The parties began to realise what was happening only after this movement of the masses had created an accomplished fact. All this had important consequences. The movement exhausted and spent itself once it had achieved the maximum that spontaneous and unguided action of this kind could possibly achieve—*i.e.*, the resignation of the Government. To exploit this success for more positive and constructive ends would have been the task of the political working-class parties. None of the existing parties was up to this task.

The Communist leaders went to Moscow in order to decide there whether or not Germany was ripe for a revolution. It took them seven weeks to arrive at a decision. Meanwhile, the leaderless Communist Party did exactly nothing.

The Social Democrats decided to join Stresemann in yet another Coalition Government. Admittedly it had not been an easy decision for the Social Democrats to join a Cabinet under the leadership of Stresemann. Whatever his personal merits, Stresemann was one of the leading men of the German People's Party, the Party of Stinnes and Vögler, the reactionary big business party *par excellence*.

The only other alternative, however, was even less acceptable to the Social Democrats such as they were. For in that situation the choice was not between joining yet another Coalition and parliamentary opposition. Conditions had become far too chaotic for any opposition to be limited to speech-making in the Reichstag and shepherding the loyal flock into the division lobbies. In the prevailing situation, opposition could not have stopped short of a real struggle for power. For this the Social Democrats were not prepared. In such a struggle they would have had to forsake their Party's most cherished tradition and principles; they would have had to rely chiefly on extra-parliamentary actions of the masses.

The risks involved in such a decision would certainly have been as great as in 1918 or in 1920, if not greater. The economic situation was worse even than that immediately after the War, and a great political struggle would undoubtedly have caused its further deterioration. The French were in the Ruhr, and it is not unlikely that they would have attempted to exploit a political struggle of this kind for a permanent separation of Western Germany from the rest of the Reich. Bavaria was in the hands of Germany's most ardent reactionaries and would in no circumstances have acquiesced in the establishment of a Socialist Workers' Government. Nor would Stinnes and his industrial colleagues or Hugenberg and his land-owning friends have pas-

93

sively watched such a development, to say nothing of the Army officers and the Black *Reichswehr*.

In other words, a political party which intended to put itself at the head of the spontaneous workers' movement in order to form a Government and carry into practice the radical programme for which the workers clamoured, had to reckon with the outbreak of a bloody civil war, the outcome of which was completely uncertain.

In view of their past record, it is not surprising that the Social Democrats shrank from taking such risks. As a matter of fact, with the exception of a few individuals, they did not even consider it as a possibility. To try to go this way would have meant a complete break with their tradition and their transformation into a party of an entirely new type. Indeed, a party shaped, not for the conquest of power and national leadership, but for the democratic representation of the workers' interests within the framework of the existing society could not go this way.

Social Democracy was, however, not the only working-class party in Germany. There was after all a Communist Party which was not handicapped by a reformist tradition or an over-scrupulous respect for the law and for parliamentary procedure. Its avowed aim was the proletarian revolution, and its self-chosen part was that of the "vanguard" of the working class. During the critical summer months of 1923 the radical socialist programme of the Communists and their revolutionary appearance had an almost magnetic attraction for an ever-growing section of organised Labour. This attraction became even greater when the Communists were showing their willingness to co-operate with Social Democrats, even with their much despised leaders.[1]

From the Communist point of view, such co-operation and the establishment of a united front with the other working-class organisations was sensible not as an end in itself, but only as a means of acquiring greater striking power and a better chance of success in forthcoming actions. But the Communists did not mean to take action. In fact, not until after the Cuno strike did they even begin to ask themselves whether by any chance the time for vigorous action had come. Far from leading the workers, the Communists were taken completely unawares and were greatly surprised by the force of the spontaneous movement.

In Moscow, whence the Communist leaders had been sum-

[1] The Leipzig Conference of the Communist Party in January 1923 had adopted a resolution demanding the formation of a "Workers' Government" as different from a Communist or *Räte*-Government. As the resolution stated it was to be "an attempt of the working class to carry out a labour policy within the framework and with the means of bourgeois democracy, supported by proletarian institutions and mass movements".

94

moned towards the end of August, the Executive Committee of the Comintern continued to discuss "the German situation". After endless debates it was finally "decided" that Germany stood on the eve of a proletarian revolution and that preparations should be made by the German Communist Party for an armed rising in October. Orders to that effect were given.

Obediently the Communist officials in Germany began to make their secret technical and military preparations, which were as feverish as they were amateurish.

The German workers knew nothing of the momentous decision which the Comintern had taken. Even sympathisers and the rank and file of the Communist Party had no inkling of the rôle they were destined to play. Ordinary Party activities went on as before. In its propaganda the Party continued to advocate a united front with the Social Democrats and the establishment of a "democratic workers' Government". Nothing could have been less like a serious political preparation for a proletarian revolution than this peaceful propaganda.

There was, however, not only propaganda. There were deeds, too. On October 5th the Communist Party surprised Germany with the decision to form provincial coalition Governments with the Social Democrats. In Saxony and Thuringia Communists occupied ministerial positions. Gone was the scorn for "bourgeois Government Socialists" and for "treacherous Labour ministers". Or so, at least, it appeared to the astonished German working class. "Something must have happened to the Communists to account for this unexpected readiness to accept Governmental responsibilities. Perhaps they have really learnt their lesson after the disastrous experience of their abortive rebellion in March 1921; or perhaps it was Russian influence that tamed the Communist shrew." That was the sort of comment generally made on the Communist decision to take part in the Coalition Governments of Saxony and Thuringia. The German workers were bewildered, and so was, for that matter, the general public. The last thing anyone suspected was that the Communists' participation in two provincial Governments coincided with their final preparations for the armed rising which had been planned in Moscow two months earlier.

The Communist position was manifestly absurd. The two policies of accepting responsibility of government, on the one hand, and of preparing for a revolution, on the other, obviously excluded each other. Yet the Communists pursued both at the same time, with the inevitable result of complete failure.

Since the overthrow of the Cuno Government the spontaneous workers' movement steadily abated. As long as the chaos of inflation lasted feeling still ran high, but by October the movement had well passed its zenith. The Communists disregarded the elementary truth that the success of a revolution does not depend on a few technical preparations. When according to the Communist time-table the revolution was nearly due to break out, they blithely entered into coalition Governments and waited for things to develop. After a little while they found that things were not developing in accordance with the decisions taken by the Comintern. The revolution, which had been planned for the end of October, was therefore called off at the last minute.

Owing to a technical mishap the Hamburg branch of the Party had not been informed in time of this sudden change of orders. On October 23rd Hamburg Communists therefore rose in arms—according to plan. A number of police stations were occupied during the night. The next morning they called for a general strike. The surprised Hamburg workers, who had no idea what all this was about, looked on passively. For three days two hundred lone Hamburg Communists fought a strange and hopeless battle against the police in the working-class suburbs of Barnbeck and Schiffbeck. They fought bravely. Many of them lost their lives. The rest were rounded up.

The Hamburg rising was a tragically grotesque finale to the revolutionary post-war crisis which had lasted exactly five years, from the Autumn of 1918 to the Autumn of 1923.

In the German Labour movement the events of the year 1923 remained a subject of endless controversies. The Communist Party Executive which had been in office at that time was later accused by its successors and by the Comintern of having "bungled" a revolution which, but for them, could have been successful. Some outstanding German historians [1] more or less share this view. Others [2] have lately developed the thesis that the political upheaval of that time tended, not towards a revolutionary Socialist, but towards a Fascist solution. The ousted Communist leaders of 1923 put the blame for the failure on the Comintern, whereas most of the leading Social Democrats denied altogether that there had been any chance either for a Communist or a Fascist revolution.

There is some truth in most of these statements. No doubt the Communist leaders had bungled whatever chances they had; nor can there be any doubt that the leaders of the Comintern had their full share of responsibility. It is also true that a powerful

[1] So, for instance, Arthur Rosenberg in his book *Geschichte der deutschen Republik* (cf. pp. 159–160 and 168–169).
[2] Cf. Franz Borkenau: *The Communist International* (London, 1938), pp. 243–256.

and spontaneous mass movement had existed which wanted a radical Socialist solution of Germany's problems. It is finally true that there had been not only a strong Left-wing working-class movement, but also a strong Right-wing nationalist and Fascist movement.[1] In other words, towards the end of Germany's revolutionary post-war crisis many different developments were possible.

A determined, intelligent and independent leadership on the Left might have turned the radical mood of the masses, their hatred and their longing, into a genuine revolutionary movement of great force. But it is almost certain that such an attempt would have challenged the counter-revolutionary Right to active and probably powerful resistance. No one can say what the outcome of such a struggle would have been.

One thing, however, is certain. In 1923 the working-class movement missed its last chance of gaining power in Germany. Twice before, in 1918 and in 1920 it had failed to make use of unique opportunities. After the defeat of the Kapp rebellion it had held all the trumps in its hands. No one could then have offered any serious and prolonged resistance because the overwhelming sympathies, not only of the working class, but of almost the entire nation, were with the Labour movement. In 1923 the nation was divided, and the task would have been infinitely more difficult, the struggle much more costly. Nevertheless, even in 1923 German Labour had yet another chance. It failed then as it had failed before, because the spontaneous revolutionary mass movement remained without leadership.

A final point to be made is this: all the political and the industrial organisations failed equally. The Trade Unions and the Social Democratic Party were essentially organisations representing sectional interests of the working class *vis-à-vis* the sectional interests of other classes. The very purpose of their existence and the structure of their organisations rendered them quite unsuitable for the task of conquering power and shaping the destiny of the nation. The Communists, on the other hand, despite their talk of "power" and "revolution", were not better equipped for this task. For one thing, their absolute dependence on orders from the Comintern, whose policy, in turn, was determined by the requirements of Soviet Russia, made them unfit for the task of leading the German Labour movement, whose problems were, of necessity, different from Russian problems. Moreover, because of this dependence the Communists were unable to attract or retain the allegiance of strong personalities and inde-

[1] On November 9th, 1923, Hitler made his first, though unsuccessful, bid or power.

97

pendent minds, who, by virtue of their character and their personal qualities, could have risen to leadership.

CHAPTER SIXTEEN

CAPITAL *VERSUS* LABOUR

In 1923, while the German Communists were still toying—half frivolously and half amateurishly—with both Revolution and democratic Government, the Social Democrats were trying to solve Germany's most urgent problems by means of indirect pressure which they brought to bear on their coalition partners in the Government. They did not achieve much in that way, and for the little they did achieve they never received the credit due to them.

Their chief political aims at that time were, first of all, the liquidation of the Ruhr conflict, and, secondly, the stabilisation of the currency. For both they could rely on the co-operation of Stresemann. Towards the end of September "passive resistance" was officially broken off and negotiations with the French began. At the same time the Government started to tackle inflation in earnest. The Minister of Finance was then the Social Democrat, Rudolf Hilferding. It was he who worked out the plan for the stabilisation of the currency which was eventually accepted, and thanks to him it was speedily carried into practice. This, however, the public never learnt because conservative pressure forced Hilferding out of the Government before his work was finished. With their negative flare for propaganda, the Social Democrats were satisfied that this most important piece of work had been accomplished by one of their men. They never bothered to destroy the legend, which later arose, that it was Helfferich who saved the country from economic ruin.

Hilferding's removal from office was actually enforced by Stresemann's party, or, more precisely, by the strong big business groups in that party. As soon as it was realised in these circles, representing Germany's heavy industry, that the stabilisation of the currency could not possibly be delayed longer, they insisted on determining at least the character of the stabilisation, and Hilferding, whom they regarded as a stumbling-block and a "difficult" man, had to go.

Naturally, the demands put forward by the spokesmen of the big coal and steel combines were designed to strengthen their own economic and political position in the country. That was possible only at the expense of Labour. Once again the attacks on the Eight Hour Day were renewed. The powerful Employers' Association and the big combines were resolved that the occasion of stabilising the Mark should not pass without another determined effort to abolish such institutions and legislation as guaranteed the worker a minimum of social security.

Their first move in this new battle was an attempt to secure the aid of the French Army of Occupation for the fulfilment of their wishes. A truly fantastic situation developed. The ultra-nationalistic coal-owners, who were constantly vieing with one another whenever it came to a public show of "patriotism" and to stirring up a venomous frenzy against Germany's former enemies, actually entered into business negotiations with the French before the German Government had officially called off the passive resistance in the Ruhr.

On October 5th, 1923, a committee of six leading Ruhr industrialists, consisting of Stinnes, Vögler, Klöckner, Janus, Lübsen and von Velsen, met the French General Degoutte at a conference in the course of which their spokesman Klöckner declared:

> "The Rhenish-Westfalian coal industry has decided to re-introduce the pre-war working time, as from Monday next. . . . *The industry is, however, not in the position to carry out its plans without the support of the Occupation Forces.*"[1]

The German coal-owners' attempt to enlist the aid of French bayonets against German workers only failed because General Degoutte refused to play. He declared that the Army of Occupation was determined to respect the German Law. As the Eight Hour Day was a legal German institution, he did not feel that he was in the position to interfere.

The industrialists were not discouraged by this rebuke. Two days later Stinnes directed a letter to Stresemann, in which he demanded among other things:—

(1) Compensation by the Government for all coal requisitioned by the French.
(2) Abolition of the coal tax.
(3) Compensation by the Government for coal delivered to the Allies under the Reparation scheme.
(4) Abolition of the Government Coal Commission.
(5) Support of the Government for the introduction of longer working hours both in the occupied and in the un-occupied zone.

[1] My italics.

99

(6) **Immediate** repeal of the laws protecting the workers against dismissal and compelling the employers to retain ex-servicemen in employment.

When the content of this letter and, above all, the demands put to General Degoutte became publicly known, a wave of disgust went through Germany. At a large protest meeting, which was attended by tens of thousands of workers, the Democrat Member of Parliament Erkelenz, amidst stormy applause, called Klöckner's proposal to General Degoutte, "one of the most shameful events in modern German history". *Der Vorwärts*, the central organ of the Social Democratic Party, published an article on October 10th in which Hugo Stinnes was singled out and bitterly attacked: "With the aid of French bayonets Stinnes tried to subject the German workers to the dictatorship of ruthless industrial exploitation (*Industrielles Scharfmachertum*)." The "Social Democratic Parliamentary Service" called the negotiations with Degoutte "behaviour bordering on high treason". In the Reichstag the Communist Party actually tabled a motion accusing the six Ruhr industrialists of high treason. Many Social Democrats supported this motion.

No practical action, however, followed these protests. On the contrary, the industrialists retained the initiative. In a reply to Stinnes' letter of October 7th, Stresemann promised the industrialists a number of concessions, in particular a very large sum of money as compensation for damage suffered during the period of passive resistance. Stresemann's colleagues in the Government were not informed of this promise. Only fifteen months later did the German public learn that the Government had presented the leading industrial combines of Western Germany with the vast sum of 715 million gold Marks as "compensation for damage suffered". Of that sum the Stinnes concern alone received about 100 million.

The working class and the lower middle classes, who had really "suffered damage", received no compensation. In contrast to the industrialists they had no spokesmen in the Government who were either willing or capable to defend in this crisis the interests of the mass of the common people as doggedly as the employers' representatives were exploiting the crisis in the interest of the few.

Financial compensation was in point of fact only one, and not even the major objective of the industrialists. Much greater importance was attached to the old problems of working hours, wage level, social legislation and the power of Trade Unions, since these were the factors permanently affecting the cost of production and the margin of profit. And even more important,

100

these were the factors determining the social and political position of the big industrialists, not as individual employers, but as a class accustomed to rule and resolved to preserve its power.

On September 30th the coal-owners had organised a meeting in Unna. At this meeting a decision was taken to increase the working hours for miners working underground from seven to eight and a half hours, and for those working overground from eight to ten or twelve hours a day without an increase in wages. This, as a matter of fact, was the decision to which Klöckner had referred in his appeal to General Degoutte. A motion in Parliament, to enable the industrialists to carry the decision into practice, had been defeated. Nevertheless, the colliery owners issued orders to increase immediately the working hours in all their mines.

The Unions issued counter-orders requesting the miners to disregard this illegal procedure. Strikes and lock-outs were the inevitable sequel. In the end the miners had to give in, at least partially. The fruitless struggle against the inflation and the equally fruitless passive resistance against the French in the Ruhr had exhausted their strength.

On October 25th the Employers' Associations published a Memorandum, in which the popular clamour for *Goldlöhne* ("sterling wages" based on a stable currency) was countered with the employers' demand for *Goldleistung* ("sterling effort"). This "sterling effort" was defined as "the maximum performance unhampered by cramping social obligations".

When the Mark was at last stabilised the employers offered an average wage of twenty Pfennigs per hour (the equivalent of about twopence halfpenny). The Unions declined to open negotiations on this basis and, as a counter-move, the employers proceeded to launch company unions, for which they established a national centre under the name of *Reichsbund Vaterländischer Arbeiter- und Werksvereine* (National League of Patriotic Workers' and Works' Associations). They then demanded recognition of an equal status for the National League of Patriotic Workers' and Works' Associations with the genuine Trade Unions. This was so flagrant a breach of the November Agreement which they themselves had concluded with the Trade Unions in 1918 that, in January 1924, the Free and the (democratic) Hirsch Duncker Unions withdrew their own signatures.

In a sense the withdrawal from the November Agreement was a recognition on the part of the Unions that they had now entered a period of open economic class struggle. But this recognition of the new situation came at a moment when the outcome of the struggle had already been decided against them. The employers had won great victories. A Decree, issued on December 21st, 1923, gave the employers licence for extensive exemptions from the Eight Hour Day. Moreover, nearly all legal restrictions of the employers' right to dismiss workers and to close down factories were removed. The main social achievements of the November Revolution had gone.

Only in one important respect did the Unions manage to hold their ground. They succeeded in maintaining the principle of collective bargaining, though the Employers' Associations tried hard to replace collective bargaining by individual agreements. The maintenance of that principle, more than anything else, enabled the Unions later to recover from the defeat which they suffered in the Autumn and Winter of 1923.

Wages fixed after the stabilisation were appallingly low, although not quite as low as the employers orginally proposed. In December 1923 the average national wage was fixed at 51·5 Pfennig an hour (about sixpence). This one figure is a better illustration of the weakness of the German Trade Unions at that time than many long descriptions.

This weakness had many complex causes. The chief cause was undoubtedly the inflation itself, which had made nonsense of all normal Trade Union activities. The struggle against the inflation and its devastating effects on the standard of living could not be fought with the orthodox Trade Union methods and on a class basis. It could only be fought in the political arena and as a national issue. The lower middle classes were as hard hit by the inflation as the industrial working class, but, unlike the workers, they had no organisation to defend their interests. What might have been a powerful struggle of all common people against a handful of unscrupulous profiteers remained an inadequately organised industrial fight between workers and their employers which had no chance of success.

The political abstinence of the Unions, so rigidly observed, was based on strong traditions. Only once, during the Kapp *putsch*, did the Unions seize the political initiative, proclaiming a general strike in defence of the democratic Republic. The disappointment over the final outcome of that action, which in itself had been so successful, thoroughly discouraged them from repeating such experiments. In fact never again did the Unions take any political initiative; not even at a time when political action was the only means of saving them from defeat, and finally from destruction.

Gradually, then, the Unions were driven into a position in which they were reduced to uttering impotent protests. As a result the workers' confidence in the Unions dwindled, while the

Communists, demanding political action from the Unions, increased their prestige. The best barometer of this development was the result of the shop-steward elections. Among the railwaymen, for instance, 70 per cent. of all votes were cast for the Free Trade Unions in 1921, but only 62 per cent. in 1924. The Communists, on the other hand, who had no separate list in 1921 and who in 1922 managed to get a bare 7 per cent. of the total vote, got almost 20 per cent. in 1924. That is a typical example, for the same trend could be observed in all important industries. Perhaps the most striking advance of the Communists (at the expense of the Free Trade Unions) was that among the Ruhr miners. In the shop-steward elections of 1924 the Communists actually got a slightly greater number of votes than the Free Trade Unions (34·23 per cent. as against 33·85 per cent.).

But even apart from these political repercussions and from their financial weakness, the Unions suffered most from the general effects of mass unemployment, which began to develop on a scale hitherto unknown in Germany as soon as the Mark was "stabilised". By December 1923, 1,500,000 men were registered as unemployed. Almost one quarter of all Union members were out of work and 47 per cent. of the remainder were working half-time.

CHAPTER SEVENTEEN

MILITARISTS *VERSUS* LABOUR

THE OFFENSIVE against the Labour movement was by no means confined to the economic and social sphere; nor were the trusts, bankers and big industrialists the only active enemies of Labour in this struggle which ended with the triumph of German reaction.

Towards the end of September 1923 the Bavarian Government appointed Herr von Kahr as a kind of High Commissioner. Herr von Kahr was a well-known Monarchist. His first act was the proclamation of a 'state of emergency and the assumption of dictatorial powers over the whole of Bavaria. The Central Government in Berlin (under Stresemann) reacted by proclaiming its own state of emergency for the whole of the Reich (which, theoretically, should have annulled the special Bavarian state of emergency) and by entrusting the executive power of the Reich to the Army.

A conflict between the Reich Government and the self-styled

Bavarian dictator soon developed. The Reich Government requested the Bavarian Army divisions to use their executive power against Herr von Kahr. Under the leadership of General Lossow, the Bavarian divisions refused to obey the orders from Berlin. On October 22nd the Bavarian troops swore a new oath of allegiance to the new Bavarian régime. This was a clear case of mutiny. But Stresemann did not order the *Reichswehr* to enforce the authority of the Reich and to deal with the Bavarian rebels accordingly.

Instead, he ordered the *Reichswehr* to march against Saxony and Thuringia, where Left-wing Coalition Governments of Socialists and Communists were in office.

In contrast to the Bavarian régime of Herr von Kahr, the Saxonian and Thuringian Governments were perfectly constitutional and enjoyed the support of majorities in their respective Diets. Nevertheless, the *Reichswehr* forced the two Governments to resign. The official excuse for this actions was as thin as the real motive behind it was transparent. The Army generals had no intentions of tolerating working-class Governments in the heart of Germany.

No hand was raised against Bavaria.

After this outrage the Social Democrats made the inevitable gesture of protest and left the Government. They did no more. The initiative was no longer theirs. It was with the nationalists and reactionary forces of the Right, flourishing after a threefold success. The Bavarian challenge had remained unanswered. The hateful Socialist–Communist coalition in Saxony and Thuringia had been suppressed by main force. The Social Democrats had been driven out of the Government. With this very considerable success most of them were content for the time being.

Only a small group among them had the illusion that the time was ripe for the immediate conquest of total power in the whole of the Reich. They were the National Socialists, led by Hitler, Röhm and Ludendorff, dreaming of imitating Mussolini's example and staging a march on Berlin. The Army leaders, however, including the Bavarian generals, favoured longer and more thorough preparations. Hitler and Ludendorff remained alone when, in the night of November 8th–9th, they staged their abortive *Bürgerbräu putsch* in Munich. Only after this failure did Hitler learn to appreciate the opportunist wisdom of the much-ridiculed words of General Lossow's: "Of course, I want to march, but I shall not do so unless there is a fifty-one per cent. probability of success".

The Hitler *putsch* had been precipitated. It was not defeated as Kapp had been defeated by a powerful movement of democratic resistance. It broke down simply for lack of support. Ten years later the Army backed Hitler to the hilt. But in 1923, the generals still believed that they could achieve their aims more safely by their own methods and without the aid of the troublesome agitator whom they only half trusted. They did not yet understand that it was necessary in Germany to preach peace in order to prepare for war, to speak of justice in order to reach out for conquests, and to propagate socialism in order to suppress Labour.

Later, the generals (as well as the industrialists) learnt that in the age of mass movements they could not rule by themselves, but could achieve their aims only by supporting a popular party that had developed demagogy to a fine art. In 1923 they still felt self-confident. After all, they had achieved one important victory after another. It was clear now, beyond possible doubt, that the generals and not the Government decided when, where, against whom and with whom the Army was to march. It was equally clear that the danger of fundamental social changes no longer existed in Germany. Words like socialisation, nationalisation, or a Workers' Militia had been struck from the German vocabulary.

In 1923 only a very mature Labour movement, under the best leadership conceivable, could have changed the course of German history. As it happened, the German working-class movement was neither politically mature, nor did it possess a particularly intelligent or courageous leadership. That is true for the Trade Unions just as much as for the Social Democrats and the Communists.

Only five, indeed only three years earlier, this movement had held all power in its hands. It did not know how to use it. For this sin of omission it was to be punished with annihilation.

PART FOUR

PROSPERITY ON CRUTCHES
1924–1928

CHAPTER EIGHTEEN

THE CRISIS OF STABILISATION

GERMANY'S AMAZING recovery after the economic and political turmoil of the immediate post-war period gave her the appearance of a giant in strength and recuperative power. But this appearance was deceptive. Neither the economic recovery nor the return of political calm was a sign of inner soundness or stability. They were merely the short-lived results of outside intervention.

Strictly speaking, Germany's recovery began only after the London Conference of August 1924 and the acceptance of the Dawes Plan. Until then the country passed through yet another period of crisis, though one very different from the mad chaos of the inflation. The symptoms of this new crisis were unemployment, low wages and a series of drastic economy decrees designed to cut down expenditure as far as possible.

The Government—since December 1923 headed by Dr. Wilhelm Marx of the Catholic Party—had been empowered by Parliament, for a certain limited period, to rule by emergency decrees. After long and heated debates the Social Democratic Parliamentary Party decided to vote in favour of these emergency powers for the Government, although the Party was once again in opposition. The Marx Government showed no reluctance to use its powers, and issued decree after decree, all of which hit the little man while protecting and favouring the property-owning classes. The Social Democrats and the Unions violently attacked some of these measures, such as the reduction of unemployment benefits, the dismissal of a great number of civil servants, the increase of indirect taxes, and the simultaneous decrease of taxes on property.

As a result of this criticism, Parliament was dissolved and new elections were held.

The Social Democrats' protest came too late. It was not forgotten that their voting in the Reichstag had empowered the Government to rule without parliament. Altogether, their record had not been glorious. In their own way, they had tried their best to end the Ruhr conflict and the inflation, but even of the limited successes which they did achieve the mass of the workers knew little or nothing. It was not surprising that they suffered for the second time a disastrous defeat in the general elections which followed in May 1924. Of their 171 parliamentary seats, the Social Democrats lost 71.

The Communists, on the other hand, made considerable gains, increasing the number of their seats from 17 to 62. Although their own failure had been as great as that of the Social Democrats (indeed greater, if measured by their own standards), the shortcomings of this "untried party" were far less obvious to the working-class electorate than those of the Social Democrats and Trade Unions. To the man in the street the Communists appeared as the victims[1] of the reactionary development, and in no way responsible for it. Their somewhat surrealist policy of 1923 had been far too complicated to be understood by the ordinary working-class people. Even the rank and file of the Communist Party never quite realised what the game had been. The wild conflicts between the various factions who competed for leadership within the Communist Party remained confined to a very small top layer. These conflicts, moreover, were invariably connected with conflicts within the Comintern, which,. in turn, reflected differences among the Soviet leaders about problems of Russian home and foreign policy.

All this was much too involved to be understood by anyone but an expert. To the average elector the issue seemed to be perfectly straightforward; to him the Social Democratic Party was the traditional party of Labour which stood for democracy, gradual progress by means of reforms, legality, and law and order. The Communists, on the other hand, whatever their "line" happened to be at the moment, seemed to be the new, tough and radical party which stood for a revolutionary fight against vested interests and reaction. Millions of German workers had become radicalised as a result of the chaotic development, and in the elections of May 1924 the Communists were to reap the harvest.

Only six months later new general elections were held. This time the Social Democrats returned to the Reichstag with 137 members as against 100 in May, whereas the Communists lost 17

[1] On November 20th, 1923, the Communist Party had been suppressed. On February 28th, 1924, the state of emergency was raised. Shortly afterwards, the Communist Party became once more a legal organisation.

of their 62 seats. Chiefly responsible for this change of the political climate was the beginning of the recovery following the Dawes Plan and the sudden influx of foreign loans into Germany.

CHAPTER NINETEEN

THE TRADE UNIONS

Pᴿᴼˢᴾᴱᴿᴵᵀʸ ᴬᵀ ˡᵃˢᵗ—or so it seemed. What was about to begin was Germany's five-year period of sham-prosperity, founded on foreign loans, short- and long-term credits, which were used for an almost complete reconstruction and re-equipment of the country's war-worn industries. Two decades later this freak recovery seems hardly more sane than the preceding chaos of inflation and civil wars. But this is very much an after-thought. At the time the first breath of prosperity, whether real or false, felt like the end at long last of the World War and like the final return to normality. It is a strange and, even more, a sad reflection that dollar and sterling loans should have been necessary to restore some of the self-confidence of the Labour and Socialist movement which had been lost in years of defeat. The longed-for "return to normal conditions" which the Unions and Social Democrats had failed to bring about when power was theirs to take was now presented to them by Anglo-American investors.

And so when commerce, trade and industry were allowed to return to "normal business", the Trade Unions, too, resumed their normal activities.

The beginning of this new period saw a great number of sharp industrial conflicts, though conflicts very different in nature from the desperate semi-insurrectionist struggles the German workers had fought in the years of inflation and starvation. They were the normal conflicts between capital and labour, concerning first and foremost the share which each class were to get of the growing national income. They were industrial rather than political conflicts, and, as a consequence, the Unions seemed to gain a new and growing importance.

Many of the disputes concerned wages and salaries. But the most serious and most frequent arose over questions of working hours. The Unions were determined to restore the Eight Hour Day as the legal maximum working day or, at any rate, to save as much of it as possible. The employers remained equally determined to remove all restrictions on the length of the working day or, at least, to fix the maximum as high as possible.

Time and again both sides resorted to their most powerful weapon, to strikes and lock-outs. More working days were lost in 1924 as a result of strikes and lock-outs than in any other year between the two World Wars, the employers' lock-outs, be it noted, causing considerably more stoppages than the workers' strikes. Altogether 13·2 million working days were lost owing to strikes, and 22·6 million working days owing to lock-outs.

As this industrial tug of war tended to end more often than not in deadlock, the conflicts were settled by compulsory arbitration. As a rule, though not in every case, the compulsory awards tended to bring about a compromise favourable to the employers, and as time went on this form of compulsory arbitration became in fact the chief means of settling labour conflicts. It need hardly be emphasised that this influenced not only the development of German Trade Unionism, but even more the attitude of the workers to their Unions.

In earlier years compulsory arbitration had been regarded as an emergency procedure, to be used in rare and exceptional cases only. In 1918 the Trade Unions themselves had promoted the idea of State arbitration. They did so because they were convinced that the Weimar Republic was their own State—a State that could be relied upon to make just and fair awards. They believed that arbitration coming from "their" State could, by definition, never really clash with labour interests.

However, the German Republic, as it eventually emerged after the series of post-war crises, was not a State which the Labour movement could call its own. After the autumn of 1923 (with the exception of a short period of rather less than two years—1928–1930) the Republic was governed by cabinets in which organised Labour had no representatives. During all these years the judiciary power of the State was firmly in the hands of the country's most notorious reactionaries. So was the executive power. This remains true although in individual Federal States, such as Prussia, Social Democrats controlled the police force. Their authority proved effective only during periods of stability or else if and when the police were ordered to act against the Left; as soon as the Social Democrat control of the police seemed to become dangerous to the Right, the police forces were placed under the command of the Army, as for instance in Prussia in July 1932.

In the economic and social sphere the power of capital had been enormously strengthened ever since 1920. From 1924 onwards this power—economic power used for political ends—grew further and more rapidly than before, in the course of reconstruction, rationalisation and the progress of monopolisation.[1]

In all essential spheres, therefore, real power lay in the hands of those most hostile to Labour; and this was much more important for the character of the Weimar Republic and its subsequent development than its very excellent and most democratic Constitution. Within the Labour movement this state of affairs came to be realised only gradually. Yet even though the illusion that the Weimar Republic was "their" State could not be easily upheld, the Unions felt nevertheless that there was no other way but to rely more and more upon co-operation with the Government and the organs of the State. To-day it may seem difficult to see why they should have thought so. The reason why was quite plainly their own weakness. The power of capital had grown so prodigiously that the Unions not only felt that they were too weak to fight their own battles, but probably were in fact too weak to fight successfully. After 1924, therefore, there was a very noticeable and rapid decline in the numbers of strikes led by the Unions.[2] That is not to say that the number of strikes decreased because there were fewer conflicts; it decreased because the Union relied more and more on State arbitration. State arbitration and the decreasing number of strikes created the false impression of a genuine, if temporary, industrial peace at that time. In reality, the conflict of interests between employers and workers had become so irreconcilable that free negotiations no longer led to workable agreements.

For the Unions this development was fatal. The less they relied on their own strength, the more dependent did they become on the State, whatever the character and policy of the Government in office. A further consequence was that the workers gradually lost interest in the Unions because they felt that it was the State, and not the Unions, which fixed their wages and decided their working conditions. This loss of interest in the Unions was further increased by the legal extension of collective agreements to all unorganised workers, as well as by the comprehensive system of social insurance and the creation of special Labour Courts for the settlement of legal disputes between employers and employed.

The crowning piece of social legislation was the Unemployment

[1] The two most powerful German trusts were formed during that period of "borrowed prosperity" which began in 1924, the *I.G. Farben Industrie* (the German Dye Trust) in 1925 and the *Vereinigte Stahlwerke* (United Steel Works) in 1926.

[2] In 1924 over 21 per cent. of the total Trade Union expenditure was spent on strikes; between 1925 and 1931 the average annual expenditure on strikes was only just over 4 per cent.

Insurance Act of 1927. The Unions had played a great part in the drafting of this Act and of social legislation in general. But this work was chiefly done by special committees and experts who negotiated and worked, as it were, behind the scenes, and the Unions therefore got very little of the political credit which they truly deserved, because the mass of the workers knew next to nothing of these activities.

The decline of Trade Union strength and influence did not become really visible before the great depression and mass unemployment began. But it is important to remember that mass unemployment was not the only cause which eventually reduced the German Unions to a shadow of their former self. The Unions' growing dependence on the State, their submissiveness and self-emasculation, were, to say the least, very important contributory causes.[1]

During the period of recovery, however, the Unions were still a factor to be counted with—though numerically they were infinitely weaker than they had been in the years 1922–1923. (Total Trade Union membership was 4·6 millions in 1924 as against 7·8 millions in 1922.) Their greatest achievement was no doubt a substantial improvement of wages and salaries. In December 1923 the average national wage had been fixed at 51·5 Pfennig per hour; by December 1924 it had risen to 69·3 Pfennig; by June 1925 to 80·7 Pfennig and by December 1925 to 81·1 Pfennig.

But the activities of the Unions were not confined to a struggle for higher wages, temporarily successful, to social legislation and a rather unsuccessful struggle for the restoration of the Eight Hour Day.

Much of their energy was spent on the creation and promotion of co-operative enterprises, social welfare and the like. The German Builders' Union, for instance, had started the so-called *Bauhütten-Bewegung* (Building Guilds), whose object it was to build good and cheap working-class flats and houses. This *Bauhütten-Bewegung* merged later on with several similar societies

[1] Many German Trade Unionists and students of Trade Unionism clearly recognised this. Johannes Wolf, the President of the German Landworkers' Union, called the reliance on State arbitration "organised irresponsibility". Frieda Wunderlich, who quotes these words, emphasises that "the workers lost all interest in their organisations when they found that wages were fixed by the State and not by their Unions" (Frieda Wunderlich: *Labour under German Democracy*). Franz Neumann, in his pamphlet on *European Trade Unionism and Politics*, also confirms this view: "The arbitration system, the legal extension of collective wage agreements to unorganised workers, unemployment insurance and the whole system of social insurance—these made it appear to the worker that he had no longer any need for the T.U. 'If the State takes charge of all these things, what use are T.U.s?' This was the stock question in Germany," (p. 32).

into the "Union of Social Building Enterprises", which was controlled by the *Allgemeiner Deutscher Gewerkschaftsbund* (the German T.U.C.). Other enterprises founded or promoted by the Unions were the German Housing Welfare Society for Workers and Civil Servants, the Workers' and Civil Servants' Bank, an enterprise for the supply of office equipment, a co-operative insurance company, the so-called *Volksfürsorge* (People's Welfare), etc.

No doubt these institutions rendered excellent services to a great many working-class families. Their effect on Germany's economic structure was exactly nil. The Trade Union urge for "industrial democracy"—once again one of the chief slogans of the movement since the Breslau Trade Union Congress of 1925—remained a pious wish-dream. The transformation of the Provisional National Economic Council into a "Proper Economic Parliament", which the Breslau Congress had demanded, never took place. But even if such an "economic Parliament" had been created, it would have remained a farce and a sham institution so long as economic power was concentrated in the hands of a small minority. Industrial democracy without basic economic equality is as nonsensical a demand as political democracy without basic political equality.

The second great demand of the Breslau Trade Union Congress had been for wholesale rationalisation of industry. Great theories were expounded proving conclusively that the workers could only benefit from rationalisation. Little did the delegates foresee that, under the prevailing conditions, unplanned rationalisation was bound to lead to chronic mass unemployment, to endless misery, and at the same time to a further weakening of the Labour movement. The Trade Union leaders took pride in being "modern" and "progressive"; no doubt they would have been shocked had anyone told them that, in a sense, they were inverted machine-wreckers. Yet it is not at all far-fetched to make this comparison. The twentieth-century Trade Unionists of Germany were active partisans of the machine age and of technical progress in the sense in which the nineteenth-century Luddites had been the active enemies of the machine—as though social problems could be solved by technical means.

CHAPTER TWENTY

HINDENBURG AND THE PRINCES

G ERMANY'S ECONOMIC recovery of the mid-twenties coincided with a rapid political recovery of the Social Democratic Party. In the Reichstag the Party remained in opposition until its great election victory in 1928. As the largest single party, it was able to exercise considerable influence on parliamentary decisions. Where the Party failed to influence policy, it could at least make effective demonstrations, and it did so, in many ways, to the satisfaction of a growing section of the working class. Only one field of politics seemed taboo for the Social Democrat opponents of Stresemann's Cabinet.

In foreign affairs the Party's opposition was non-existent. It fully subscribed to Stresemann's "policy of fulfilment". It had voted for the Dawes Plan; Thoiry, Locarno and Germany's eventual admission to the League of Nations were hailed in the Labour press as the beginning of a "new era". In fact the Social Democrats claimed, not entirely without justification, that it was not they who subscribed to Stresemann's foreign policy of international understanding, but that, on the contrary, Stresemann was merely carrying out their own Social Democratic policy.

The desire of the Social Democrats to emphasise their agreement with Stresemann in questions of foreign policy and their fear of disturbing the continuity of his efforts cramped their style as official opposition party and took the sting out of their opposition in home affairs. Stresemann's success, on the other hand, was also their success and was widely recognised as such by the people in Germany.

In home affairs the Social Democrats concentrated their energies on raising the general standard of living and securing a greater share of the national income for the working classes. For these aims the Party fought a long and stubborn parliamentary guerilla war. And in the course of these battles the Party tended to become more and more the parliamentary mouthpiece of the Unions, concerned not so much with political as with social questions. The Social Democrats fought the introduction of high tariffs, they fought for a reducion of indirect taxation and of wage taxes and for an increase of property taxes and death duties. In the tariff question they suffered an absolute defeat, in the question of taxes they carried some of their points. Altogether their successes were modest and limited, but the mere fact that they had

113

energetically fought for their programme went a long way to restore lost prestige.

In other spheres they showed no such enterprise. On the whole, the Social Democrats were content that the Republican State-form and the democratic Constitution had survived the series of crises and abortive rebellions since 1918. They were a great deal more concerned with conserving what they had gained than with attaining what they had not yet got.

The new programme of the Party, adopted in 1925 at the Heidelberg Conference, still retained much of the traditional Marxist terminology. But neither the authors nor those adopting the programme regarded that as more than a matter of form and a reverence for the great past. A programme that was to be displayed on festive occasions like a beautiful string of pearls. In everyday life it was not much use. Phrases such as this occurred in the Heidelberg programme:—

"The number of proletarians is growing; the conflict between exploiters and those who are exploited increases in violence; the class warfare between the capitalist rulers of economy and those whom they oppress is becoming fiercer. . . ."

In practical politics the Party was very far removed from the rôle of the champion of "fierce class war".

There were, in those few years of comparative stability and prosperity, not many occasions for big political fights involving important issues. All the more significant, as a test of strength and of political wisdom, were the few occasions which called for far-reaching decisions.

One of these occasions came with the death of Ebert in February 1925 and the necessity of electing a new President for the Reich. No less than seven candidates were presented for the first ballot. Social Democrats, Communists and Democrats, the Catholic Centre Party, the Catholic Bavarian People's Party, and the National Socialists—each had their own candidate, whereas the large Conservative parties, the German People's Party and the German Nationalists, together with the so-called "Patriotic League", put up as a joint candidate, Dr. Jarres, Burgomaster of Duisburg, a moderate Conservative who had once entertained mild sympathies for the Rhenish Separatists.

The solid bloc of the Conservative forces achieved its purpose; their joint candidate received the greatest number of votes (10·7 million), although he was far from having won an absolute majority. A second ballot became necessary. Next to the Conservative candidate the Social Democrat, Otto Braun (then

Prime Minister of Prussia), had received the largest vote (7·8 million). The purpose of the second ballot, so it would seem, could only be a decision between the two strongest candidates. If the Social Democrats managed to win the support of some of the other parties, confronting the Conservative bloc with a progressive democratic bloc headed by a popular candidate, they might have had a chance of gaining the additional 3 million-odd votes necessary to beat their Conservative opponent. So it was widely thought. But the case was never put to the test.

Afraid of being unable to attract a sufficient number of bourgeoisie votes for a Social Democratic candidate, and thereby indirectly helping their Conservative opponent, the Socialists decided to withdraw their own candidate and to support instead Dr. Wilhelm Marx, candidate and leader of the Catholic Centre Party.

In the first ballot Dr. Marx had received exactly half as many votes as Braun (3·9 million). From the point of view of purely formal democratic procedure, therefore, it was very strange indeed that the Social Democrats should have agreed to withdraw their own candidate, who had received twice as many votes as the man in whose favour he was to resign. Even more important was the fact that Wilhelm Marx was anything but a progressive or popular personality. Only one year earlier Marx had been the Prime Minister of a Cabinet which had become notorious for its unpopular and anti-social emergency decrees. The name of Wilhelm Marx was connected with the increase of indirect taxes and the decrease of taxes on property, with the reduction of unemployment benefits and a reactionary law reform (the virtual abolition of trial by jury).

To support this man meant probably to make sure of the votes of the moderate bourgeoisie parties. But it was impossible to win for him the support of the more radical sections of the working class or to arouse from their apathy potential voters who would not bother to go to the polls simply because none of the candidates had sufficient personal appeal. The Conservative bloc, too, had changed its candidate. Dr. Jarres was dropped and the parties concerned agreed on the candidature of Paul von Hindenburg. A terrific press and general publicity campaign for Hindenburg was launched by the nationalist press-lord Hugenberg, in which the aged Field-Marshal was advertised as "the Saviour", while the Social Democrats went about canvassing for Dr. Marx under the slogan "the lesser evil"—an unfortunate phrase which many German Social Democrats lived to regret.

Even if Marx had been elected, it is highly doubtful if he would really have proved to be a "lesser evil". Marx, no less than Hindenburg, "would have respected the will of the generals and the capitalist magnates in every crisis".[1]

Hindenburg was eventually elected President of the Republic. The Social Democrats blamed the Communists for having split the Left vote and thus indirectly supported Hindenburg. It is quite true, of course, that the maintenance of an independent Communist candidate (Ernst Thälmann) had no other purpose than that of a demonstration, and objectively every Communist vote was a gain for Hindenburg. But it is equally true to say that the Communists had hardly another choice. To support Marx, as the Social Democrats suggested they should, would have been political suicide for them. Of all reproaches of the Communists this was probably the least justified.

The Socialist support for Wilhelm Marx was merely the first important instance of the "policy of the lesser evil" which was to have such fatal consequences during the years of the pre-Hitler crisis. It was not really a new policy. It was perfectly consistent with the main Social Democratic trend of thought, which hoped to safeguard the democratic Republic by an alliance with the democratic sections of the middle classes. There was nothing wrong with the idea of such an alliance. Indeed, an alliance of this sort was as necessary as it was inevitable, in view of Germany's social and political structure. But such an alliance is never one of complete equals, and its character is always determined by the partner who assumes the rôle of leadership, takes the political initiative and works out the policy to be pursued. On all these scores the Social Democrats surrendered to their "allies". Their "policy of the lesser evil" or, as it was also called, their "policy of toleration" merely meant that the leadership and initiative in this alliance were left to a "partner" who, unlike the Labour movement, had no vested interest either in democracy or in social progress, and who was therefore quite ready at the critical moment to desert its ally and join forces with stronger battalions which seemed to know what they wanted and to be determined to get it.

In the period between the first Hindenburg election and the great slump it was by no means so clear as it is to-day that this policy was leading straight to self-destruction. On the contrary, it appeared—outwardly at any rate—as though Social Democracy was making steady headway. Its successes in social legislation, in the general raising of the standard of living, in municipal and educational reforms were very substantial, and compared with these achievements the election of Hindenburg as President of the German Republic seemed to be an incident of no major importance.

[1] Arthur Rosenberg, *op. cit.*, p. 208.

Had the economic stability lasted, this view might have proved correct. But German prosperity was built on precarious foundations. Foreign indebtedness increased until it amounted to about one half of the national income. Exactly one half of the foreign credits given to Germany up to 1931 (Mk. 10,300,000,000 out of a total of Mk. 20,600,000,000) were short-term credits, which remained unconsolidated.[1] It was a "borrowed prosperity", and the policy of the Social Democrats consisted mainly of an endeavour to share out the fruits more justly. As long as it lasted, they were not unsuccessful, though extremely short-sighted not to have foreseen that this state of affairs could not possibly last. No preparations of any sort were made by the Party Executive for the economic catastrophe that was bound to come sooner or later.

The catastrophe could have been prevented only by the methods of a fully planned economy. But how was it possible to plan, in any real sense of the word, without the existence of a central authority with overriding powers over vested interests and sectional egotism? The emergence (or non-emergence) of an authority with such powers was therefore the one crucial issue on which, in the last instance, German democracy depended. The true measure of Labour's success or failure was therefore not this or that piece of social legislation, not this or that wage agreement, nor this or that housing scheme, but the extent and the speed with which it acquired—or lost—a position of real power.

If seen in this light the significance of the Hindenburg election lay chiefly in the fact that it showed, in a flash, how far removed from power the genuinely democratic and socially progressive forces were in the mid-twenties. The lack of self-confidence, and the essentially defensive spirit which had induced the Social Democrats to support Wilhelm Marx, had their counterpart in the aggressive attitude of the Right. To choose Hindenburg as their presidential candidate was as much a challenge to the Allied Powers[2] as to the German working class. It was a test case that would indicate what sort of reaction might be expected to an even more serious and threatening challenge for which the Hindenburg

---

[1] "On the eve of the international crash the condition of the German banking system was such that most of the investments of the 'rationalisation era', the building and modernisation of plants, the drilling of coal mines, the building of department stores and power plants, were financed by short-term bank deposits of which a large percentage was due to foreign creditors and was ready for repatriation at the first intimation of an approaching slump." (Gustav Stolper: *German Economy 1870–1940*, London, 1940, p. 187.)

[2] Stresemann had tried vainly to prevent Hindenburg's nomination. Although not opposed to him for internal reasons, he feared that the election of a Prussian World War general as Germany's supreme representative might destroy the chance of international understanding.

candidature was merely a preparation. His supporters were re-assured. Nothing happened. With the Field-Marshal's election the power of the *Reichswehr* generals was considerably strengthened. They and their associates could now calmly bide their time until opportunity came for "the next step".

For once the next move did not come from the Right. For once it was the Left which took the initiative by organising a referendum for the expropriation of Germany's former ruling Princes. In 1918, when Germany's Emperor, Kings and Princes abdicated in panic, the question of their property had been left unsettled. As long as the country stumbled from one crisis to another, not much was heard of them. But as soon as the currency was stabilised and economic recovery began, they came forward with exorbitant demands for compensation. Apart from landed property, they claimed enormous cash payments from their former subject States.

When these States did not hurriedly comply with their wishes, the Princes went to law. With few exceptions, the higher judges were ardent Monarchists of the old school, and pronounced judgment in favour of the royal claimants. A prolonged quarrel ensued between the Prussian State and the House of Hohenzollern over the question of compensation, which finally ended in a public scandal. Eventually, Social Democrats and Communists agreed to join forces in order to settle this question once and for all, by a general plebiscite.

Whatever the outcome of this plebiscite, very little depended on it for the destiny of the Weimar Republic. Nevertheless it aroused almost as much political passion as the last fateful elections before Hitler's advent to power. The outward impression was that of an issue between Monarchists and Republicans. In point of fact it was a contest between the classes owning property and those who did not.

The demands formulated by the Socialists and Communists now acting in unison were straightforward and uncompromising—complete expropriation of Germany's former ruling Princes; no right to compensation; and the establishment of a fund from the proceeds for the support of war invalids, unemployed, old age pensioners and others who, through no fault of their own, were unable to earn their living.

For many millions the demands of this plebiscite corresponded exactly to their own idea of that rough social justice for which they had vainly been waiting since 1918. Moreover, the unity of Social Democrats and Communists, so suddenly achieved, gave the members and followers of both parties a new feeling of self-confidence and growing strength. For a moment it looked as though a completely fresh start was about to be made by the German working-class movement.

This impression was shared by their opponents on the Right, who were deeply worried, not so much about the property of the Hohenzollerns, as about the danger to their own social position should a precedent of this kind be created. They used every means, fair and foul, to prevent the success of the plebiscite. For example, the parties of the Right did not ask their followers to vote against the plebiscite, but to abstain from voting altogether. They did so in order to circumvent the secrecy of voting. Everyone going to the polls would thus be known to be in favour of expropriation. In many rural areas the social pressure of the landowners was sufficiently strong to frighten the population into abstention.[1]

To strengthen the popular appeal of their case the parties of the Right enlisted the aid of the President of the Republic. A most extraordinary situation arose when Hindenburg lent the authority of his high office to support his personal and political friends and stated in a letter that was widely quoted during the plebiscite campaign:

"By exciting the instincts of the masses and by exploiting the misery of the people with regard to the individual case now in question, there may arise the method of continuing on the road of expropriation, with the aid of a similar plebiscite, which would rob the German nation of the very foundations of its cultural, economic and State life."

The Social Democratic Party sharply rebuked the President for this letter. It published a long declaration which culminated in the question:

"What connection is there between justice or morals and the fact that Wilhelm II, who possesses property in Holland worth many million, now demands a further 300,000 *morgen*[2] of German land together with castles and other valuables worth 183 million gold Mark?"

The plebiscite did not win the necessary absolute majority. Nevertheless, the result was not a defeat but, on the contrary, a

[1] In East Prussia, the home of the Junkers, only 20 per cent. of the electorate voted, whereas in big industrial centres, such as Berlin, Hamburg or Leipzig, there were absolute majorities in favour of expropriation. In most rural areas the total number of votes registered in the plebiscite was lower than the combined working-class vote in normal elections. In urban areas the opposite was the case.

[2] 300,000 *morgen* equals 180,000 acres.

great success for its initiators. In the last general elections of December 1924 Social Democrats and Communists had polled between them ten and a half million votes. In the plebiscite of 1926 they gained fourteen and a half million. To have attracted four million new voters, in spite of a regular election terror in the rural areas, and within the short period of eighteen months, was a considerable success. It was due to two equally important factors: on the one hand, the clear simplicity of the issue, and, on the other, the co-operation of the two working-class parties.

There had been only few occasions in the history of the Weimar Republic when the two parties decided to forget their differences and join hands in common action. Three occasions, to be exact: during the strike against Kapp in 1920; in the protest movement against the Rathenau murder in 1922; and lastly, in the plebiscite of 1926. In every instance their joint action produced a response far greater than the sum total of the support they had been able to muster when acting separately. The plebiscite demanding the expropriation of Germany's former ruling Royalties was the last occasion of such successful co-operation.

CHAPTER TWENTY-ONE

RECOVERY OF THE LABOUR MOVEMENT

Less THAN two years later the German Republic elected its fourth Parliament. No significant changes had taken place in the meantime. Social Democrats and Trade Unions had somewhat increased their prestige, notably through the adoption by Parliament of the Unemployment Insurance Act of 1927 and the creation of special Labour Courts in the same year.

The German electors who went to the polls in May 1928 were a moderately contented people. Economic recovery had been rapid; its precarious basis was not apparent to the mass of the people. The standard of living was rising. Unemployment figures were low. Wages and salaries had been increased. Decent working-class houses and modern schools had been built. Green belts, recreation and sports grounds had been constructed. Social legislation had been greatly improved. The Locarno Treaty had been concluded. Germany had been admitted to the League of Nations. The Dawes Plan was functioning without difficulties. War, inflation and the Treaty of Versailles were a distant past and virtually forgotten. It seemed as though at long last Germany was beginning to live at peace with herself and with the world.

It was only natural that the Social Democrats should benefit most from the situation. For it was their policy which, both in home and in foreign affairs, had met with comparatively so much success. Now that democracy appeared to be functioning and social reforms to be bringing results, their former failure was quickly forgotten and their policy seemed amply justified.

In the elections the Social Democrats polled over nine million votes, gaining 1·3 million compared with the previous elections. All non-working-class parties lost heavily, although the losses suffered by the more moderate and democratic middle-class parties were less pronounced than those of the extreme German Nationalists.

The Communists, too, increased their vote to 3·2 million, attracting over half a million new voters. Together with the Social Democrats they were the only winners in that election. Although they did not again reach the high vote they received in the joint plebiscite of 1926, the two working-class parties together held just over 42 per cent. of all parliamentary seats—that is, almost exactly as much as the Nazi Party gained in the terror election of March 1933, after Hitler had become Chancellor and after the burning of the Reichstag.

It may seem strange that the Communists should have made progress in an election that was so clearly a victory for democracy, social reform and the League of Nations policy. The answer is that at that time Communist policy did not differ essentially from that of the Social Democrats.

The Communists had gone through many metamorphoses since their *débâcle* in 1923. Very soon after that "bungled revolution" the old "Right-wing" set of leaders had been replaced by the so-called "ultra-Left" wing. Under this new leadership the Party had begun to organise separate "red" Trade Unions, with the result that most Communists who wished to remain members of the Free Trade Unions were duly expelled. The inevitable effect of this policy had been a rapid isolation of the Communists from the main force of organised Labour and the loss of over one million votes in the general election of December 1924. At the Trade Union Congress of August 1925 they had no more than four delegates, as compared with eighty-eight at the preceding Trade Union Congress of 1922. The "ultra-Left" policy of 1924 had quite obviously led to even greater failure than the see-saw policy of 1923.

Another "change of line" was due. At the request of the Comintern the "ultra-Left" leaders were expelled and replaced by a set of leaders who had neither a "Right Wing" nor a "Left Wing" nor any other policy of their own, but who were able and willing to adapt themselves smoothly to the varying and changing demands of the Comintern leadership.

In 1925 the demand happened to be for Trade Union unity. It was prompted partly by the hopeless position into which the German Communists had manœuvred themselves. But its chief motive was the necessity of bringing the German section of the Comintern into line with the policy of the Russian Unions, which had just come to an agreement with the British Trade Unions.[1]

For the next three years—that is to say, from 1925 until 1928 (when the decisions of the Sixth World Congress of the Comintern required yet another turn)—Communist policy resembled in many ways that of their rivals, the Social Democrats. Differences there were, of course. The language of the Communists was more violent, their propaganda more vigorous and their instinct for working-class mentality less cultivated. But in other respects the differences did not seem very marked. More often than not the two parties voted together in Parliament, they worked side by side in the Unions for the improvement of labour conditions, they co-operated in the organisation of the Plebiscite of 1926. In view of all this, it was not surprising that the Communists, too, should to some extent have benefited in the elections which came after a series of common achievements and common opposition in Parliament.

Opposition in Parliament had been an important source of strength for the Social Democrats. The purely negative fact that, as a party in opposition, they could not be held responsible for the shortcomings of the Government, but could attack it before and during the election campaign, had done much to restore their prestige. Since the early days of the Weimar Republic their popularity rose and fell in direct proportion to the vigour and militancy of their opposition. Every time they accepted office, they failed. How could it be otherwise? To accept office without sufficient power to carry out a programme, or a reasonable chance of winning power quickly, is suicidal for any party, except in very special circumstances. German Social Democracy never even began to learn this lesson. They did not understand that in their situation "opposition was, had they but known it, a condition of power, office a cause of impotence".[2]

After the 1928 election they decided to try once more the

---

[1] Foundation of the Anglo-Russian Committee for Trade Union Unity after the joint London Conference of April 1925.
[2] R. T. Clark: *The Fall of the German Republic*, p. 230.

experiment of the "Great Coalition".[1] Hermann Müller became Premier.

One of the first actions of the new Government developed into a *cause célèbre*, the so-called affair of the Pocket Battleship A.[2] This unfortunate Pocket Battleship figured prominently in the election campaign. It had been an important item in the budget for the year 1928, voted by the previous Parliament. Before the election this budget, and in particular the naval programme, had provided the chief target for attack by the working-class parties. The main slogan of Socialist propaganda had been: "Battleship or feeding centres for children?"

After the election of the new Reichstag and the formation of a Government led by a Social Democrat, it was generally assumed that the plan for the construction of the battleship would be dropped. But the *Reichswehr* and its friends in the Government insisted on the construction being carried out. Once more the Socialist Ministers were faced with the alternative of either acquiescing or provoking a Cabinet crisis and leaving the Government before it had begun to govern. The latter they did not want to do. They tried to take a middle course—*i.e.*, protest against the construction of the battleship, but take no further action should they be out-voted, as they assumed they would be. The following brief drama does not lack comic aspects: To their extreme discomfort and surprise, the Social Democrats discovered that the Democratic Ministers had decided to support the Socialist protest against the construction of the Pocket Battleship, so that there was no chance at all of being outvoted when the matter came up. Hermann Müller was thus in the unexpected and to him most disagreeable position of having the majority of the Cabinet behind

[1] Various coalition governments with different party compositions became known under special names. Thus, the "Weimar Coalition" consisted of Social Democrats, Democrats and the Catholic Centre. The "Great Coalition" consisted of the Weimar Coalition plus the German People's Party. The "Right Coalition", also called the "Bourgeoisie Bloc", consisted of the Centre Party, the Bavarian People's Party, the German People's Party, the Business Party (*Wirtschaftspartei*) and the German Nationalists.

[2] The construction of this battleship violated none of the clauses of the Treaty of Versailles, and had nothing to do with the so-called "secret rearmament" of the Weimar Republic. The "secret rearmament" of the Weimar Republic has been vastly exaggerated for propaganda purposes. It is quite true that the *Reichswehr* did a certain amount of rearming which was illegal under the terms of the Treaty of Versailles, although it hardly deserved the description "secret", because the whole world knew about it, largely thanks to public protests against secret rearmament and the "Black *Reichswehr*", published in Carl von Ossietzky's *Weltbühne* and in the German Labour press generally. The scope of this secret rearmament was extremely limited. For the purposes of modern warfare, Germany was and remained disarmed until Hitler came to power.

and not against him.[1] Owing to the decision of the Democrats, the Socialist protest against the battleship would have been carried in the Cabinet by a clear majority vote. It would have meant not Hermann Müller's own resignation and that of the other Socialist Ministers, but the resignation of the Ministers who belonged to the Centre and the German People's Party. Hermann Müller had not nearly sufficient confidence in his own ability and in that of his Party and Ministerial colleagues to risk splitting the "Great Coalition" and thus earn the undying hatred of all nationalists and militarists. He felt, in particular, that he could not do without Stresemann, who appeared to conduct Germany's foreign affairs so successfully. He and his colleagues therefore bowed to the wishes of the *Reichswehr*. The protest against the construction of the battleship was never made.

A wave of disgust and fury went through the ranks of the Labour movement, when this story became known. Violent articles were printed, passionate speeches made, enormous protest meetings organised. The wave of anger spread through the entire working class and large sections of the middle classes. Anti-militarism was still in its hey-day.

The Battleship affair had yet to be closed. Fierce public protests compelled the Parliamentary Socialist Party to disavow its own Ministers and to table a motion in the Reichstag demanding that the construction of the battleship be discontinued. The motion was defeated by a narrow majority. All four Socialist Ministers were absent when the vote was taken.

For a long time the Battleship remained one of the most-discussed controversies in the German Labour movement. The ambiguous attitude of the Socialist Ministers made them an easy and favourite target for Communist attacks, but attacks from their own Party comrades were hardly less pronounced.

At the Magdeburg Conference of the Social Democrats in 1929 the whole complex of "the military question" became once more the subject of heated debates. In the end, a general anti-war resolution was adopted, demanding a further voluntary reduction of German armaments. Another paragraph of the same resolution referred to the necessity for the Republic to maintain a defence force "for the protection of its neutrality and of the political, economic and social achievements of the German working class".

In its abstract and non-committal form this resolution was per-

[1] The Cabinet consisted of four Social Democrats, two Democrats, two Catholics, two members of the German People's Party and the Defence Minister Gessler, who belonged to no Party but was the instrument of the politically "neutral" *Reichswehr*.

fectly acceptable from the Party's point of view. There is no conflict whatsoever between the principles of Socialist internationalism, on the one hand, and the desire to defend one's country
against attacks from without or within, on the other. In practice,
however, the German *Reichswehr* was as well suited for the rôle of
the protector of "the political, economic and social achievements
of the working class" as a tiger for the rôle of the protector of the
sheep. Those who wanted to defend Germany's neutrality abroad
and political and social liberty at home could not possibly do so
with the support of the German Army, but only against it. It
did not need the experience of Hitlerism and the second World
War to learn this lesson.

The strength of the *Reichswehr* may have been under-estimated
by the German Labour movement, but about its character there
could never have been any doubt. Indeed, there was none.
There was no German worker who did not know that the
Reichsweht was the very embodiment of reaction and counter-
revolution.

At one time some of the Social Democratic leaders had believed
in the possibility of reforming the *Reichswehr*. They actually
thought that there was a chance for the old Prussian officers to be
able and willing to "improve" the *Reichswehr* and to transform it
into a reliable defence force of the Republic. This school of
thought was chiefly represented by Ebert and Noske. They soon
were proved wrong.

The only alternative, of course, would have been to try to
break the dangerous power of the Army. But the fight against
the military hierarchy was never taken up, not even after the
Kapp *putsch*, when its defeat would have been a foregone conclusion. None of the three working-class parties, which then
existed in Germany, proved capable of taking up this fight.

Sure in their instinct, but left without a lead, the German
workers spontaneously choose a third way. They boycotted the
Reichswehr. A worker who joined the armed forces was regarded
as a traitor and outlaw. The Trade Unions and the Social Democratic Party tacitly followed suit. It was by far the easiest way.
After 1923 the issue was more or less decided. The Social Democrats had not taken up the fight; on the other hand they no longer
believed in the possibility of co-operation after the disastrous
experience with the Ebert–Noske policy. So the *Reichswehr* was
simply boycotted and silently disregarded—and left alone. Now
and then periodic scandals brought it into the news, and Socialist
members of Parliament would raise their voices in protest.
Thereafter the matter was again allowed to drop.

All this does not mean that the Social Democrats or any one of their responsible leaders were engaged in a silent and sinister conspiracy with the *Reichswehr* or supporting secret rearmament. Nothing could be farther from the truth. The fact is that they were simply not interested—which, in a way, is perhaps just as bad or worse. They buried their heads in the sand in the ostrich manner, convincing themselves that there was no danger, for no better reason than that they did not know how to meet it.

The resolution of the Magdeburg Conference did not mean, therefore, that the Party pledged its support to the *Reichswehr* such as it actually was. On the contrary, the chief shortcoming of this resolution was that it refrained from referring to anything that was at all real.

PART FIVE

INTO THE ABYSS
1928–1933

CHAPTER TWENTY-TWO

"RELATIVE STABILITY"

THE TENTH anniversary of the November Revolution was celebrated by none in Germany except the Social Democratic Party and the *Reichsbanner*.[1] Nothing could have been more characteristic of the state of the German Republic ten years after its foundation. The fact becomes even more significant if one recalls that this anniversary occurred at a moment when the economic boom had just reached its peak and when post-war Germany was politically more stable than ever before or after. Political stability and economic prosperity only just succeeded in calming down Right-wing and Left-wing opposition to the Weimar Republic and in taking the sting out of their attacks. But there was nothing to arouse in the mass of the German people any feeling of love or pride or enthusiasm.

Even at that period of relative stability the majority of Germans thought of the Weimar Republic as of something essentially transitory. One section, on the Left, regarded the Republic merely as a transitory stage on the road to socialism; other sections, on the Right, regarded the Republic as an equally transitory stage on the road towards recovery of military power and a German domination of Europe.

In 1928 economic recovery and the relative success of Stresemann's foreign policy had temporarily pushed these issues into the background. The slightest blow to the precarious stability of the Republic was bound to revive the passionate internal strife which had torn and shaken the country ever since the defeat in

[1] The *Reichsbanner* was a para-military non-party organisation founded in February 1924 by the Social Democratic Party as a republican and democratic counterweight to the numerous military organisations on the Right. The bulk of the *Reichsbanner* members consisted of Social Democrats and Trade Unionists, but there were also among them a number of men from the Democratic and Catholic Centre Parties. Its task was to protect the Republic and Germany's democratic institutions against attacks from within.

1918. The blow that was to come with the devastating slump was so forceful that it became the death blow of the Republic of Weimar.

CHAPTER TWENTY-THREE

"SOCIAL FASCISM"

THE COMMUNISTS had been the first to sense the approaching crisis, although they completely misunderstood its character. In 1928 the Sixth World Congress of the Comintern met in Moscow and passed a resolution which predicted "the end of relative stabilisation" and the approach of the "third" period.[1] The policy that went with this theory was a new swing to the "Left"—that is to say, chiefly a move away from and against the Unions and Social Democracy. Once again the Trade Unions were split, separate Communist Trade Union organisations set up, separate Communist lists for the shop-steward elections composed. Collaboration with the Social Democrats became the worst conceivable crime for a Communist. Indeed, after a short period Social Democracy was denounced as a Party of "Social Fascists", deliberately "deceiving the working class", and therefore its chief enemy.[2]

Because of this new policy, a number of Communists, including many of their better known "Right-wing" leaders, broke away from the Party, forming an organisation of their own, the so-called Communist Party Opposition (*K.P.O.*). They were in favour of maintaining Trade Union unity and of a united front with the Social Democrats. In many ways their general line of policy was much more realistic than that of the official Communist Party. Nevertheless, as a splinter group, they were doomed to remain an insignificant political sect unable to attract mass support.

Three events of great momentary importance helped the Communists considerably to convince their members and sympathisers of the apparent correctness of their new anti-Social Democratic policy. One of these events was the great labour conflict in the

[1] The "first" period, according to the Comintern, had been the revolutionary post-war period. The "second" period was the period of "relative stabilisation". The "third" was supposed to be another period of wars and revolutions.

[2] In an undated Communist pamphlet (probably published early in 1930) German workers were called upon to concentrate their energies on "the struggle against Fascism in its present most dangerous form, *i.e.*, its Social Democratic form". (*Was ist Sozialfaschismus?*, published by the *Internationaler Arbeiter-Verlag*, Berlin, p. 26.)

Rhein–Ruhr district which broke out in the early Winter months of 1928; the second was the bloody battle between Berlin workers and the police on May 1st, 1929; the third was the so-called Sklarek scandal that occurred later in the same year.

In the Autumn of 1928 the iron and steel workers of Western Germany demanded an increase in wages. The employers refused. Negotiations failed. As in all similar cases, the arbitration board was called in. In its award it proposed to grant the workers a wage increase amounting to about two-fifths of what they had originally demanded. The Trade Unions accepted this award, but the Employers' Association did not. The arbitration board declared the award to be legally binding. However, the Employers' Association remained adamant and called a lock-out which, in the circumstances, was illegal. Through this lock-out more than 200,000 workers of the iron and steel industry became unemployed, and, in addition to them, masses of miners and other workers in the district whose employment depended on orders from the iron and steel industry.

During their enforced idleness the locked-out workers received financial support from the State. The Government then made another attempt at reconciliation. This time the Home Secretary intervened. His award was eventually accepted by both parties. The workers got a slight increase in wages, but this increase remained considerably behind the one originally awarded by the arbitration board. The employers were content. The workers were embittered. For this award, which represented a clear victory for the Employers' Association, had been made by Severing, a Social Democratic Minister. And the Communists had fresh ammunition in their fight against Social Democracy.

The Winter 1928–1929 was unusually cold. Seasonal unemployment added to the number of those thrown out of work by the oncoming depression which was beginning to make itself felt, and to the large number of those who had become permanently unemployed as a result of the rationalisation of industry. By February 1929 the total number of unemployed had passed the three million mark. Of these more than half a million were excluded, for one reason or another, from full unemployment benefits. A new wave of radicalism swept over Germany, a wave of protest against a Government which allowed the nation once more to face chaos and economic misery.

The Communists organised unemployment demonstrations and hunger marches and incessantly called for strikes. Being outside the Unions, they were incapable of organising successful strikes. But they were less concerned with the success of a strike than with the strike action itself. In their own way they had come to accept the words of their great theoretical opponent, of the Revisionist Eduard Bernstein: "The movement is everything, the aim is nothing".

The inevitable result of this activity for activity's sake was a further isolation of the Communists from the main force of organised labour. Trade Unionists considered "partial strikes", which were bound to lead to defeat, as crimes against the cause of Labour, and detrimental to the immediate interests of their men. Yet, the Communists continued to propagate "partial strikes". The result, in almost every case, was the dismissal by the employer of the Communists who had organised these strikes. The advancing depression gave the employers a welcome opportunity to get rid of the most troublesome workers. Rapidly, therefore, the Communists were becoming a party of unemployed.

General tension grew. In order to prevent clashes between political opponents, such as had begun to occur during the winter months, chiefly as a result of the increasing unemployment, Zörgiebel, the Social Democratic Police President of Berlin, prohibited all open-air demonstrations on May Day, 1929. It was to be foreseen that the radical Berlin workers, including many old Social Democrats, would not easily forego their May Day demonstration, for which they had fought in the past against the laws of Bismarck and the Kaiser. The Communists called them out into the streets in defiance of the prohibition, and their appeal had an overwhelming success. In the main centres of the Berlin working-class districts streets and squares were packed by a seething mass and for hours all traffic came to a standstill. The police were sent out against the demonstrators with orders to enforce the law at all costs. That proved utterly impossible for most of the day, as there were no demonstrations in the strict sense of the word, but just a huge mass of angry people filling the entire street from one side to the other, moving slowly forward and back again without any other aim than to defy the police orders to clear the streets. The police handled the situation in the worst possible manner. They opened fire against the unarmed demonstrators. The outraged workers defended themselves as best they could. Regular street battles went on throughout the night of May 2nd, and for two days barricades remained erected in the Wedding and Neukölln.[1] On May 3rd the police had at last enforced order, at no cost to themselves, but at the cost of twenty-five workers killed, thirty-six severely wounded, of whom some died later in hospital, and numerous others slightly injured.

[1] Wedding and Neukölln are, or, as one should now say: were, two of Berlin's most densely populated and at that time politically most radical working-class districts.

To make the worst of a bad situation, Police President Zörgiebel issued a statement, a few days after the event, in which he tried to justify the shooting by allegations that the police had been shot at first. According to Zörgiebel's statement fourteen butts of police rifles had been shattered or pierced by shots from the crowd, although, fortunately, the police suffered no casualties. For months to come there was no end of sarcastic comment and bitter jokes about the excellent marksmanship of the Berlin workmen.

The "Zörgiebel-May-Day", as it came to be known, has never been forgotten in Berlin. It was largely responsible for the swing of the working-class vote from the Social Democrats to the Communists in the general election of 1930. Within the Social Democratic Party itself the behaviour of the police, in particular their use of firearms against unarmed demonstrators, no matter how illegal the demonstrations, was severely criticised. It is true that it was the commanding police officer who gave the order to shoot, and not the Social Democratic Police President nor the Social Democratic Ministers. Their very reason for prohibiting the demonstration had been to avoid bloodshed and certainly not to cause it. Nevertheless, the Social Democrats in charge of the Prussian police force could not escape responsibility.

There was a sprinkling of individual Socialists and Democrats in the Prussian police force. But as a whole the Prussian police were as little reliable as guardians of Republican order as the *Reichswehr*. The Prussian Government, and in particular their Social Democratic Prime Minister, Otto Braun, had earnestly tried to reform the police. But he was only a little more successful than Ebert had been with the *Reichswehr*. With the intensification of the economic crisis and the growing political radicalism which accompanied it, a large section of the police sided more and more openly with the Right against the Left. To millions of German workers—and by no means only to Communists—the police became gradually an open enemy from whom they could expect persecution, but never protection.

The nominal responsibility of Social Democratic Police Presidents and Ministers of State for this police force added more fuel to the Communist hate propaganda against the Social Democrats. With few individual exceptions, not only the Social Democratic Party as a whole, but even their responsible Ministers and civil servants, were quite innocent of the outrages committed. They were nevertheless found guilty. And in a sense they really were guilty, though guilty of a different crime than the one of which they were commonly accused. Their real "crime", if one chooses to call it so, was a political and not a moral one; it was not born of wickedness, but of political blindness and weakness. It consisted in the acceptance of responsibility without having first secured the power to act responsibly.

After May 1929 the name of Zörgiebel became a symbol as ominous as the name of Noske had been in the early post-war period. For some time Communist propaganda even went so far as to refer to rank-and-file members of the Social Democratic Party and the Free Trade Unions as "the little Zörgiebels". That sort of propaganda naturally produced the opposite effect from the one desired. It helped to forge a new solidarity between the Trade Union leaders and those of the Socialist Party, on the one hand, and the more radical section of their rank and file, on the other. Critical though they were of their own leadership and of the policy of their Party and Unions, Socialist workers were driven to rally more closely around this leadership by the viciousness of the Communist attack. The two great sections of the German working-class movement kept drifting farther apart until mutual hatred became so intense that it rendered them both equally impotent to meet the mortal danger of the rising Nazi movement.

By the Autumn of 1929 the excitement over the "Zörgiebel May-day" had given way to a new political sensation, the "Sklarek Scandal". A private commercial firm, headed by the brothers Sklarek, was discovered to have committed a big fraud, largely at the expense of the Berlin municipality. A number of city councillors, among them some Social Democrats, were found to be involved in the fraudulent transactions. The Sklarek brothers, too, were members of the Social Democratic Party. This unfortunate affair gave rise to a wild agitation against the Party. Communist and Nationalist papers vied with each other in lurid descriptions of its inner rottenness and corruption. Earlier scandals of a similar kind were recalled, in particular the "Barmat affair", another case of corruption in which some individual Social Democrats had been involved and which had excited the German public early in 1925.

As a Party, the Social Democrats were as little responsible for the one case as for the other. Yet these scandals did them enormous harm, because they occurred at periods when growing misery made the poor and impoverished particularly susceptible to agitation against the real or alleged financial corruption of the "political bosses". Owing to the progressing depression, the visible contrast between the way of living of the poor and the wealthy grew sharper. With the really rich minority of the Upper Four Hundred the impoverished masses had no contact at all. What they did see, however, was the comparative wealth displayed by those with a slightly higher income and those with whom, for political reasons, they were in constant touch, the Trade Union and Party bosses, city councillors, burgomasters, managers of public corporations and municipal enterprises, who were, of course, particularly closely watched if they had come into these positions on the strength of their party ticket. None of them had made a fortune out of their positions, and hardly one of them had ever abused his office in a dishonest way and for personal advantages. Yet, when unemployment increased and the standard of living rapidly declined, people in such secure and comparatively well-paid positions were simply regarded as corrupt *Bonzen*,[1] who had become the enemies of all destitutes.

All failures and mistakes with which the Social Democratic Party, rightly or wrongly, was publicly associated, temporarily helped to increase the Communist prestige. The swing from the Social Democratic to the Communist camp would undoubtedly have been far greater had it not been for the crazy Communist propaganda against "Social Fascism" and all its practical consequences.

The majority of the Social Democratic workers felt that the shortcomings of their Party were chiefly due to weakness and not to wickedness, as the Communists alleged. They were even confirmed in their loyalty to their traditional movement by the very viciousness of the Communist attacks, but at the same time they were also more and more despairing of the effectiveness of their own movement. Thus, they were torn in their feelings and frustrated in their action at the very moment when only initiative and action, unity and self-confidence could have warded off the fate that eventually overtook them with Hitler's advent to power.

CHAPTER TWENTY-FOUR

THE NATIONALIST LEGEND

In the Autumn of 1929 the National Socialist danger still seemed so remote that the movement was taken seriously by no one except Hitler himself. The issues that divided the nation were social issues, and the violent nationalist tirades of the extreme Right-wing parties aroused but little interest. At that period Hitler was still regarded as a troublesome and rather absurd

[1] *Bonzen* is an untranslatable term of abuse for lazy, corrupt or parasitical bureaucrats—especially paid party or Trade Union officials.

agitator who, together with his followers, need not be taken more seriously than a gang of irresponsible criminals. In the general election of May 1928 the Nazis had gained no more than 12 out of 475 seats in the Reichstag.

In September 1929 they put their strength once more to the test. Together with the German National Party, now under Hugenberg's leadership, and the "Steelhelmet",[1] they initiated a plebiscite against the Young Plan and the War Guilt Clause of the Versailles Treaty, demanding that German Ministers (or their deputies) who had signed the Young Plan or any other treaty based on the recognition of Germany's war guilt be punished for high treason.

Despite the frenzied agitation which accompanied the campaign for the plebiscite and the practically unlimited funds now at the disposal of the Hitler Party, the plebiscite was a failure. The German people were not yet miserable enough to fall for the nationalistic appeal of Hitlerism. Not more than 5·8 million out of a total electorate of almost 45 million voted for the plebiscite— that is to say, almost exactly the same minority which, in the last general election, had voted for the parties supporting the plebiscite.

If anything, this plebiscite is evidence against the alleged uninterrupted preoccupation of the German people with "national" issues in general and with the Versailles Treaty in particular. In reality, German nationalism was not so much the cause of Hitler's rise to power as its result. Naturally, Germans felt that they had been badly treated by their conquerors in the immediate postwar period; but they also realised that international readjustment was on its way. The national indignation against the Ruhr occupation had been an absolutely genuine feeling, and was shared by the entire German people. But the jingoist frenzy whipped up by the Nazis after 1929 had little or nothing to do with real German grievances. No German felt friendly towards the Versailles Treaty, but neither was this Treaty and its implications the subject of universal concern and hatred before the Nazis exploited it for their own ends.

A nation bent on revenge and aggression would in its overwhelming majority have supported the plebiscite against the Young Plan. Only 13·8 per cent. of the electorate did support it. Yet less than nine months after the plebiscite, in the general elections of September 1930, Hitler scored his first astounding success, as the result of which his party suddenly rose from insignificance to be the second strongest party of the Reichstag.

[1] "Steelhelmet" was a Right-wing military organisation of ex-servicemen, led by Seldte, which counted among its honorary members the then President of the German Republic, Field-Marshal von Hindenburg.

Nothing had happened in the world during these nine inter-vening months that could in any way account for a sudden revival of German nationalism. Indeed, if one tried to explain the Hitler victory of September 1930 as a response of the national pride to some real or imagined provocation from outside it could not be explained. There had been nothing like a provocation. In fact, there was at that time no issue disturbing relations between Germany and other nations. Hitler's election victory was caused exclusively by Germany's internal crisis, which followed the Wall Street crash, and by the complete and obvious failure of all other parties to deal effectively with the crisis.

CHAPTER TWENTY-FIVE

HITLER'S RECRUITS

THE FAILURE to find a solution for Germany's social prob-lems was first and foremost the failure of the German Labour movement. There was only one alternative to Hitler's brand of economic solution, of a vast programme of rearmament as a preparatory stage for war, and that was planning for mass con-sumption, ruthlessly overruling the claims of industrial and agrarian vested interests. There was no third way. In particular, there was no possibility of solving anything by "muddling through"; not so much because the German mind is apt to revolt against the very idea that "muddling" or improvisation can ever achieve anything, but because the crisis itself soon reached over-whelming dimensions, because social and political antagonism was becoming ever more violent and because the suffering of the people had already become much too intense to be cured by haphazard improvisation.

From 1929 onwards unemployment increased steadily until it reached and passed the six million mark in January 1933. That was the official figure of registered unemployed. Actually between eight and nine million wage and salary earners were out of work. Among them were almost 50 per cent. of all Trade Union mem-bers.[1] At the same time, wages and salaries were reduced, un-employment benefit was cut and, owing to the rapid decline of the workers' purchasing power, millions of small shopkeepers,

[1] In certain industries this percentage was even higher. In the building industry 90·6 per cent. of all organised building workers were unemployed when Hitler came to power.

tradesmen, artisans and peasants were ruined. The agricultural population had been hit even earlier by the international agrarian crisis. Large sections of them became overburdened with debts which they could not hope to repay. The slump Germány suffered at the beginning of the 'thirties would have been a catastrophe for any country. But in Germany, which had known little but hardship and chaos since 1914, the crisis had a much deeper effect. There had been altogether too much misery and altogether too many failures. Too long had the patience of the German people been tried. Now frustration and passive suffering turned into despair.

A radical solution—never mind of what sort so long as it was sufficiently radical and effective—that was what an increasing number of Germans demanded in those years until the phrase: *So kann es nicht weitergehen*[1] was as current as *Grüss Gott* and *Guten Tag*. They did not know what they wanted or what could or should be done. They merely knew that something ought to be done.

It was in those years that the majority of Germans came to identify the Weimar democracy, and then democracy in general (because the Weimar Republic had been their only practical experience), with sheer misery and inefficiency. It was in those years that notions like "liberty", "freedom" and "independence" lost their meaning in Germany, because liberty was an empty phrase to a man who could not use it to help himself; freedom and independence became mere catchwords in a situation in which anonymous social forces did their destructive work while the individual looked on in utter helplessness. To fight and over-come this blind, undirected social fate was becoming a passionate desire. Hitler very aptly described this desire as the "anti-capitalist longing of the masses", and directed his propaganda accordingly.[2] It has been said that during the crisis three-quarters of the German nation turned Socialist. That was certainly true if the word "Socialist" is understood chiefly in its negative sense—as the opposite of capitalism and *laissez-faire*.

Indeed, after 1929 there was but one issue left in Germany: Which of the allegedly Socialist movements would eventually win the support of the nation?

[1] "Things can't go on like this."
[2] The official programme of the Nazi Party was full of "Socialist" demands, which were never carried into practice. With the growing intensity of the crisis the "Socialist" demagogy of the Nazis became more and more outspoken. In October 1930, the Nazis tabled a motion in Parliament demanding the immediate expropriation, without compensation, of all property held by bankers, financiers, Jews and foreigners as well as the immediate socialisation of all banks.

Between them, the two "Marxist" parties succeeded in holding the allegiance of their traditional supporters up to the very last moment, although there was a shift within the Labour movement away from the Social Democrats towards the Communists. Both parties, however, failed to catch the imagination of those millions of common people whose means of independent existence had disappeared, but who dreaded nothing more than the nightmare of "proletarianisation".

For this class—a class very large in numbers—the Labour movement had no message at all, no hope, no offer of a solution that allowed them to remain what they were. What the working-class movement had to say to the frightened *petit-bourgeois* was in essence a prediction of his doom. "Go on struggling for your existence—it won't help you. Your class is finished. You cannot fight historical necessity. You will become proletarians anyhow. You might as well give in and support us now." This type of approach had only one effect: it turned the people to whom it was directed not against the causes of their misery, but against those who told them that they were destined by history to be miserable. It turned them not against the causes of their "proletarianisation", but against the proletarians.

The mass of the German *petit-bourgeois* turned to Hitler, who promised them not decline but new glory and social security in a national renaissance. They did not remain the only supporters of the new creed of National Socialism. Hitler recruited followers in all classes of German society, though least of all amongst the workers. Followers of Hitler were, in fact, chiefly those who had lost their traditional position in society and their security without a chance of regaining it through personal effort.

In the working class Hitler found his followers among the permanently unemployed who had given up hope of ever again finding work in the "normal" way. These men were the victims not so much of the new slump as of industrial rationalisation, which had made them permanently "superfluous".[1] As for the intellectuals, National Socialism found its recruits in the "academic proletariat", among the sons and daughters of an impoverished middle class who had no chances of ever rising to responsible and secure positions. Among the peasants and big landowners the Nazi supporters were those most hopelessly in debt. Last, but not least, a large and important section of the capitalist class cast in its lot with Hitler right from the beginning. Outstanding among them were the well-known leaders of German heavy industry, who were on the verge of bankruptcy.

[1] Even during the boom year 1927–1928 the official unemployment figure never fell below 1·4 million.

Bankruptcy in the widest sense of the word, social bankruptcy, was the one common denominator of those who gathered under the Swastika flag. The one common interest uniting people of such widely different social background and personal fortunes was their wish for a strong authoritarian State that would create work for the unemployed, subsidise industry and landed interests, "save the middle classes"—in short, do for them what they were unable to do for themselves. Their man was Hitler, their creed Fascism, setting out to merge modern capitalism with Governmental absolutism, guaranteeing profits to industry, work to the workers, responsible positions to scientists and bureaucrats, rent to the landlords, protective guilds to the craftsmen, power to the army, and glory to them all.

Hitler carefully avoided the difficult task of explaining in detail exactly how he intended to establish his paradise on earth. Untroubled by a tradition of "scientific Socialism", he did not bother to propose specific cures to heal the thousand ailments from which the German people were suffering. He simply said: "Give me the power and I will do everything for you that you cannot do yourself".

It sounded incredible. But still—what else was there to hope for? The Communists? No. A Party that takes its direction from a foreign country can never rise to the rôle of a freely and universally accepted national leadership in its own country. The Social Democrats? No. They had failed abysmally at every critical moment. The slump had started with the Socialists in office. They had proved quite incapable of doing anything about it. All other parties were finished, anyhow. Only Hitler had never failed as yet because—he had never been tried out. His party seemed a strong and determined body, bent on action, guided by one central will, strikingly different from all other parties, which had proved hopeless failures.

Of course, Hitler's propaganda was not only concerned with social demagogy. Its violent nationalism and anti-semitism played at least as great a part. Yet, without his ruthless social demagogy, nationalism and anti-semitism could never have constituted a sufficiently strong appeal to the mass of the people.

Wild nationalists and anti-semites there always were in Germany. Ever since 1918 they had remained in a minority because it was only too obvious that their alleged patriotism consisted of nothing but the pursuit of narrow class interests in their crudest form. In the German language the very word "national" had come to be identified with the ultra-reactionary, sectional interests of a small clique.

If patriotism means to put the interest of one's country above the interest of individuals or minority sections, then the most wildly nationalistic Germans were the least patriotic. But no political party claiming national leadership could afford to neglect genuine patriotism. It would have been of tremendous importance for the German Labour movement to give expression to this genuine patriotism and to prevent gutter-patriots posing as the only "good Germans". In this the Labour movement failed as in so many other things. It allowed its nationalistic enemies to disguise their policy of reaction at home and aggression abroad as "German patriotism".

As long as the advocates of nationalism were exclusively found among the landowning aristocracy, the industrial magnates and the army officers, the majority of the common people remained immune to their appeal, and the situation did not seem dangerous. Things became different when Hitler came, appealing not only to an outraged sense of social justice, but also to the frustrated sense of patriotism which the old Right-wing parties had so openly abused and the Left-wing parties so completely neglected.[1]

Indeed, what made Hitler so irresistible was the combination of his appeal to these two basic emotions of patriotism and social justice. No other political party of the Republic was able to make this dual appeal, though most of them tried. The unnatural situation of a citizen forced to make his choice between being a good German and being a Socialist simply dissolved into nothing if only he accepted the Hitler creed—and with it disappeared the dead-weight of confusion and frustration. Suddenly everything seemed quite simple: That Germany was not a Socialist paradise was the fault of other countries, the fault of the *Versailler Diktat*, the fault of Bolshevism, the fault of World-Jewry. Everything else followed easily and naturally.

In all its absurdity, baseness and deliberate falsehood, the Hitler creed seemed to millions like a revelation. That this was possible is certainly a proof of Germany's political immaturity. It was also a symptom of the depth of her despair, which, in millions of people, destroyed the capacity for sober judgment and straight thinking.

For many years the world regarded Hitler as a kind of political magician, and even the most hardened rationalists had to admit

[1] Among both Socialists and Communists a number of individuals felt uneasily that here was a problem to be solved. Some of them began themselves to confuse nationalism with patriotism and to make concessions, in theory as well as in practice, to their jingoist opponents, whose cause they strengthened while adding to the demoralisation of their own movement. People of this type always remained, however, a small minority and cannot be regarded as typical of either of the two parties.

that Hitler's personal appeal and his power to influence his fellow-men were nearer the miraculous than anything else in modern history. No one can or should deny it: but it is as well to remember that Hitler came up against a barrier which, right up to his victory, he never succeeded in breaking down. This barrier which Hitler could not overrun was the organised Labour movement, which proved a thousand times stronger in a stubborn, passive, almost dullish defence of its own traditions and ways of thought than it had ever been when called upon to act. It was a clear frontier. Hitler never won followers in the camp of organised Labour, an insignificant number of individuals apart. If this comparison can be made at all, it will be found that German Labour produced not more Quislings before or after January 30th, 1933, than the oppressed peoples of Europe. Hitler did not even win the allegiance of a minority, and this in spite of the suicidal policy which both working-class parties continued to pursue to the bitter end. Only after the National Socialist *Machtergreifung* was the régime strong enough to defeat and suppress the German working-class movement.

Even a superficial analysis of election figures clearly shows that the rapidly growing number of Nazi voters were deserters from the middle- and upper-class parties, with the exception only of the Catholic Party. During the fourteen years of the Weimar Republic the Centre Party moved politically from the moderate Left to the conservative Right. In its social composition it remained fairly stable. Apart from the Nazis, the Centre was the only German party which counted among its adherents members of all social classes. The working-class section of the Centre Party was organised in the Christian Trade Unions. They proved as immune to Hitler propaganda as the two so-called Marxist parties.

Taken as a whole the working-class electorate remained solid, while Hitler scored his amazing successes among the middle and upper classes. This can be clearly seen in the chart on page 141, covering the five general elections between 1924 and 1932. Of course, Socialists and Communists made considerable gains and suffered considerable losses at various elections; but these gains and losses invariably cancelled each other out. The middle- and upper-class parties, on the other hand, suffered an almost equal decline, while Hitler scored success after success. Their losses were his gains.

The second category of Nazi voters and supporters was that large section of the German nation which, in the past, had been more or less politically indifferent. They were the non-voters whom Hitler succeeded in mobilising, the men and women who

Parties	1924	1928	1930	July 1932	Nov. 1932
	[in Million Votes]				
"Bourgeois" Parties (except Centre Party) .	13·2	12·9	10·3	4·0	5·3
Social Democrats and Communists . .	10·5	12·3	13·0	13·1	13·1
Catholic Centre Party .	4·1	3·7	4·1	4·5	4·2
National Socialists .	0·9	0·8	6·4	13·7	11·7

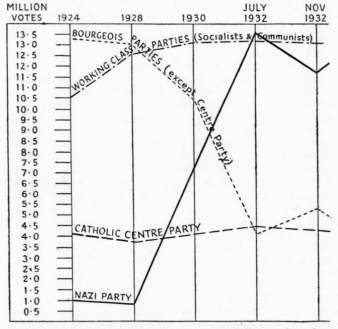

called themselves "unpolitical", that essentially passive element in politics which invariably follows the strongest force.

A united and militant working class might have attracted them. A working class split into two rival organisations, each condemning and denouncing the other, was the embodiment of impotence.

CHAPTER TWENTY-SIX

NO LESSER EVIL

THE DECLINE and fall of the German Labour movement has often been attributed to its disunity. Undoubtedly the split into a Social Democratic and a Communist camp has been a permanent source of weakness. Nevertheless the split was not the primary cause of the eventual collapse. The continued co-existence of the two working-class parties was itself only a sign of the imperfection and limitation of each. Every member of the German Labour movement realised how tragically the movement was weakened by its lack of unity. And yet it seemed utterly impossible to overcome the split as long as its original causes continued to be operative.

Each of the two parties saw the weakness of the other through a magnifying glass without finding a way to remove the causes of its own failure. From the point of view of both parties, the mutual denunciations seemed justified; and the idea of a merger, or at least of close co-operation, was discarded by both because it seemed like a "betrayal" of the most sacred principles. The justice of many of the mutual accusations made it impossible for either party to attract the members and the followers of the other. There was, of course, a certain amount of fluctuation between the two parties, and between 1929 and 1932 the Communists made some gains at the expense of the Social Democrats, just as in 1923. But this shift did not alter the balance decisively. For the ordinary German worker it became increasingly difficult to decide which of the two parties deserved more support. If anything, this was clearly a case for choosing "the lesser evil", for the policies of both parties were so obviously hopeless that the choice between them became a matter more of temperament than of conviction.

Until March 1930 the Social Democrats remained in office. In the end the Great Coalition split over a conflict concerning unemployment insurance. Conservatives and Nationalists were pressing for what they chose to call a "reform" of the Unemployment Insurance Act, demanding increased contributions and smaller benefits. The Socialist Ministers refused to give in, and the Cabinet resigned. The stiffer attitude of the Socialist Cabinet members and their refusal, for once, to compromise were in fact due to the heavy pressure of the Trade Unions, to whom unemploy-

ment benefits were a vital issue. With the resignation of Hermann
Müller and his Socialist colleagues the last Social Democratic
Ministers had left the Government of the Reich. Came the "era
Brüning", and with it the end of the Weimar democracy.

Brüning's rule by emergency decrees was unconstitutional.
What was worse, his decrees made the devastating slump even
more unbearable for the mass of the people. Salaries, wages, unemployment benefits were ruthlessly cut. Indirect taxation was
increased, new general taxes were introduced, imposing the same
payments on the poor as on the rich.[1] At the same time import
duties on grain and other agrarian products were greatly increased; in some cases by as much as 500 or 1000 per cent. This
measure was quite inadequate to bring the agrarian crisis to a halt,
but effective in preventing the urban population from buying
cheap foreign foodstuffs. Hindenburg's friends, the East Prussian
Junkers, were presented with enormous sums from public funds,
which did not rescue them from their bankruptcy, but encouraged
them to clamour for more. The result was a public scandal, the
notorious *Osthilfe-Skandal*, and an endless play of intrigues began
which eventually caused the fall first of Chancellor Brüning and
later of Chancellor Schleicher.

Most of Brüning's emergency measures were part and parcel of
a general policy of deflation, designed to support German export
industries and export trade and thereby economy as a whole.
That end was never achieved. But in the process of trial Germany's shrinking wealth was thoroughly redistributed in favour
of the property-owning classes.

In spite of all this, the Social Democrats decided to "tolerate"
Brüning and his policy of emergency decrees, holding that, bad
though Brüning was, he was the "lesser evil" compared with what
might come after him. Having started, they continued to tolerate
every new blow as part of the "lesser evil", until the last spark of
fight had died in them and they had become the hopelessly frustrated spectators of their own defeat.

They were violently attacked by the Communists on account
of their "toleration" of Brüning. The Communists argued that
starvation under Brüning was no better than starvation under anybody else and that one could not pacify the devil by giving him
a little finger; he is apt to take the whole hand. This sort of
criticism was received with much approval by a growing section
of the Socialist and Trade Union rank and file. But the Communists did not leave it at that. They forfeited all chances they

[1] The most hated of these taxes was the so-called Citizen-tax, popularly
called "nigger tax", which imposed the same fixed sum on every German citizen,
millionaire and beggar alike.

might have had of winning the majority of the Labour movement for a more militant and effective policy because they were much less concerned—and said so openly—with warding off the supreme danger facing Socialists and Communists alike than with their ardent desire to "unmask" the Social Democrats and Trade Unions as "traitors". Most of their energy and of their extremely vitriolic propaganda was used to try to prove that virtually *all* parties were "Fascists" of one sort or another except, of course, their own party. The Social Democratic Party was "Fascist", the Trade Unions were "Fascist", the Brüning Government was "Fascist"—why on earth should the working class be afraid of Hitler?

As a matter of fact, for a time, they took it for granted that a Hitler victory would only hasten their own revolution. Was there not a law of the "dialectic" development of all history that greater pressure must also produce greater counter-pressure? In a Reichstag speech of October 14th, 1931, Remmele (after Thälmann the best-known leader of the German Communist Party) said:

"Herr Brüning has expressed it very clearly; once they (the Nazis) are in power, the united front of the proletariat will emerge and make a clean sweep of everything. . . . We are not afraid of the Fascists. They will shoot their bolt sooner than any other Government."

In their blindness to reality the Communists not only believed that a Hitler dictatorship would take them nearer to their own victory—they even strengthened the nationalistic appeal of the Nazis by suddenly launching a programme of "National and Social Liberation" and denouncing the Nazis as waging a mere sham fight against the "Versailles slavery", whereas they, the Communists, were the true advocates of "national liberation". In August 1931 the Communists participated actively in a Nazi plebiscite against the Social Democratic Government of Prussia.

By the beginning of the year 1932 it slowly dawned on them that their policy was leading straight to the abyss. They did not change their line radically, but they began to concentrate their main attack on the Nazis instead of on the Social Democrats. Yet when they called for a more vigorous fight against "Fascism", their supporters had already been so confused by previous propaganda that most of them did not know exactly where "Fascism" began and where it ended. Both the Socialists and the Brüning Government had earlier been denounced as Fascist. Yet Brüning had to make room for the "more Fascist Cabinet of Barons", headed by Herr von Papen. And when Papen "dismissed" the constitutional Social Democratic Government of Prussia, the Communists suddenly proposed a united front to the Social Democrats and Trade Unions. They suggested a general strike against Papen's *coup d'état* in Prussia and in defence of the same Braun–Severing Government which they had tried to overthrow only eleven months ago by supporting the Nazi plebiscite. After all that had happened, this united front proposal was too much of a surprise to be taken seriously anywhere.

Communist irresponsibility gave the Social Democrats an easy excuse to continue their suicidal inactivity while, on the other hand, their failure to take action seemed to justify all Communist accusations against the Socialists. Not to take action when the Social Democratic Government of Prussia was overthrown by Papen's *coup d'état* was tantamount to political resignation. In all German cities formations of the *Reichsbanner* and the Iron Front were standing by, polishing their rifles and waiting for a call to action. If ever there had been a moment to defend the Republic it had come on July 20th, 1932, when Herr von Papen entrusted the Executive Power in Prussia to General von Rundstedt.

There was no call to action. The only message that came from the Executive of the Social Democratic Party was an appeal to vote Socialist in the forthcoming elections.

The Communists were satisfied once again to "unmask" the "Social Fascist traitors". They did not attempt to do more. Both parties therefore not only pursued the worst policy imaginable at the most critical moment of their history, but each, by its own failure, pushed the other farther and farther in the wrong direction, until there was a world between them, and reconciliation had become impossible.

The economic crisis went from bad to worse. At the time of the general election in September 1930 the number of registered unemployed had been well over three million. One year later it had risen to five million, and was still far from having reached its peak.

Trade Unions and the Social Democratic Party published a number of plans designed to distribute the burden of the slump more evenly and to improve the economic situation in general. But all these plans were conceived in a defensive, indeed in a defeatist frame of mind, without vision, determination or fighting spirit. They caused some heated debates among a handful of experts, but were singularly unsuited to create a new confidence, to say nothing of enthusiasm. They were soon forgotten.

The Party and the Unions were not more lucky in a belated

attempt to create an anti-Fascist defence force, the so-called "Iron Front" (founded in 1931). The "Iron Front" was composed of members of the Social Democratic Party, the Trade Unions, the *Reichsbanner* and various Labour sport organisations. If it was to have any purpose at all, it could only have been that of preparing for a civil war which the Nazis would launch sooner or later. But both Party and Unions were convinced that democracy and the Constitution would be destroyed in a civil war, and they were determined to avoid it. There was therefore not much point in forming the "Iron Front". All the same, for a short time it gave the rank and file fresh hope and confidence. They were all the more disappointed when this organisation created for active defence was never called upon to act or to defend.

In the same year a minority section broke away from the Social Democratic Party. They formed the so-called Socialist Workers' Party (*S.A.P.*) and drew a number of former Communists into their ranks. The new party did not achieve great importance, mainly because most workers were by instinct reluctant to support a "splinter" party that increased further the tragic rivalry and disunity within the movement. It did not help the new party to declare itself in favour of unity because, whatever its programme and proclaimed policy, its practice had been that of further splitting the movement.

The year 1932 was Germany's great election year. There were two general elections for the Reichstag, elections for the Prussian and other Diets and a Presidential election with two ballots. It has been said that in 1932 German democracy elected itself to death. That is true enough, provided one regards these elections not as the cause but as a symptom of the death-struggle of German democracy.

In the first of the five 1932 elections Germany re-elected Hindenburg as her President. He was elected by the parties of the Great Coalition, including the Social Democrats, who considered him as a "lesser evil" than Hitler, much as, seven years previously, they had regarded Wilhelm Marx as a "lesser evil" than Hindenburg. The Communists once again put up Ernst Thälmann as their own candidate; he received, however, considerably fewer votes than his Party three months later in the general election. Many Communist sympathisers were obviously afraid of splitting the vote which might inadvertently put Hitler in power.

At that time two-thirds of the German nation still voted against Hitler. The Nazi vote of 13·4 million increased in the next general election (July 1932) to 13·7 million. The German electorate being at that time about 45 million, the Nazis had actually conquered rather less than one-third of the national vote. This was the highest vote they ever got in a free election. It is important to remember this fact in judging German public opinion at that time. If election figures have any meaning, then it is quite clear how unfounded the Nazi boasts are that Hitler was swept into power by the will of the overwhelming majority of the German nation.

Indeed, in the last free elections held before Hitler's advent to power, in November 1932, the Nazis suffered a considerable setback, losing 2 million votes, which were recaptured by the German Nationalists. At that time it was widely assumed, both in Germany and outside, that this election marked the beginning of the decline of the Hitler movement. In reality, however, Hitler had merely temporarily lost the support of some middle-class sections who had become frightened by the radical language of the Nazis. They had become frightened, above all, by the Nazi participation in the Berlin transport workers' strike called by the Communists on the eve of the November election. Social demagogy in propaganda speeches was one thing, but social demagogy actually carried into practice was more than Hitler's capitalist supporters could stand, even if it was only an electioneering stunt designed to capture the working-class vote.

The story of the Berlin transport workers' strike is perhaps the saddest illustration of the agony, disunity and disintegration of the German Labour movement. It was the last time before Hitler's advent to power that the working class became active. The strike had been called in order to prevent a threatened cut in wages. In the strike ballot a large majority of the workers had voted in favour of a strike; but the necessary majority of 75 per cent. had not quite been reached. Insisting on the strict observation of their rules, the Trade Unions refused to sanction the strike, while the Communists called the men out. From their point of view, the action was highly successful. Practically all the transport workers came out and for a time Berlin transport was completely paralysed. The strikers enjoyed widespread sympathy and active support from the Berlin population, which was all the more remarkable as a strike of busmen, tram and railway men inevitably caused great inconvenience to all inhabitants.

Nevertheless, the strike was doomed to failure because the Trade Unions refused to support it and to pay relief. The Nazis saw a unique opportunity to feather their own nest. Thus, to everybody's surprise, they came out in favour of the strike. Street collections were organised for strike funds, and in some districts of Berlin the unique spectacle could be observed of a Communist and a Nazi standing arm in arm and shouting in an agreed rhythm, while they were shaking their collection boxes: "For the strike fund of the *R.G.O.*" [1]—"For the strike fund of the *N.S.B.O.*" [2] The sight of this perverted united front was so repulsive to most ordinary Trade Unionists, Socialists and even many Communists, that the initial sympathy for the strike and the strikers turned into disgust and hostility. After five days the strike was called off.

The Nazi experiment of trying to catch the working-class vote by their participation in the strike proved a failure. They never repeated the experiment. On the other hand, they had managed to frighten off a considerable section of their middle-class supporters. It almost looked as though Hitler would be unable ever to redeem his promise of gaining power by exclusively legal methods. Of course, the success he had already achieved in gaining almost one-third of the national vote was tremendous; but it was difficult to see how he could get much farther. It looked very much as though he had reached the limit of what he could hope to achieve by his methods. It seemed impossible that he could get the whole nation behind him in his bid for absolute power, or even the majority of the nation. Thus, he decided to go the opposite way—*i.e.*, to get into power in order to get hold of the nation. From the November elections onwards until January 1933, Germany's history was reduced to one long chain of manoeuvres and intrigues between Papen, Hitler, Hugenberg and the men around Hindenburg. This story has often been told and need not be retold here. No doubt more details will one day be known when the archives of the Third Reich are opened. Only this needs saying: The German nation at large, especially the common people, knew little of the intrigues that were hatched in the feudal *Herrenklub*, in the Hotel Kaiserhof (then Hitler's Berlin Headquarters) and in Hindenburg's Palace. The mass of the people had simply become a pawn in the game for power. This rôle of passive onlookers to their own doom was in strange contrast to the wild agitation of many parties seeking the political support of the masses and to the growing tension and the atmosphere of civil war that was beginning to creep over the whole country.

The civil war atmosphere was created by a sort of three-cornered fight between Nazi bands, chiefly the S.A., working-class groups and the police. Armed raids of Nazi formations on political meetings of opponents or on workers' settlements had become an almost daily occurrence since the early summer of 1932. The growing number of street demonstrations organised

[1] *R.G.O.*—Revolutionary Trade Union Opposition (Communist).
[2] *N.S.B.O.*—National Socialist Factory Cell Organisation.

by the Nazis as well as by various working-class organisations ended, as a rule, with bloody clashes. Police intervention usually led to more bloodshed. As the tension grew worse, many policemen in the big cities got so nervous that they became unfit for further duties there. They had to be exchanged for new police recruits, who were generally taken from the country districts and, as often as not, were open sympathisers with the Hitler movement. As a result their intervention in street fights developed more and more into a one-sided attack on the Left. The workers of Berlin and of other big cities had more than one opportunity of seeing mounted police charging into hungry crowds, trampling down passers-by as well as demonstrators, and attacking women and children as well as men. The victims of these, often quite unprovoked, assaults, and many who witnessed them, soon came to hate the very sight of a policeman just as much as the sight of an S.A. man in a brown shirt and jack-boots.

As Autumn and Winter came, people grew accustomed, on Monday mornings, to look in their newspapers almost mechanically for the accounts of deaths which had occurred during the week-end as a result of Nazi assaults on Communists, *Reichsbanner* men and other political opponents. In many districts an average of half a dozen deaths per week became quite the rule. On special occasions, particularly on the week-ends preceding the numerous elections of 1932, the figure rose much higher. By far the greatest number of victims were Communists and *Reichsbanner* men.

The various Governments which followed each other in rapid succession were quite incapable of dealing with this situation. In April 1932 the S.A. had been suppressed, chiefly on the insistence of Otto Braun, the Social Democratic Prime Minister of Prussia. Two months later the Government of Herr von Papen again restored the S.A. to its legal existence. As a result the Nazi terror raged as never before. According to a statement by the Prussian Government, 99 cases of violent death and 125 cases of severe injuries were registered in Prussia alone within one month after the restoration of the S.A., not to mention the large number of people slightly injured as a result of the terror.

By August even the Papen Government felt that something had to be done. By emergency decree the death penalty was introduced for assaults on policemen or on political opponents. Although a number of Nazis were thus condemned to death, these sentences were not carried out in a single instance—not even in the notorious Potempa case, in which five Nazis were tried and found guilty of the murder of a Communist landworker into whose cottage they broke at night and finding their victim asleep

149

in his bed literally trampled the man to death before the eyes of his mother.

It is important to recall these facts if one is to understand at all why the German working-class movement which regarded Hitler as its deadly enemy never moved a finger when he came to power. The fury of the Nazi terror before Hitler came to power does not explain all, but it certainly helped to create and maintain that paralysing attitude of "things-cannot-become-worse-any-more". When, on January 30th, 1933, Hitler was made Chancellor of Germany, the terror did, of course, increase beyond all measure. However, it *increased* and was not altogether a new and hitherto unknown thing, and therefore appeared to be at first a mere change in quantity.

To-day one is accustomed to regard January 30th, 1933, as the first day of totalitarian Nazi rule over Germany. But at the time this was not at all clear to most people either inside Germany or outside. There was in fact no sharp dividing line between the Hitler régime and its predecessors that could be recognised at once by every man and woman. The Nazis stormed no barricades, they did not assault Government buildings nor did they stage a spectacular march on Berlin. In the Reich Capital January 30th was as dull and miserable and grey as any other day of the month. There was no rebellion, no *putsch*. Hitler was simply asked to be Prime Minister of a coalition Government, exactly as before him Brüning, Papen and Schleicher had been asked.

German democracy was dead, killed by the crisis, long before Hitler buried it. The three last Governments of the Weimar Republic had been so reactionary in their legislation and had based their reign to such an extent on unconstitutional emergency decrees that the fundamental novelty of the Nazi Government was at first hardly visible. Moreover, all these semi-dictatorial Governments had so often been denounced (chiefly though not exclusively by Communist propaganda) as "Fascist" Governments that millions of workers felt it did not really make any difference whether their Fascist ruler was called Brüning, Papen, Schleicher or—Hitler.

Hitler began his rule with the dissolution of Parliament and the order for general elections to be held in March.

Another election! What difference was there from previous Governments? What did Governments matter anyhow? Six million registered unemployed. In addition at least two million "invisible" unemployed. A hard winter. No bread. No coal. No work. Endless queues in front of the employment exchanges for a miserable dole. Nazis shooting or beating up Communists and *Reichsbanner* men. The police charging into excited crowds maddened with hunger and despair.

All that had been "daily life" before Hitler. What could Hitler take away that had not been lost long before? It was in this mood that the German working class silently witnessed the birth of the Third Reich.

PART SIX

THE SURVIVORS
1933–1945

CHAPTER TWENTY-SEVEN

DESTRUCTION OF THE LABOUR MOVEMENT

On February 1st, 1933, Göring issued a decree against Communist propaganda. On February 4th the new Government drafted and Hindenburg signed and issued an emergency decree "for the Protection of the German People", which was directed against all anti-Nazi forces. On February 7th Göring appointed National Socialist officials to the Ministry of Interior. On February 9th all police officers who did not whole-heartedly support Hitler were requested to resign from their posts. On February 13th all Republican civil servants in high positions were dismissed. On February 15th Nazis were appointed as police officers in place of such Republicans as had been forced to resign. On February 17th the terror was officially sanctioned by a Göring order to the police to use their firearms at their own discretion.

In the meantime almost the entire Communist and Socialist press had been suppressed, in some cases indefinitely, in others for three months or only for days. After such a period they were again allowed to reappear for a day or two in order to be suppressed anew. Labour literature was destroyed, Labour meetings were banned. Anti-Nazi posters were torn from the walls. Banners and flags of the working-class movement were hauled down and torn to pieces. For the forthcoming election of March 5th the Labour movement had been robbed of all its propaganda means.

Still, the Social Democrats preserved a touching and indeed pathetic faith in the continuity of the rule of law. During the last open-air meeting which the Socialists were allowed to hold in the Berlin *Lustgarten*, Otto Wels, chairman of the Party, gave his estimate of the situation by quoting the comforting proverb: "*Gestrenge Herren regieren nicht lange*".[1] Even the monstrous Nazi pro-

---

[1] "Strict masters don't rule for long."

vocation of February 27th, the burning of the Reichstag, did not entirely succeed in destroying the stubborn and wishful belief that after a while "things will be normal again".

Whilst this was the average view of the Socialist and Trade Union leadership, the Communists were hardly more realistic. The two wings of the Labour movement differed only in that the Socialists believed that "things could not really develop quite so disastrously" as some "pessimists" would have it, whereas the Communists maintained that "things could not possibly become worse", seeing how bad they had been all along, under previous Governments.

The first wave of terror was particularly directed against the Communists. The Communist Party was banned on the day of the Reichstag fire, which provided the excuse. During the next few days thousands, if not tens of thousands of its active members, including parliamentary deputies, were thrown into prisons, concentration camps, or murdered in cold blood. In the course of the next few months the Socialists were to experience exactly the same fate. But they were given a short spell of grace during which their Party organisation was allowed to continue a sham legal existence although their press was prohibited, their meetings dissolved or raided, their election posters torn from the walls and their Party and Trade Union offices ransacked.

The general election of March 5th, in spite of the tremendous wave of terror against all organisations of the Left and despite Nazi intimidation, particularly in rural districts, still ended with as many as 120 parliamentary seats for the Socialists and 81 for the Communists, as against 288 Nazis, 73 Catholic Centre and 52 German Nationalists. The Communist vote having been declared "illegal" by Government decree, the Nazis could now claim an absolute majority.

Even the month of February 1933 was not impressive enough to open the eyes of the German workers, who watched and suffered their fate in a horrified bewilderment that was paralysing. They were just waiting. Waiting to awake from a bad dream, or waiting for a lead for action which never came, either from the Socialists, or from the Communists. The Socialists went on proclaiming that "we must wage our struggle on the basis of the Constitution", which had long been abolished. They emphasised that "undisciplined procedure by individual organisations or groups on their own initiative would do the greatest harm to the entire working class".[1] That call for discipline remained their one and only message to the workers who awaited a call to

[1] From the Manifesto issued by the Executive and Parliamentary Party of the Social Democrats, *Vorwärts*, January 31st, 1933.

action. Previously, they had spoken of "fierce resistance", but the pledge was only remembered when it was too late.

The Communists had used even stronger language, but no acts followed their words. Later they argued that "the betrayal of the Social Democrats" had rendered any action impossible. Even from their own point of view this argument was untenable. They had so often proclaimed themselves as the only "vanguard of the Proletariat" that it would have been up to them to give a lead, and not to wait for this lead to come from a party whom they consistently denounced as "Social Fascist". However, the Communist Party was not in the least perturbed by its failure to take action. According to its own subsequent verdict, the lack of resistance did not signify anything, for "the strength of the Communist Party expressed itself in the fact that, at the critical moment, the Party remained homogeneous. During the critical weeks there were no 'discussions' going on in the German Communist Party." [1]

Thus, the political and organised life of the working-class movement came to an end. In the early days of Spring 1933 contact between the Central Executives of both the Communist and the Social Democratic parties and their local and district organisations was broken off. The rank and file vainly sought guidance from their former leaders. They got nothing but examples of retreat or hollow, meaningless phrases.

Deceived by the fact that the Nazis advanced only step by step and did not destroy all democratic institutions at one blow (although achieving in months what had taken years to achieve in Fascist Italy), some leading Social Democrats believed up to the very last minute that they might be able to save their Party from illegality. Consequently they concentrated all their energies on preserving at all costs the Party and its legal status. They went far to achieve this end. Towards the end of March, long after the Socialist and Liberal press of other countries had published full accounts of the atrocities committed by the German Nazis, several members of the Social Democratic Party Executive volunteered to go abroad and were given facilities by Göring to do so, in order to stop this publicity, on the ground that it was "apt to harm the position of the anti-Fascists in Germany" who were being held responsible by the Nazis.[2] On March 30th, Otto Wels, Chairman of the Social Democratic Party, demon-

---

[1] *The Communist International*, German edition, No. 10, July 7th, 1933.

[2] In fact, some of them took this opportunity to inform their Labour friends in London and elsewhere of the true state of affairs in Germany; but since this had to remain secret it could not destroy the demoralising outward effect of their official mission.

stratively resigned from the Bureau of the Second International. Wels' subsequent explanation that this resignation had been nothing but a tactical move and that he had never really contemplated giving up his and his Party's international affiliation is, no doubt, correct. However, the attempts of Social Democrats to adapt themselves, if only outwardly, to the new German spirit of narrow nationalism, certainly played into the hands of the Nazis. Whatever its secret motive, the demonstrative abandonment of working-class internationalism added considerably to the already existing demoralisation.

Neither concession nor compromise could save the Labour organisations from their fate. Piece by piece, the basis of their legal existence was destroyed. The most shameful attempt at a voluntary "self-adaptation" to the régime was that of the Trade Union leadership. Still hoping that they might be able to save their organisations by a display of what they continued to call "political neutrality", they even went so far as to give their full support to the Nazi transformation of the First of May, the traditional day of international working-class solidarity, into a "National Labour Day". The *Gewerkschaftszeitung*, official organ of the A.D.G.B. (the German T.U.C.), published for May 1st an article by Walter Pahl of which one paragraph read:

> "We certainly need not strike our colours in order to recognise that the victory of National Socialism, though won in the struggle against a party which we used to consider as the embodiment (*Träger*) of the idea of Socialism (*i.e.*, the Social Democrats), *is our victory as well*; because, to-day, the Socialist task is put to the whole nation." [1]

This declaration, which caused much indignation among the rank and file of the Trade Union and Socialist movement, failed to impress the Nazis. On May 2nd—that is, immediately after this moral surrender—all Trade Union buildings were occupied by detachments of the S.A. and S.S. The most prominent Trade Union leaders, Leipart, Grassmann and Wissel, were arrested. On May 13th all Trade Union property was confiscated. The German working class had lost its industrial organisations. The only Union to escape the enforced *Gleichschaltung* was the *AFA-Bund* (the union of clerical workers), which had voluntarily dissolved itself in order to spare its members the shameful subjection.

In the meantime the Social Democrats had split into several groups. A part of the Executive emigrated to Prague to continue activities from there. A section of the Parliamentary Party, led

[1] My italics.

by Paul Löbe (President of the German Reichstag), made further and further concessions to the new régime, vainly hoping that Hitler might reward such submissiveness by recognising a distinction between "good" and "bad" Social Democrats, and tolerating the "good" ones. A third group finally decided to go underground, and of them more will be said later.

On May 17th Hitler made the first of his famous Reichstag speeches on foreign policy. That was the last Parliamentary session in which Socialists were to participate, although only about half the Parliamentary Party was represented.[1]

Hitler's speech of May 17th, 1933, it will be remembered, was the first of many occasions when he used the full register of his rhetoric and eloquence to convince a somewhat suspicious though, on the whole, indifferent world that PEACE was his only desire and aim. Peace and reconstruction at home—peace and co-operation in foreign affairs. "Germany", said the *Führer*, "will strictly observe the treaties she has concluded. Her only desire is to settle peacefully all outstanding problems concerning other nations."

That was the key-note of the whole speech to which one half of the Social Democratic Reichstag faction were listening in utter bewilderment. What were they to do? If words meant all and the man speaking them nothing, were the Social Democrats—hopelessly defeated, and yet anxious to save what was lost long ago—to vote against as passionate a declaration of world peace as any labour leader ever made? They chose to bury their heads and to listen to the words only—not to the man. And in a last pathetic attempt "to save the Party" the Social Democrats said "Aye" to the National Socialist motion on foreign policy which was thus unanimously adopted. This was unconditional surrender. By it the leaders might conceivably have hoped to save their lives, but never their Party. The Nazis, naturally, showed nothing but contempt for their internal appeasers—and little leniency.

On June 23rd the Social Democratic Party was officially banned; the leader of the policy of appeasement, Paul Löbe, was arrested, together with many others. The Nazi régime had tolerated Löbe's line of compromise exactly as long as they considered it useful for their own ends—that is to say, until confusion and demoralisation had worked havoc amongst the members of the Labour movement and killed the last spark of self-confidence.

All this came to an end when the decree prohibiting the re-organisation of political parties, issued on July 14th, 1933, made

[1] Of the remainder, some had gone into exile, some were in prisons and concentration camps and others had stayed away in protest.

the National Socialist Party the only legal political party in Germany.

Thus, in less than four months, the great German Labour movement, educated by Marx and Engels, proud of its tradition and achievements, burst like a huge toy balloon. The totalitarian State was established. The Labour movement had vanished from the surface.

For a long time German workers were as stunned and bewildered and unable to believe what they saw as were the people of France after the surrender of their Government in 1940. How had it all been possible? Many of them began to despise themselves and their defeated organisations as much as only their fiercest enemy could. But, worst of all, not even then did the responsible leaders in exile try to understand what had happened and to seek new ways and means to rebuild the beaten movement. They refused to face up to reality, and buried their heads in the sand.

At the time of the worst defeat, when everybody was wondering: "How could this have happened? What was the cause? What are we to do now?" the Communists, for example, persisted in self-delusion:

> "All signs point to one thing, namely, that in the very near future violent class struggles must be expected. . . . Will the Party (the C.P.) be able to give a sufficient lead to the *present revolutionary movement of the masses*?" [1]

Blithely, the Communists went on to speak of the "increasing revolutionary activities of the masses", etc., while at the same time continuing to direct their main attacks against the Socialists. It is true, the end of the Social Democratic Party and the Trade Unions had been inglorious and shameful; but all efforts to appease the Nazis had been the work of only a few, though prominent individuals. The Communists knew that as well as anybody, but it did not prevent them from claiming that "the complete elimination of the Social Fascists (the Social Democrats) from the State apparatus and the brutal suppression of the Social Democratic organisation and of its press do not alter the fact that they represent now as before the main social buttress of the dictatorship of capital". [2]

The Social Democrats were just as eager to attribute all responsibility for the defeat to the Communists.

[1] A few remarks on the illegal activities of the C.P.G., *The Communist International* (German Edition), No. 14, September 1st, 1933.
[2] Fritz Heckert, Member of the Central Committee of the C.P.G., "About the fight of the C.P. in Germany", *Rundschau*, No. 23, July 7th, 1933.

"The fact remains that Communism has been one long crime and a terrible fate for the German working class. Communism paralyses the parliamentary influence of the Labour movement. . . . Thus Social Democracy was defeated; and with it, the Republic and the working class were defeated by the assault of counter-revolution." [1]

These mutual recriminations did not vindicate their authors. Why should they? Were they not all in the same boat? Together they had been defeated. Together they had failed to offer resistance. Together they were responsible. Most German workers felt this. And it is fair to say that nine out of ten Communists or Social Democrats were much more impressed by the practical failure of *all* working-class organisations than by the feeble explanations and excuses of their former leaders. That was the mood of the defeated enemies of Hitler in the Summer of 1933.

Meanwhile Hitler was speaking golden words. He had asked for four years in which to do away with economic misery, to abolish unemployment and to restore "German honour". Had he not been right when he scorned the working-class parties? Had they not really and shamefully failed? Perhaps he was more right that one had thought—perhaps he was right, too, in other respects. . . . Should one not give him the fair chance for which he was asking? Such were the thoughts of the overwhelming majority of the German people when Autumn approached.

The result was the unique Nazi victory in the election of November 1933. 92·2 per cent. of the total electorate voted for the Nazis. And the anti-Nazi opposition? 3·3 million election cards were deliberately rendered invalid and 2·1 million voters had the courage to abstain—in all 7·8 per cent. of the electorate. These, of course, are the official figures. No one can say to what extent the election results were falsified. There was, of course, no public or impartial control. Faking of the actual results is no doubt one explanation of Hitler's first "Over-Ninety-Per-Cent." victory; but it is not the only explanation. There was terror too, wholesale terror and intimidation, but even that does not explain all. The terror could be so effective only because a general demoralisation among the anti-Nazis (in particular among the members of the former working-class movement) came to its aid. The dual effect of terror *and* demoralisation is best illustrated by the following instance. A polling booth had been set up in the notorious Nazi concentration camp at Dachau, where, at that time, all prisoners were political opponents of the new régime, mostly Communists.

[1] " Break the Chains", *Neuer Vorwärts*, Prague, No. 1, June 18th, 1933.

After the November elections it was officially announced that the majority of the prisoners had voted for Hitler. . . .

The exiled German Social Democrats in Prague celebrated the election results almost like a victory:

". . . these millions are not an 'opposition' in the normal sense of the word; they are an army, hostile to the system, a nucleus battalion for the coming Socialist revolution." [1]

The Communists went even farther:

"The election result . . . represents a great victory of Thälmann's Party. . . . This army of millions of brave anti-Fascists confirms the correctness of the statement, made already in October by the Central Committee of the German Communist Party, that a new revolutionary upsurge has begun in Germany." [2]

CHAPTER TWENTY-EIGHT

FIRST UNDERGROUND ORGANISATIONS

WHILE THE "revolutionary upsurge" and the Socialist revolution against Hitler remained a wish-dream of those who were either unwilling to face facts or incapable of understanding the fearful power of the new totalitarian régime that had been set up in Germany, it is, of course, true that there have been active anti-Fascist minorities in Germany from the first day of the Hitler dictatorship. In 1933, 1934 and even 1935 it was fashionable to spread the most romantic tales about their activities—stories which were just as far from the truth as the assertion, which became fashionable after 1939, that there has never been such a thing as an active opposition of Germans within Germany.

In the early days of the Hitler Dictatorship, while the working-class parties were breaking up, thousands and thousands of their former members not only refused to betray their convictions, but were determined to carry on the struggle in spite of the dangers involved.

Yet, what were they to do? They lacked all experience, all

[1] " Four Million German Revolutionaries", *Neuer Vowärts*, November 19th, 1933.
[2] "The Meaning of the Elections of November 12th in Germany", *Rundschau*, No. 43, November 17th, 1933.

preparation for the new kind of work. Moreover, they were faced with a completely new political phenomenon which they failed to understand. They did not even see how radical were the changes that had taken place. How could they work without those organisations which had been their only strength, their only weapon? Who was to guide them after their old leaders had so obviously failed and disappeared?

They knew no better than to continue their former activities as well as they could. The methods and activities to some degree varied according to the different political background of these first underground workers. But they had still many things in common, although they developed independently of each other.

Common to most of them was the concentration of their activities almost exclusively on what may be called illegal mass-propaganda. That is to say, they all chalked up anti-Fascist slogans on pavements and walls; they all printed or duplicated newspapers, periodicals, broadsheets and leaflets, which they distributed as widely as possible. Even the contents of this literature was, on the whole, rather uniform.

To all of them it was obvious that the Hitler Government was a catastrophe for Germany. And against it they did what they had done in the democratic past: they tried to "enlighten" the people and to "unmask" the Nazis. That was the essence of their propaganda. They were convinced that mass-propaganda of this sort, if continued persistently, would eventually open the eyes of the German people, break the spell and undermine the Hitler régime.

Yet, unfortunately, the eyes of the German people were not so easily opened as these first propagandists seemed to believe. These initial activities were very largely based on illusions about the "weakness" and "instability" of the new régime, with the consequence that, after the elections of November 1933, the disappointment even affected the nuclei of the illegal workers. The *Rote Stosstrupp* (one of the numerous illegal Socialist groups which were formed after Hitler had taken over) wrote immediately after the November elections:

"The election result has called forth uncertainty and discouragement here and there among our comrades! We no longer fight against a party, but against the whole people, they say. To some this fight seems hopeless and they would rather avoid the sacrifices which it implies."

The disappointment in the ranks of the *Rote Stosstrupp* was by no means an exception. All organisations had similar experiences, for the elections were bound to shock those who had based their hopes on illusions.

These illusions expressed themselves not only in the contents of their writings but also in their methods of work. For a certain period there was much talk in the international Press of "mysterious groups of five" which the Communists more than the rest had organised to cheat the Gestapo. The grain of reality in those reports was the simple fact that under Fascism mass meetings cannot be held and that the gathering of even a dozen people may arouse the suspicions of the police. Any illegal meetings could therefore take place only in private houses or flats and be attended by a very small number of people. That had been the time-honoured practice of conspirators throughout the ages, a practice which the German anti-Fascists were forced to copy after they had been reduced to the status of conspirators.

The Communist Party had actually organised itself into such groups of five or ten even before Hitler came to power. Unfortunately for them that re-organisation had been so widely advertised and so many of its members were so well known—to enemies as well as to friends—that these much-talked-about conspiratorial units provided not even a minimum of protection. They would not even have been a match for a much less clever and ruthless police force than the Gestapo turned out to be.

The fierce determination of tens of thousands of German Communists to defy all dangers and to carry on at all costs should certainly not be underrated. The heroism displayed by many of them will not easily find its equal. But by their gross self-delusion, which mistook the actual defeat for a "revolutionary upsurge", they were driven into a wild activity for activity's sake, so that, during that first period of underground work, they destroyed more than they built up.

The most active and most courageous among them were the first victims. One set of illegal workers after another disappeared into the cellars of the increasingly efficient Gestapo. Each time there remained enough men and women to replace them. Still the third, fifth, tenth, umpteenth group that took over was noticeably less qualified than the previous ones had been.

The Social Democratic Party developed on somewhat different lines. It lacked the revolutionary background of the Communists just as much as their tradition of extra-parliamentary activities. Quite naturally, most Social Democrats found it even more difficult to adapt themselves to the new situation and to cope with the new tasks. Moreover, as soon as their organisations were suppressed the Party dissolved itself into a number of independent groups much more rapidly than the Communist Party, which had always been a strictly centralised body.

After the failure of the Social Democratic Executive to organise resistance had become obvious to all, these independent groups formed themselves very quickly all over Germany. It is not by accident that the first attempts were made chiefly by the younger generation. The "groups" often developed out of no more than a circle of friends who, in many cases, had belonged to one or another of the opposition wings of the Party. Common to them all was an unbroken energy due to their youth, which also exempted them from the terrible burden of responsibility for the past and made it psychologically much easier for them to survive the general shock and depression.

Many of these first attempts at illegal re-organisation remained, however, purely local and anonymous without affecting anything but their immediate surroundings. Others attempted to create proper organisations with branches in many districts. Among these were the *Rote Stosstrupp*, mentioned above, the *Proletarischer Pressedienst* and others.

This does not mean, however, that the elder generation of the former Labour movement had gone over to Hitler. Yet during that first period most of them had lost all self-confidence and the hope that anything could be done at all or was worth a trial. Nevertheless, many of them quietly maintained their former contacts. At night they used to gather at the old meeting-places, in their pubs, beer-gardens or cafés. They had nothing to do with underground work. They could be seen by all and everybody, whispering together, exchanging recollections of "better times", telling one another of the horrible fate of this or that Comrade, discussing wage cuts or the latest police raids in their street. They were glad to keep these contacts, in fact they were their only consolation. They were even happy, now and then, to get hold of an illegal leaflet or newsheet which expressed what they felt themselves, or to see the words "Down with Fascism" chalked on a wall. But they did not go farther and did not want to, at least not at that time.

Slowly and only half-consciously a few of them have since made their peace with Hitler. The majority lost all interest in politics. Others became again active for the cause of Socialism at a later period. However, by their passivity, during that first period, they enabled Hitler to boast of the support of the entire German people.

Some of the smaller, rather sectarian and doctrinaire working-class organisations which had traditionally stood between Socialists and Communists—"too radical for the Socialists and

162

too independent for the Communists"—gained a temporary importance during that first period of underground struggle which was altogether out of proportion to their size and their real or potential influence. Notable among them were the *Sozialistische Arbeiter Partei* (Socialist Workers' Party), the *Internationaler Sozialistischer Kampfbund* (Militant International Socialists) and the *Kommunistische Partei Opposition* (Opposition Communists). All of them benefited from the fact that, in the past, they had remained outside the limelight of the political battle. As a result their members were less well known to the police. Perhaps even more significant was the fact that, thanks to the relatively small part they had previously played in politics, they were not held responsible, and did not regard themselves as responsible, for the breakdown of the movement to the same extent as the two main working-class parties. That was, no doubt, their greatest moral asset. Finally, they never suffered the consequences of a wide gap between an active and dominating central bureaucracy, on the one hand, and a passive rank and file following more or less willingly and feeling more or less frustrated, on the other. What held them together were strictly dogmatic—often narrow—principles which, in those times of general confusion, proved a very firm bond. In fact they had all the advantages and all the shortcomings of a political sect.

All this explains the sudden importance gained by these small sectarian bodies—an importance which was further increased by the simple fact that, numerically speaking, the big Labour organisations such as Trade Unions, co-operatives, parties, etc., had themselves been reduced to sects, without having the advantage of sectarian fanaticism.

Later on, however, the smaller organisations were to suffer as much as the rest. They merely escaped very largely the early terror waves which were directed in the first place against the most prominent former working-class leaders, officials and better-known members. Once the police set out to hunt down the illegal groups, all shared the same fate.

Most of these first attempts at organising underground anti-Nazi opposition failed in all but one respect: they provided the German movement with legions of heroic martyrs whom the free world has no right to forget. Whether Communists or Socialists, these first underground workers—with only few exceptions—were rounded up by the police, man by man. Thousands were murdered by Hitler's henchmen; the majority of those who survived were still suffering in prisons and concentration camps when war came in September 1939. Some managed to escape abroad. Many of them were fighting in the International

163

Brigades in Republican Spain, continuing there the struggle against Fascist oppression which they could not complete in their own country.

One Social Democratic organisation had developed from the beginning on somewhat different lines. From the title of its first pamphlet, published in 1933, it got the name *Neu Beginnen* (New Start).

The history of this organisation goes back to the year 1931, when small discussion circles formed themselves in Berlin, consisting of Socialists and Communists who were critical of their own parties, who realised the danger threatening the German working-class movement and who agreed that the only chance of averting the danger lay in the unification of the two hostile wings of that movement. They were much too small a group to have any substantial success in the short space of time before Hitler's victory. Nevertheless the *Neu Beginnen* organisation can rightly claim to have shown considerably greater foresight than many other German Socialists.

Aware of the danger of the threatening Nazi dictatorship, they began to prepare for it by building up an underground organisation designed to weather the coming storm. After Hitler's advent to power, *Neu Beginnen* became increasingly the centre for young active Social Democrats who were determined to carry on the struggle against the dictatorship inside Germany herself.

In the first period of Hitlerism, this organisation found itself in sharp conflict with most other underground and refugee groups because of its "long view" which others decried as superpessimism and even defeatism. In particular, *Neu Beginnen* emphasised

(1) That the Hitler Government was not merely one of the many ultra-reactionary Governments which would disappear as quickly as it came, but that Fascism meant a fundamental transformation within the capitalist society, which for a long time to come would render the chances of Socialism exceedingly small.

(2) That one of the most important differences between Fascism and other reactionary régimes was the fact that the former was carried to power by a broad mass movement recruiting its members from all sections of society.

(3) That as long as the stability of the Fascist régime was guaranteed by a genuine mass support, anti-Fascist mass-propaganda (as carried out by other groups) would only demand senseless sacrifices without achieving any visible results.

(4) That the essential task was to build up a strong organisation of carefully selected members, each of whom should be qualified for independent political judgment and be capable of assuming responsibility. The members should all be well trained, theoretically as well as practically, with contacts and "spheres of influence" in as many important workshops as possible and preferably also in other sections of society.

(5) That the task of such an organisation was essentially that of active preparation for times of general crisis when the newly awakened spontaneous mass opposition could and should be co-ordinated and guided.

(6) That for the eventual victory the re-unification of the mutually hostile working-class parties was an essential prerequisite. Although "unity" had meanwhile become the foremost slogan of most of the clandestine organisations, *Neu Beginnen* held that it was essential to take the first practical steps immediately by co-ordinating all militant forces within the framework of a revived Social Democracy, arguing that despite all its failures in the past, millions of German workers continued and would continue to preserve their loyalty to this party which they had helped to build and which in their eyes continued to be the embodiment of working-class tradition. Besides, the democratic structure of the Social Democratic Party (as different from the C.P.) would ensure the possibility of a free development of new and progressive ideas.

(7) That continuity of organised opposition to the Nazi régime was of utmost importance in order to preserve the tradition and experiences of the working-class movement, which, left to themselves, were bound to fade away; and that therefore an "illegal technique" had to be consciously developed to cope with the extremely thorough and methodical procedure of the Gestapo.

Many of these ideas have later become common property of all underground groups. They were not generally accepted in the early days.

The intellectual equipment with which the shattered remnants of the German Labour movement began the unequal struggle against Nazism consisted of little more than a few romantic ideas based on a vague and imperfect knowledge of other underground movements, such as the Socialist movement in Tsarist Russia, the German working-class movement under Bismarck and the international minority movement against the Great War. There was hardly any knowledge or understanding, for example, of the clandestine opposition to Italian Fascism—the only experience

165

that might have been of some practical value to the German underground struggle.

To understand their problems and their development it is necessary to appreciate above all, that the greatest psychological handicap for the underground groups was not the ever-present danger of discovery, with all its fearful implications for the people concerned, but rather the acute consciousness that no amount of personal sacrifice and heroism could in any way alter the course of events. They were not only under the permanent shadow of imprisonment and death, but in constant doubt as to the purpose of their existence and the practical value of their activities.

Endless discussions took place among them as to what could and should be done. Whatever they began soon turned out to be about as effective as trying to stop a tank with a shot-gun. The result was a feeling of utter helplessness which, more than Gestapo terror and persecutions, caused the decimation of the movement.

Early in 1934 the following report was smuggled out of Germany; its author was an exceedingly well informed person who had enjoyed a long-standing reputation in the old German Labour movement and who, after January 1933, was actively engaged in underground work:

"One year only after the collapse, most of the remnants of the old organisations have largely been annihilated. I am not suggesting that their members have given up their faith or that all organised connections have ceased to exist. But it does mean that the movement and its activities have been reduced to microscopic size.

"The Communist movement seemed to be better prepared and, on the whole, more willing to offer resistance than the rest. They never questioned whether or not they should continue their work. Of course, they, too, had traitors in their ranks, and men who willingly and quickly made their peace with Hitler—at least as many as any other section of the movement. Communist illusions as to their own exaggerated significance persisted also under the new conditions.

"For the many tens of thousands who actively worked within the ranks of the Communist movement, the effect of these illusions was as devastating as the effect of reformist sluggishness had been in the Social Democrat camp. Nothing remains which resembles a coherent movement. Central as well as district and local headquarters have been hunted down by the police, time and again.

"The basic units are, of course, the most active ones, the cells and the little groups of purely local character, the so-called street-cells. They produce their own material, write it and duplicate and distribute it themselves in the houses of their districts or at the Labour Exchange. Increasingly they are reduced to maintaining contacts only in their closest vicinity. They have had too much bitter experience. Many, only too many, are caught—as recently in the *Chaussee Strasse* in Berlin— in the course of surprise raids on the huge working-class tenements. In that case as in most, every single person present, men, women and children, were questioned and searched by the Police.

"Camouflaged as study-circles for foreign languages some groups continue their theoretical political discussions, usually on a deplorably low level; they seem to have learnt as little as they have forgotten. Still, they are the most advanced section of the old Communist movement, trying to remain politically alive and to serve the cause. Some are more than critical of the official Comintern line, but under the new conditions it seems no longer so dangerous to be a critical Communist.

"Even more bitterly they all complain of the failure of the central leadership in regard to organisation problems. In the case of Alfred Kattner, who was to be chief witness for the prosecution in the forthcoming Thälmann trial, it was found out that he had contacts with one of the illegal central headquarters. Two or three headquarters with whom he maintained contact were caught. Even after that he remained in his position until later he was shot.

"Kattner's betrayal of Johnny Scheer (a member of one of the central headquarters which were taken), of Steinfurt and others, has very seriously undermined morale—nothing is discussed more in illegal Communist circles than the spy plague; still, they go on with their work.

"There are instances of great heroism and devotion. A funeral of a comrade was attended by many workers. Within hearing of the police the widow said at the grave: 'I know you were not shot in an attempt to escape.' And a worker said: 'You fell for the worker's cause, you shall be revenged.' The police did not intervene—they merely took photographs of a number of those present. . . .

"Of the former Social Democratic movement it is, above all, the young who maintain contacts. Numerically, extremely few are left. In the borough of a large town which used to have an organisation of several thousand members, there is to-day a group of eight or nine younger party members. They maintain contact with a similar group in the neighbouring borough, consisting of only three. For protection they have joined one of the tolerated charity organisations to cover their frequent meetings. They are on the look-out for 'illegals' who, they understand, have firmer organisational relationship. Persons who are supposed, rightly or wrongly, to be associated with the 'illegals' are approached for advice and help. They are looking for an experienced instructor who could help them with their study circle and whose political views would be on the Left of the former Party. Without knowing very much what it is all about this group distributes a duplicated broadsheet issued by one of the illegal organisations. This then is the remnant of a formerly strong Party organisation. It is a typical example—typical for its attitude, for the isolation of the individual, but also for the chance to reorganise the best elements, few though they may be in numbers.

"In another district regular meetings actually take place in the flat of a formerly well-known comrade. Here, too, an organisation once numbering many thousands can now assemble without difficulty in one room. They have many discussions, and are seeking a new way in serious political talks among young people conscious of their responsibility and aware of the possible consequences of their actions: concentration camp, torture and even death.

"In a third district meetings are held regularly in private houses and flats. Here they are more careful and therefore have far fewer casualties. They have refused to distribute material smuggled from abroad. 'They don't know, anyhow, what conditions in Germany are like nowadays; that stuff isn't worth risking your head for.' They also learnt from the sad experiences in their neighbouring district of Y. There a badly organised attempt to recommence the work resulted in many arrests. Among those who were left there was abject depression and an atmosphere of mutual suspicion, general anxiety and fear. Now they say: 'The last arrests have shown that you cannot trust even your oldest comrades.' Or, 'It's no use; none of the former comrades will go on doing anything.'

"In one of the districts mentioned above, they believe that to-day as of old, activities can be increased and strengthened by success. But under present conditions success means above all not to be discovered, to expand as fast as one's own forces can 'digest' and not to try doing things with which one cannot fully cope and which tend to get out of control. They think it vital to give all comrades as much security as is humanly possible, to avoid senseless sacrifices and to assure steady progress by careful selection of the best individuals.

"Many of those who with courage and energy took part in some badly organised activities have never recovered from their depression following the arrests of their friends. The mere news that the police got hold of a list of names has meant for many a complete break-down in which some lost their nerves so completely that they even, though without malice, betrayed their friends to the Gestapo.

"The younger ones of course learn quickest of all. A year ago they merely kept in contact, met for outings or social evenings and went out hiking through the country. In the meantime, many of them have learnt more than they could have learnt during many years under normal conditions. Slowly they are acquiring political maturity and organisational skill. They are but few compared with the millions of German youth. But these few are the core of a new generation which can defeat Fascism. . . ."

That is the picture of the German underground movement at the beginning of 1934 as it presented itself to one who actively took part in it.

A few months later the world learned of the bloody events of June 30th, 1934, when Röhm, Strasser, Schleicher and hundreds of other so-called conspirators were killed by order of Hitler. After several weeks the German press published a list of seventy-seven victims. According to unofficial but careful estimates the actual number of victims of this "purge" well exceeded one thousand.

These mass killings of well-known Nazi leaders provoked a host of fantastic speculations and utterly unfounded prophecies suggesting that now the "beginning of the Nazis' end" had definitely come.

It is perhaps not surprising that most of the international Press misjudged the German development so completely. But one might have thought that the German anti-Fascist organisations would have known better, being almost exclusively occupied with the observation of conditions in Germany. However, with the exception of those few who, from the beginning, had emphasised the need for a truly critical analysis and a realistic approach free from illusions, they were all as thoroughly misled as the foreign journalists.

The *Sozialistische Aktion*, illegal central organ of the Social Democratic Party, printed abroad and smuggled into Germany, published an article on July 12th, 1934, headed "Suicide of the

Dictatorship", which maintained that there can be no doubt that "the shots in Munich and Berlin mark the beginning of *the self-destruction of dictatorship*". The next issue of the same paper contained this sentence: "*The 30th of June is the beginning of the end of National Socialism*".[1]

For once, Socialists and Communists were in complete agreement. An official publication of the Comintern, the German edition of the *Inprekorr*, said of the Röhm purge:

> "June 30th is the beginning of the end of the Fascist dictatorship in its National Socialist form", and remarked that: "The crisis which broke out on June 30th is only another aspect of the revolutionary upsurge of the working class."[2]

Unanimity in this question was reached by practically all German anti-Fascist organisations. Only very few dissenting comments showed a more realistic estimate of the bloody events and their consequences; they were shouted down as "pessimists" and "defeatists".

Yet, the so-called pessimists turned out to have been the only realists. June 30th—far from being the "beginning of the end"—was merely a stage and an instance of the "growing pains" of German Fascism. In no sense could it be taken as evidence of its decay, but merely as evidence of the régime's determination to overcome initial difficulties which were still barring the way to 100 per cent. totalitarianism—and with methods peculiar to the Nazi régime. After the working-class organisations had been defeated and annihilated, after the liberal and the conservative organisations had been "brought into line" and incorporated into the Fascist system, there remained one final blow to be dealt to all those ambitious and—actually or potentially—hostile forces which might try successfully to challenge Hitler's leadership in times of acute difficulties. Both Röhm and Schleicher represented such forces, different though their background and their aims were. With their "removal" the road was freed for Hitler's unchallenged rule.

[1] Italics in the original.
[2] *Rundschau*, No. 30, July 5th, 1934.

CHAPTER TWENTY-NINE

REVOLUTIONARIES IN HIDING

THE STABILISATION of the Nazi dictatorship after the Röhm purge was, in a sense, an even greater and more unexpected shock for Hitler's enemies than his original access to power. For almost a year they had been trying to convince themselves that "this can't last". But instead of weakening and collapsing, the Hitler régime was evidently growing stronger. And when, in the following years, Hitler marched triumphantly from success to success, with the tacit support of the entire world, it needed almost superhuman strength to continue an apparently hopeless struggle against such tremendous odds.

For Hitler's internal opposition, hundreds of broken pledges and promises mattered far less than the fact that there was one promise which he had not broken—the promise to liquidate unemployment. That he had succeeded in this made such a tremendous impression upon Germans of all classes that it stifled a great deal of the initial opposition to his régime. For unemployment had become *the* problem of Germany; and it was Hitler who had performed the apparent miracle and solved it. The uneasy feeling that rearmament could lead to war only was somewhat balanced by Hitler's passionate peace proclamations and, above all, by the success of his policy of "peaceful" blackmail and "peaceful" penetration. Indeed, Hitler's successes in the field of "peaceful" foreign policy were greater even than his success at home. The list of these successes—and their sequence from the German-Polish Agreement in 1934 to the occupation of Prague in 1939—is only too well remembered.

Hitler's blackmail worked like a charm. Inside Germany the phrase *IHM gelingt ja alles* . . .[1] became universal, as an expression of either exasperation or admiration or of both. Outside Germany the free world acquiesced, although millions of free men were alarmed and outraged and indignant. It acquiesced in Hitler's rearmament as in the Fascist conquest of Republican Spain, in Mussolini's conquest of Abyssinia and in Japan's undeclared war on China. It acquiesced in Hitler's annexation of Austria and Czechoslovakia. It acquiesced in the horrors of the German concentration camps and in the anti-Jewish pogroms in Germany in November 1938. It acquiesced because it dreaded war. Statesmen from all over the world travelled to Berlin or Berchtesgaden and shook Hitler's blood-stained hand. Without

[1] "HE succeeds in everything. . . ."

them, without their non-intervention, their acquiescence and appeasement Hitler could never have acquired the strength to start the Second World War.

These facts are recalled here with deliberate disregard of all reasons why and how it so happened; because whatever reasons and circumstances there were which could explain—though not excuse—the democratic acquiescence in Hitler's crimes had to remain hidden to the small circles of revolutionaries in Germany. To them these events came as a succession of blows and appeared as acts of incomprehensible folly and betrayal. To them it looked as though they had to fight not only against Hitler, but against the entire world. For the world seemed bound in conspiracy to keep Hitler in power, to strengthen his might and to give him everything he liked to ask for. To the German opposition the acquiescence of the world in Hitler's crimes and in his open preparation for war was even more incomprehensible and exasperating than the acquiescence of the German people in Hitler's crimes has been to the United Nations since the outbreak of the War. For the free nations of the world had the power to act, had they but used it; the German opposition was powerless.

From whatever angle one looks at it, the task of this opposition has all along been infinitely more difficult than for instance that of the oppressed nations of Europe has been during the War. A comparison between their respective efforts cannot fairly be made.

The anti-Fascist German revolutionaries had no one to look to in the whole world, no one to support them except a few individuals. Undesired and hunted refugees were their only spokesmen abroad. They had neither an exiled Government nor a National Committee to represent their interests, nor powerful allies for whose victory they could hope and from whom they could expect deliverance. Theirs was not the fight against a foreign aggressor whose acts of oppression naturally rallies the entire nation against him—but the lone and seemingly hopeless struggle against the law and the State power of their own country. They were not secretly admired by their own countrymen as heroic martyrs and patriots. At best, they were pitied; at the worst, they were despised as contemptible traitors. They could not count on the spontaneous help of their unknown neighbours in case of need, becaue they would never know who of their neighbours, indeed who of their own family, was a genuine Nazi or perhaps even a Gestapo agent, and who only feigned loyalty to Hitler. They were not protected from spying ears by barriers of language, nor did they have the advantage over their enemies of a better knowledge of local customs and local geography. They were not only watched and persecuted, but every one of them was coerced into active service in one or several of the countless Nazi organisations which reduced their privacy to a few hours of sleep.

The organised opposition in Germany has never been large in numbers. In pre-war days it numbered perhaps some tens of thousands. Certainly not more. It could not have been larger, because in any country and in any generation only comparatively few individuals have the moral strength which a struggle of this kind requires. I do not mean the moral strength to defy death and Gestapo torture, but the moral strength to fight for what looks like a lost cause, the strength which a David needs to fight Goliath, without the prospect of help coming from anywhere.

The vast majority of the active opposition had been members of the working-class movement. Of necessity their activities remained largely invisible. Their only witnesses are Hitler's silenced victims—the dead and the inmates of overcrowded gaols and concentration camps. No one but the Gestapo knows for certain how many political prisoners there were in Germany before the war and how many there have been since. Even the most reliable estimates differ vastly. A fair number of reliable reports have been published or privately circulated by men and women who managed to escape after having spent years in German concentration camps and gaols. But even the best of these reports cannot be generalised, as conditions vary greatly from camp to camp and gaol to gaol and, what makes estimates even more difficult, they often vary from month to month.

Since January 1933 there have been several distinct "waves of terror" leading to mass arrests and mass trials of which only an insignificantly small proportion has ever been reported in the press. After every such action, concentration camps and prisons became even more overcrowded than they normally were and, as a rule, large-scale exchanges of prisoners between various camps, prisons and gaols followed.

Whatever their actual number, until the outbreak of the war in September 1939 it was certainly no less than half a million, possibly far more; and no matter how small its effectiveness, their struggle was no less heroic and no less part of the general fight for the liberation of mankind than that of the Polish, Czech, Norwegian, Yugoslav, French, Russian or Jewish martyrs.

Throughout the years of the Hitler régime there have been millions of ordinary Germans who never became reconciled to the dictatorship, hating everything only remotely connected with the Nazis, and expressing their disgust and deep discontent by what Dr. Göbbels calls "grumbling and grousing". But this discontent and grumbling is not the same as active political opposi-

173

tion, and it has had very little if anything to do with organised resistance against the régime, carried on by small anonymous groups.

Thus, the main question remains: What has been the form, the content and the positive purpose of organised resistance in Hitler's Germany?

There is no simple answer to this question, and it is even less obvious than simple to people who, in the course of the war, have become accustomed to identify quite automatically all forms of political resistance with two things: propaganda and sabotage. But these two things—propaganda and sabotage—could not succeed under prevailing conditions.

The active opponents of the régime learnt fairly early that their activity could not possibly consist of propaganda in the accepted sense of the word. With the primitive means at their disposal it would have been, at the very best, a ridiculously feeble answer to the giant propaganda machine of the State. The number of people that could be reached by duplicated news-sheets and an occasional leaflet was so minute that the positive effect they could hope to achieve was grotesquely out of all proportion to the dangers involved. How many people who light-heartedly criticised the absence of anti-Hitler propaganda in Germany have ever stopped to think out in detail what was involved in the production and distribution of a single illegal leaflet inside Germany? Again, there can be no comparison with conditions in occupied countries. In Germany the Nazi organisations had ample opportunity to study their opponents long before Hitler came to power. A card index of names, addresses and the personal history of every known opponent had been carefully compiled by every local Nazi organisation. These black lists covered millions of names, constantly brought up to date by professional Gestapo agents and amateur denunciators, Labour Front officials and the *Blockwarte* who were attached to every block of flats.

Every suspicious move of any of these black-listed persons and their associates would immediately be noted and investigated. For example: for a worker to own or use a typewriter would be quite enough to attract the attention of the police. For a clerk to use a typewriter after office hours would be equally suspicious. The unmistakable noise of a duplicating machine or a printing press heard from a neighbouring flat through a thin wall would certainly lead to police investigation. The purchase of large quantities of typewriting paper or duplicating ink by any individual not connected with a legitimate business would involve the danger of denunciation. These are only some of the most obvious technical difficulties which the producers of illegal literature had

174

to face. Even greater difficulties and risks were, of course, involved in the process of distribution.

The danger of discovery existed not only for those who produced and distributed underground literature, but also for those who received it. An illegal leaflet found in the house or flat of a person would lead to many years of imprisonment even if the person concerned had nothing to do with its production and simply found it in his letter-box. The whispered accounts of the horrible beatings and tortures of the Nazi opponents in Himmler's Gestapo cellars and in the concentration camps made almost every one tremble at the mere sight of an illegal leaflet that had been pushed under his door or into his coat pocket. People got annoyed if they were involved in risks without having been asked; by no means only people who sympathised with the Nazis or who were politically indifferent, but also many of Hitler's staunchest opponents who, in other ways, were themselves taking great risks. "Am I to risk my head or liberty to read in a leaflet that Hitler is a swine, that he suppresses liberty, that he prepares for war—as though I had not always known that! It is irresponsible to risk one's own or anybody else's life for that sort of thing. . . ."

Gradually therefore, though only after many bitter experiences, most of these propaganda activities ceased—at least until the outbreak of war. They were stopped, first by the Gestapo and then by those who had escaped capture because they had learnt the lesson that as long as conditions remained what they were, activities of this kind were ultimately senseless.

Much the same applied to individual sabotage—as different from mass sabotage—involving even higher risks without the slightest chance of any serious material or political effect. The struggle against the totalitarian State is not a romantic Hollywood game of people chasing through the night with loudspeaker vans, or of professional Scarlet Pimpernels who kidnap Nazi victims from under the eyes of the Gestapo, or of disguised workers who throw bombs at Hitler meetings.

But if both propaganda and individual sabotage were more or less excluded, of what, then, did the underground struggle consist? It consisted very largely of the painstaking work of building up illegal organisations and keeping them alive as political bodies. These words, perhaps, convey very little of the importance of this task and even less of the tremendous difficulties involved in carrying it out. But the "political organisation" is and must always be the ultimate purpose and aim of any underground movement fighting not a national enemy, an invader or an old-fashioned tyranny, but a modern totalitarian dictatorship.

In the Third Reich this task became supremely important

because the strength of Hitler's régime rested, above all, on an absolute and total monopoly in two spheres, the sphere of information and education and the sphere of social organisation, both of which would be equally threatened by a non-Nazi political organisation.

About the poisonous effect of Nazi propaganda and education so much has been written and explained that no repetition is warranted in this context. But it should be recalled that the large popular movement which supported Hitler during and after his rise to power did not do so because of what he was and what he planned, but because of what he was believed to be and believed to plan. People followed him not because they wanted war, but because he spoke of justice; not because he aimed at world domination, but because he promised social security. They followed him because politically they were not sufficiently mature to see through his blatant lies and ambiguous half-truths, and because misery and despair had reduced their reasoning power to a state in which they could become the easy prey of unscrupulous demagogy, which deliberately set out to confuse. As Jean Paul once wrote: "A tyrant assaults the spirit before he attacks the body; I mean that he seeks to stultify his slaves before he reduces them to misery; for he knows that people who have minds use them to guide their hands and to direct them against the tyrant".

No one has understood this more profoundly than Hitler and no one has acted upon it with a greater singleness of purpose, allowing neither concession nor loop-hole. To break through the monopoly of propaganda and education, to gain and provide independent information and true knowledge and understanding of facts and events therefore is to win half the battle.

Perhaps of even greater significance (although in a sense the two are inseparable) is the Nazi monopoly of all social organisation; from State planning of national economy down to the most intimate aspect of human life. For the stability of the Nazi régime, the total monopoly of organisation has been even more important than its secret police, which essentially exists to safeguard this very monopoly and to prevent the rise of any organisation that might grow to challenge the régime in power. In that society the individual is powerless. But every political organisation of individuals, outside the sphere of the totalitarian State, no matter how insignificant this organisation may be in fact, is a challenge to the ruling régime, which may well be flexible in its own policy, but which cannot afford the slightest compromise wherever the principle of its total monopoly of organisation is concerned.

This may sound abstract and even like over-stating the case. But the experience of more than a decade of National Socialism has proved it to be true. The National Socialist leadership has always been aware of the fact that a substantial minority of the nation remained inwardly, and as individuals, hostile to the new régime; it has never shown itself to be unduly troubled by this knowledge. At the same time, this régime has always reacted with almost neurotic sensitiveness to all forms of independent organisation. It instinctively felt threatened by an obscure illegal factory organisation of fifteen or twenty workers or a small parish of the Confessional Church, while it felt quite strong enough to disregard the individual hostility of millions.

Totaliarian organisation means, in plain English, that it is all-embracing and all-penetrating. Its purpose is a double one, though at first sight the two supplementary functions may seem contradictory. The first function is that of *Gleichschaltung*—that is to say, the compulsion of every individual to act (and, ideally, to think) in accordance with the official philosophy and practice of the régime. The second function, no less important but less obvious, is the isolation of every individual from the social, political and spiritual section of the community to which he would naturally attach himself if left alone. All Nazi organisations follow this pattern. Take, for example, the Hitler Youth. Its function is not only that of making good Nazis out of German boys and girls, but equally that of preventing these boys and girls from setting up their own and diversified groups—be it a Catholic youth organisation, a boy scout movement or a Communist League of Youth. Similarly, the function of the Labour Front is not only that of supervising and controlling workers, but also that of preventing them from organising Trade Unions, independent shop stewards, factory councils and the like.

Theoretically there may be two ways of destroying social groups and their spontaneous tendency towards combination (without destroying the material basis of class and group distinction). One of them would be the physical isolation of every individual. This obviously is not practical. The other way would be to mix all social elements so thoroughly that the original elements, eventually, lose their social individuality. That is what National Socialism tried to achieve with the creation of mammoth organisations designed to wipe out all natural distinctions and varieties of political conviction or religious faith, of education, manner, taste and social standing. The result has not been the much-advertised "people's community"—that is to say, the genuine unity and oneness of the German nation—but a complete atomisation of society in which all natural structures have

177

been destroyed. Imagine a mixture of tea, coffee, flour and pepper in one big jar, tightly closed and well shaken. There will still be individual tea-leaves, coffee grains, etc. However, there will no longer be tea or coffee or flour, but just a mess. Totalitarian organisation has produced much the same effect. By enforced membership of the State's "one organisation for all" the individual becomes both isolated and powerless.

Thus, to break the Nazi monopoly of organisation is to break the Nazi régime itself. Revolutionary struggle against the totalitarian State means the struggle against this monopoly. Consequently active resistance to the Hitler régime has been first and foremost the business of creating and maintaining underground anti-Nazi organisations. After an initial period of aimless and costly activity Hitler's opposition discarded the motto " Action at any price!" and, gradually and, in many cases only half consciously, adopted the maxim: "The Organisation in Being".

No responsible general would dream of wasting the lives of his soldiers by sending them individually and armed simply with shotguns against powerful tank divisions. If he has only a small brigade and no modern equipment at his disposal he will try to avoid battle until he has received sufficient reinforcement in men and material to have a chance against the enemy. In the meantime he will not sit back and do nothing. He will train his soldiers and keep them fighting fit; he will watch the enemy and learn as much as possible of his secrets; he will camouflage his little force as well as possible to escape discovery in a period of weakness; he will actively prepare, but he will not tolerate precipitate and foolhardy action.

The underground struggle against Hitlerism has in all essentials been identical with the work of such a general. It has been war between a tiny and ill-equipped force and a giant army, but, for all these reasons, it has been the preparation for battle rather than the battle itself.

Obviously no work of this kind could be carried on without running risks. To my knowledge not a single German underground organisation has escaped Gestapo persecution. Even the most carefully organised activities have involved the loss of many lives and the liberty of countless individuals.

Inasmuch as the means of suppression and mental enslavement employed by Hitler's twentieth-century *tyrannis* were about a thousand times more effective than those practised by earlier autocracies, the technique of opposition, too, had to be advanced if there was to be any chance of survival.

The actual, though not always conscious and deliberate, acceptance of the formula "the organisation in being" meant that constant efforts to maintain and enlarge the existing organisations and their network of contacts began to take the place of more elementary—and suicidal—forms of direct and open resistance to the régime. Out of the shambles of Germany's defeated Labour movement, decimated almost to the point of physical extermination in the first two years of underground work, developed gradually what has been called Germany's first revolutionary *cadre* organisations. Naturally, this new type of organisation and activity also favoured a new type of revolutionary : the calculating organiser, the political instructor, the "contact-man", and, accordingly, new principles became operative in selecting prospective members, especially among the young who had seen democracy only in decay.

While personal courage and integrity obviously remained the most important characteristics of any member of these illegal *cadre* organisations, courage and integrity alone were no longer sufficient qualifications for a man whose job would be above all to organise new groups or cells or *cadres* and who would be asked to deny himself the satisfaction of revealing his true feelings in the most harmless manner.

If it is true to say that National Socialism has created a new brand of "scientific oppression and deception of the masses", then it is also true that the régime created a new brand of revolutionaries.

Anyone who has ever had personal experience of or contact with these *cadres* will readily confirm this. The men and women who stood the test of ten years of isolation and persecution were not recognisably the same individuals they had been before. These years of struggle against the most powerful enemy any political opposition ever had to encounter were a unique school of character and ability. These men and women learned to combine the qualities of true leadership with the modesty of the unknown soldier, and incorruptibility of character with the cunning of the conspirator.

These men and women realised, of course, that no matter how perfect their organisation, the revolutionary underground *cadres* were not an aim in themselves, and that they could neither replace nor create democratic mass movements, which alone would be able to carry a revolution to victory. But they were convinced that democratic mass movements could arise very quickly, even suddenly, as soon as the totalitarian structure of the régime suffered its first real cracks, revealing its inner weakness and mortality. They did not expect such spontaneous mass movement to take the form of properly organised parties or unions, complete with rules, regulations and card indexes, standing committees and executive councils. They knew that such a movement —if it developed—could, at the best, express itself through rough and primitive *ad hoc* organisations, such as the Russian Soviets of 1905 and 1917 or the German Workers' and Soldiers' Councils of 1918. They took courage from their knowledge that the Russian Revolution of 1917 was victorious although there was no ready-made mass organisation in existence prepared to take over where Tsarism left off; and they also remembered that the German Revolution of 1918, although large working-class parties and Trade Unions were then in existence, had not been "made" by either the parties or the Unions, and that that Revolution, too, had sprung from the *action directe* of the masses who spontaneously created the *Räte* as their own peculiar instrument of revolutionary action.

The existence of revolutionary organisations is not necessarily a prerequisite for the outbreak of a revolution. Every revolution creates its own organisations. But, on the other hand, there can be no doubt that such organisations as do exist, their political views and the quality and maturity of their members will most decisively influence the course of the revolution once it has broken out. In 1918 there existed in Germany no organisation either prepared or qualified for revolutionary leadership. That was the chief reason why the Revolution eventually fizzled out and why the powers of reaction and aggression could once again become triumphant in Germany. Preparation, therefore, for the task of leadership in any future German revolution—that was the ˌeal *raison d'être* of the underground *cadre* organisations operating in Germany.

If it is asked, what then was the creed of this small underground movement comprising former Communists, Social Democrats, Catholics and many who were children when Hitler crushed the free Labour movement, what were the convictions held in common by the men and women who fought Hitler many years before the Second World War broke out? then this answer may be given:

There appeared to be a deep and passionate conviction common to most of them that the past cannot and must not be resurrected and that the way to defeat Hitler is not to re-establish the very conditions which once allowed him to grow strong. There appeared to be unanimity, too, in the condemnation of past disunity and of fratricidal strife which so hopelessly weakened the German Labour movement. Shared by all was the desire to take revenge on the Nazi tormentors and oppressors and the determination to do away not only with Hitler and his gang, but with all who supported and helped him, who made common cause with him and profited from his conquests—in short, the determination to destroy the root of the evil of German reaction and aggression, the power of the military and the power of vested interests. And, finally, there appeared to be fundamental agreement that enslavement is too high a price for security as starvation is too high a price for liberty, and that a new society must be created in which the individual can be free and in which the State, by planning and direction, will master blind social force making for senseless and unnecessary human misery.

This may be a somewhat laborious description of what one of the German underground circles in Silesia once described as the general view held there: "We want a democracy, but a tough one!"[1]

CHAPTER THIRTY

GERMANY AT WAR

IT TOOK the National Socialist régime about two years to convince the vast majority of the German people, and people in other countries, that it had come to stay. After its successful mastering of the Röhm crisis it seemed to have demonstrated once and for all that it was "crisis-proof" and that nothing short of outside intervention would ever be able to destroy it, or at least provide the opportunity for such destruction from within. The active and most politically minded underground circles were the first to realise this. They knew from their study of history that the material power of any modern State is sufficiently great to be proof against any popular rising unless it has been smashed or at least seriously weakened by outside intervention. Neither Russian Tsarism,[2] nor the Ottoman Empire, nor the Hapsburg Empire, nor the Hohenzollern Empire could be overthrown without defeat in the field, even though these nineteenth-century autocracies possessed nothing comparable to the might of the German totalitarian State.

There arose therefore the strange paradox that those who were most violently and most actively opposed to Hitler and all he stood for were, in their own way and for their own purpose, awaiting the outbreak of the war almost as impatiently as the

[1] *Wir wollen eine Demokratie—aber eine scharfe!*
[2] Even the abortive Russian Revolution of 1905 did not take place until after the calamitous defeat of Russian arms in the Japanese War of 1904.

most fanatical group of Nazi warmongers; because only war, it seemed to them, and defeat in war as they confidently expected, would give them the opportunity for which they had been working day in day out, risking their lives in years of defiance. In this they were as different from the mass of the German people as were the Nazi enthusiasts at the opposite end. A flood of propaganda tales spread in the Allied countries during the war has given the impression that almost the entire German people had enthusiastically backed Hitler's war, at least until the moment of his first major defeat. The apparent justification for this widely accepted view was the total lack of any mass opposition to the war; but the absence of active mass opposition—in itself an undisputed fact—does not mean at all that the people approved of the war into which they had been led without being asked. The assumption that people *do* something about things they dislike or fear or even hate would be wrong even in democracies; it is totally wrong in the circumstances created by Fascism.

Nor would it be true to say even that disapproval, fear and hatred of the war have been the product only of defeat. This has been implicitly denied by every serious observer who lived in Germany during the period immediately preceding and following the outbreak of the war.

An astonishing degree of unanimity is my excuse for quoting the observations of three American journalists of repute whose work in Germany gave them a unique opportunity of studying German reaction and public opinion.

William Shirer for instance made this entry in his diary during the days of the Munich crisis when war seemed inevitable:

September 27th, 1938.

"A motorised division rolled through the city's streets just at dusk this evening in the direction of the Czech frontier. I went out to the corner of the *Linden* where the column was turning down the *Wilhelmstrasse*, expecting to see a tremendous demonstration. I pictured the scenes I had read of in 1914 when the cheering throngs on this same street tossed flowers at the marching soldiers, and the girls ran up and kissed them. The hour was undoubtedly chosen to-day to catch the hundred of thousands Berliners pouring out of their offices at the end of the day's work. But they ducked into the subways, refused to look on, and the handful that did stood at the curb in utter silence unable to find a word of cheer for the flower of their youth going away to the glorious war. It has been the most striking demonstration against war I have ever seen. Hitler himself reported furious. I had not been standing long at the corner when a policeman came up the *Wilhelmstrasse* from the direction of the Chancellery and shouted to the few of us standing at the curb that the *Führer* was on his balcony reviewing the troops. Few moved. I went down to have a look. Hitler stood there, and there weren't two hundred people in the street or the great square of the *Wilhelmplatz*. Hitler looked grim, then angry, and soon went inside, leaving his troops to parade unreviewed. What I've seen to-night almost rekindles a little faith in the German people. They are dead set against the war."[1]

And this is what Joseph C. Harsch had to say about the actual outbreak of the war:

"The German people were nearer to real panic on September 1st, 1939, than the people of any other European country. No people wanted that war, but the German people exhibited more real fear of it than the others. They faced it in something approaching abject terror."[2]

Wallace Deuel writes on the same subject:

"The war is a nightmare to the Germans and Italians even more than it was to the French."[3]

None of the authors of these statements believes in the existence of what is now commonly called "the other Germany". Nevertheless, they and all other truthful reporters agree that the Germans—not a small minority, but *the* Germans—were "dead set against the war", that the war is "a nightmare" to them and that they faced its outbreak in "something approaching abject horror", its outbreak and not only the period of the first setbacks and defeats.[4]

It is equally true, of course, but in no way contradictory to these statements that Hitler's early victories were acclaimed with wild enthusiasm by all but the convinced anti-Fascist minority. However, they were so acclaimed not because these victories had any positive meaning to the mass of the fighting or hard-working people, but because they seemed to lead one step nearer to the one goal that mattered supremely—the end of the war. Certainly, the majority of the people were not defeatist in the early days of the war. Certainly, if given the choice between ending the war by military victory or military defeat they would have chosen victory. But there is very little doubt that as the war dragged on

[1] William L. Shirer: *Berlin Diary* (London, 1941), p. 119.
[2] Joseph C. Harsch: *Pattern of Conquest* (London, 1942), p. 37.
[3] Wallace Deuel: *People under Hitler* (London, 1942), p. 245.
[4] Cf. p. 17.

and as the number of its victims grew into millions, both in the army and among the civilian population, as the prospect of victory grew faint, as city after city were turned into rubble-heaps, as people were reduced to the existence of cavemen, hourly trembling for their lives, there were millions, if not almost the entire population, who would have chosen defeat rather than continuation of the war if given a choice. This choice they were not given.

There is no shred of doubt that, ever since the winter of 1942, the vast majority of the German people have known that Hitler could no longer hope to win the war. Ever since Stalingrad Germany has known that she would eventually be defeated. The number of ordinary people who after that still believed in the possibility of military victory was small enough to be negligible. The number of those who believed in the chance of at least a compromise peace was rapidly dwindling. There have been hundreds and hundreds of reports from neutral sources (mainly from Sweden and Switzerland) describing the prevailing mood of the German nation after that period as a state of utter exhaustion, deepest gloom and growing despair.

Simultaneously the prestige of the Nazi Party and of the leaders of the country sank so rapidly that national as well as local Party leaders again and again publicly complained that any lying rumour, no matter how absurd, was spread like wild fire, and un-questionably believed so long as it served to discredit the Party and its leaders.

Yet throughout that period the German army went on fighting, and fought well. The German civilians went on producing, and the horror of life in the gutted towns, in overcrowded reception areas with millions of homeless people perched together in bar-racks and tents, did not bring about the widely expected collapse of the régime. Neutral observers emphasised again and again the complete absence of panic and revolt even during and after the most devastating air raids.

A number of factors combine to explain this paradox. First of all, the terror apparatus of the Gestapo and S.S., supremely pre-pared for this very situation, has been most ruthlessly and efficiently employed to prevent the transformation of a rapidly growing passive mass-defeatism into active defeatism and rebel-lion. Secondly, there are all those factors which might be termed the "material difficulties" of active defeatism. Soldiers who are prepared to surrender may have to wait months or even years until they get an opportunity of doing so. As a rule, they do not get this opportunity until and unless they are surrounded, a fact that those familiar with actual warfare readily appreciate. The civilian population, on the other hand, is less and less likely to rise against the régime and its war the more directly and continuously it is exposed to the physical horrors of the war. Where people are forced to concentrate all their energies on saving their naked lives and those of their children, relatives, friends and neighbours, where whole cities are burning and no transport is available to take people away, where houses are gutted and foodstores destroyed, there arises such a desperate urgency of dealing with the immediate catastrophe, of extinguishing the fire, of getting some food, finding shelter, caring for the wounded and all the hundred and one tasks connected with the mere struggle for survival that there is literally no time, no breath of energy left for action that might be the beginning of revolt.

Finally, there is the supremely important psychological victory which the Nazis have snatched in the last hour before their approaching doom. They have succeeded in instilling into the minds of the German people such pathological fear of the consequences of defeat that this fear itself has been turned into the greatest moral asset of their last attempt at desperate resistance. They could not have achieved this merely through clever propaganda tricks. They have achieved it because, in this case, their propaganda has for once got hold of something that was real and existed anyhow and which it was merely clever and skilful enough to exploit for its own purposes.

"The Germans", wrote Howard K. Smith as early as 1942 in his book *Last Train from Berlin,* "are terrorised by the nightmare of what will happen to them if they fail to win the war, of what their long-suffering enemies will do to them, of what the tortured people of their enslaved nations, Czechoslovakia, Poland, France will do when there is no longer a Gestapo to hold them down. The German people are not convinced Nazis, not five per cent of them; they are a people frightened stiff at what fate will befall them if they do not win the mess the Nazis have got them into."

One might add that this fear of the fate that will befall them had much less to do with the fate of Germany as a nation than with the fate of Germans as individuals. They were haunted by the nightmare of mass-deportation as slave labour or mass-expulsion from their native soil, by the nightmare of not being allowed to rebuild their devastated cities and industries, of being unable to make a living, however primitive and modest, or of ever again resuming anything like a normal family life. They were haunted by these very real and intense personal fears which the Göbbels' machine untiringly kept alive, confirming, making vocal, underlining and exaggerating what had originally been perhaps only half-conscious. From the moment the war turned into a series of unmitigated military disasters these haunting fears became Hitler's strongest weapon. And while the Allied Powers employed their best scientists and technicians to counteract and defeat flying bombs, rockets and what other "secret weapons" German military science put at Hitler's disposal, nothing was done to counteract and defeat the one moral weapon that was of greater value to Hitler in the latter part of the war than all the V-weapons combined—the weapon of fear.

The persistent refusal of the Allied Powers to tell Germany in precise and concrete terms what fate, however harsh, she can expect after defeat greatly helped to achieve the well-nigh impossible: to provide Dr. Göbbels with the appearance of truthfulness and Hitler's power of making war with a new lease of life. What German could doubt that his own worst fears, cleverly put into frightening words by the past-masters of propaganda, will come true if the silence of the Allies on all questions concerning his future seemed daily to confirm and reinforce the fears?

"According to right military discipline, *you must never drive your enemy unto despair*. For that such a streight doth multiply his force, and increase his courage, which was before broken and cast down. Neither is there any better help for men that are out of heart, toiled, and spent, than to *hope for no favour at all*."

Rabelais wrote these words more than four hundred years ago; there is little if anything that to-day could be profitably added.

CHAPTER THIRTY-ONE

WAR-TIME RESISTANCE

FOR THE underground movement the war brought both many new and difficult problems and also fresh opportunities that had not existed before. The greatest difficulties were created by the interruption of many carefully built contacts and groups which mobilisation and later air-raids, compulsory evacuation and transfer of workers to new industrial centres made inevitable. The growing general hostility to the war, on the other hand, even though it remained passive, gave the underground circles a greater scope for activity than they had had before the war, more sympathy among the population and the beginning of a new self-confidence. Although the vigilance of the secret police was increased and the draconic laws for the protection of the safety of the State were made even more draconic, the underground circles had less to fear from "voluntary" spies and denouncers among the ordinary people.

By and large, as far as can be judged from the scanty and sporadic information available at the time these pages are written, underground groups appear to have increased numerically in the course of the war and to have become more active. There is evidence, too, of a much greater variety of different types of opposition groups than there were prior to the outbreak of the war. There are, first of all, the very same small circles—perhaps meanwhile enlarged—that were formed in the early days of Fascism. Some of them were discovered and exterminated, such as the group of fourteen Mannheim workers (thirteen men and one woman) who were arrested in March 1942 and later executed. An official report described them as "former Communists or Marxists some of whom had previously served sentences for high treason". Friends abroad identified them later as belonging to an underground group of young Social Democratic workers which had been formed in the early days of 1933. How many of such groups will actually survive the war it is impossible to guess, but that many of them have been active during the war in different parts of the country is quite certain.

Secondly, there are groups of older workers, former Social Democrats as well as Communists, who had become completely passive and disinterested in politics during the six years of pre-war Nazi rule and whom only the war itself awakened to new activity. The short period of leisure which they used to spend in their gardens or allotments or over their hobbies, were, after the outbreak of the war, devoted to fresh attempts at renewing old, almost forgotten, political "contacts", at organising small groups which together listened to the forbidden broadcasts from London or Moscow, at discussing and spreading the information received and exchanging local news. One can be morally certain that the many cases of death sentences for "radio crimes" (listening to forbidden foreign broadcasts) were, without exception, cases in which whole groups of people had listened together in an organised fashion, or where the broadcasts served as a source of news for an organised illegal information service.

Only in very rare cases have official German sources provided sufficient information to prove that this was indeed the case. But since listening to foreign broadcasts has become a "crime" of which millions of Germans, including convinced Nazis, have been

187

guilty, one must assume that the striking difference between court sentences for this crime (varying from a few weeks of imprisonment to the death penalty) is an acknowledgment of the difference between occasional listening out of mere curiosity and listening as a deliberately sought source of alternative information and a starting point for anti-Nazi activity and organisation. One of the rare cases in which the German press gave more than the usual scanty information was that of Johannes Wild of Nüremberg, executed in May 1941 "for having produced an illegal pamphlet based on material from enemy broadcasts". This is what the German News Agency had to say about the case of Johannes Wild:

"Wild had been an active member of Marxist organisations both before and after the Great War. After the (Nazi) seizure of power he had listened to foreign broadcasts, thus placing himself systematically under the influence of the propaganda launched against Germany by the Marxist warmongers. When England and France declared war on the Reich, Wild hoped for the downfall of the new Germany which he hated. Mentally he thus sided with the enemies of the German nation to whose vicious and fiercely anti-German broadcasts he listened regularly. These enemy broadcasts supplied him with material for a pamphlet that contained libellous statements against the Führer and other leading personalities of the State as well as against the Army. He also incited his wife to listen to foreign broadcasts and to spread the lying news. . . ." [1]

Apart from the highly political underground circles which had continued to function throughout the years of the dictatorship and the reconstituted opposition groups based chiefly on older members of the working-class movement (including many who spent a period of time in jail or concentration camp), there have come into existence, as far as can be judged from information available before the end of the war, three other types of opposition groups.

One of these is the type of group that was discovered and destroyed after July 20th, 1944, a group that can be described as a broad coalition representing almost all the political tendencies that had existed in pre-Hitler Germany, but dominated by Conservatives and middle-class elements rather than by Socialists and workers. Almost without exception they were men of some standing who, while never reconciled to Hitler, grudgingly acquiesced in his régime and refrained from active opposition until their

[1] *D.N.B.*, September 27th, 1941.

patriotism bade them stake their lives rather than allow Hitler to continue his war and drag the entire nation with him into the abyss. Among these men were the moderate Conservative Goerdeler as well as the former Social Democratic leader Wilhelm Leuschner, who had twice spent long periods in concentration camps and who was one of the very few well-known leaders of the former Labour movement who had survived in Nazi Germany. Whether and how far these men were actually involved in the Generals' anti-Hitler plot of July 20th, 1944, it is impossible to say, but it is quite likely that they were indeed concerned in trying to get an armistice for Germany and forming a first post-Hitler "National Government". There may be other groups of this kind in Germany, although the terror wave that followed the abortive Generals' revolt of July 1944 lead to mass arrests and mass executions all over Germany on a larger scale than any other punitive action since June 30th, 1934, involving thousands of people who, under the Weimar Republic, had ever played an active part in any of the non-Nazi parties, from the Conservatives to the Communists.

Of greater potential importance than these circles of Conservative diplomats, civil servants and industrialists, who represent the past rather than the future and are concerned with "saving something" rather than with rebuilding and renewing, are opposition groups of very young people who have grown up under National Socialism and were, from their tenderest age, fed with its slogans and pervaded with its doctrine. If opposition to the régime grows among the young generation that knows of no tradition other than that of the Hitler Youth and Nazi schools and organisations, it is far more significant as a positive portent for the future than the more efficiently organised and more practically effective opposition circles of older men in responsible political and social positions.

Such youth groups have come into existence in particular in the Universities, which, in the early 'thirties, were the citadels of the most enthusiastic core of the Nazi movement. As in so many other cases of underground opposition, the outside world learned of the existence of such groups only after one of them had been caught and its members executed. But the very circumstances of the first war-time trial of opposition students which became known outside Germany made it clear that this was not an isolated case.

The case began in February 1943, when three students of the Munich University (Hans Scholl, Maria Scholl and Adrian Probst) were sentenced to death for high treason. Two months later another thirteen students were tried. Three of them, also of the University of Munich, were sentenced to death because "together with the Schools, they encouraged sabotage in armaments factories and also spread defeatist ideas". At the same time two students from Ulm who assisted in the distribution of highly treasonable leaflets "were sentenced to only five years' imprisonment in view of their youth". Five others were sentenced to terms of imprisonment varying from six to eighteen months. In connection with the activities of these young people three elder men, two from Freiburg and one from Stuttgart, were sentenced to many years of penal servitude. Two of them were accused of having failed to report these treasonable activities to the police, the third of having financed the activities, without, however, knowing the particulars.

A Swedish paper later reported that the treasonable leaflets in this case extolled "free self-determination without which no spiritual values can be created", that they had protested against the suppression of free speech and against the Nazi practice of putting young people "into uniform and crippling their intellect during the most fruitful period of development", and that they finally spoke of "a new faith in freedom and honour about to be born".

There is no need to stress the great significance of such developments, which is all the greater as the case of these young Munich students was not an isolated one. This was officially confirmed by the German authorities who, only a week after the second trial, announced that all University students would be subjected to a new test for political reliability. Only those who worthily passed the test would be allowed to continue their studies, all others would be sent to the front. Nothing short of desperate necessity could have induced the German authorities to initiate a purge of this sort in April 1943.

There is evidence finally of yet another type of youth opposition which has developed outside the Universities in the very ranks of the Hitler Youth organisation itself. In the sixth year of the war this youth opposition has become so widespread that it has grown to a fair-sized movement all over the country, but chiefly in the larger cities. It consists mainly of Hitler Youth lads between the ages of fifteen and nineteen who, in many different places, have formed groups, or perhaps it would be more appropriate to call them "gangs", which oppose the authority and strict discipline of the State and the compulsory Nazi organisations in every conceivable way. The Nazis presumably look on them as at some kind of "Dead-End Kids" or *bezprizornye*; yet they are not the children of the slums and of neglect, not waifs and strays, but young people of all classes who desperately long for freedom and who, in their own way and with the methods they have learnt from their teachers and "leaders", protest and fight against totalitarianism. The most widespread of these opposition gangs calls itself *Edelweiss Piraten*; other have chosen names such as *Bismarck Klicke*, *Texas Bande* or *Pfennig Club* (members of the Pfennig Club wear an almost surrealistic badge—a penny with a hole in the middle to which a dead may-bug is attached—all of which, for some impenetrable reason, is supposed to be a symbol of freedom). Although fiercely anti-Nazi they are essentially non-political, and if one should try to describe their (consciously non-existent) philosophy it would be a mixture between a romantic kind of anarchism and a disillusioned nihilism, in which the longing for some private pleasure and relaxation from the unbearable strain of rigid discipline plays as great a part as the readiness to use physical violence and the adoration, on principle, of anything anti- or even non-Nazi.

Some of these groups started simply as circles of friends with similar tastes and interests, and only slowly developed into "gangs" that specialised in a curious mixture of things. One of these is the beating-up, and in some cases even killing, of Nazi bosses who have made themselves particularly disliked through their corruption, cowardice and cruelty; another is the organisation of raids on local party offices or burglaries in the houses of unpopular leaders. Other no less important characteristics are their passionate cult for forbidden swing and jazz music and for smart clothes, as near as possible to the English or American style, and a great deal of drinking and sexual libertinism. Mixed with all this, at least in some of the groups, are things such as the organisation of listening parties to foreign broadcasts, the monitoring of the B.B.C. German service, the exchange and distribution of forbidden foreign news and even the production of occasional general anti-Nazi leaflets. As far as is known these groups have not been organised from one centre. They appear to have been formed spontaneously in very many different localities and from a variety of beginnings, and merely the fast-travelling rumour that in some other town "there is also a secret gang which calls itself *Edelweiss Piraten*" is presumably responsible for this name, with all its romantic allusions, having been adopted by so many different groups which otherwise are not linked through any organisation.

Although this movement has been more widespread presumably than opposition groups of a different kind, it has not been a menace to the Nazi régime so much as a symptom and indication of its decline and disintegration. There is too much of a *Götter-dämmerung* mood in the defiance of these young rebels to constitute a serious challenge to the régime and, with their utter lack of faith in anything, with their deep disillusionment and lack of any positive purpose, they are likely to be a greater problem for the post-Hitler "re-educators" of Germany than for the Hitler Government itself. These young boys, on the other hand, whom only a tragic fate that was not of their making has prevented from putting their energies, enthusiasm and potential idealism to some more positive purpose, will nevertheless have to be among the pioneers of a new regenerated Germany—provided that Germany is to be given any chance at all to recuperate and regenerate after the war.

Leadership cannot come from them. Leadership cannot even come from the type of highly idealistic students who risked—and some of whom paid with—their lives for some great and simple ideas like faith in freedom and honour. They will be among the invaluable creators of a new Germany, but leadership in the real sense of the word can come only from those who have a programme as well as courage and integrity, and who can show a way out as well as condemn the existing order.

There are men and women of this type in Germany. They are to be found among the small circles of the political underground movement which kept alive the tradition of the pre-Hitler Labour movement, and yet have learned enough from past mistakes and from the experience of Fascism to be the nucleus of a new movement rather than the relics of the past.

Obviously, if Germany were to be totally destroyed, without being given the chance of recuperation, if the country were to be carved up or held in permanent prostration and abject poverty through the destruction of its industries and "pastoralisation", problems of re-education, of democratic regeneration and popular movements (other than ultra-nationalistic movements of revenge) would not arise. However, if such insanity is not allowed to reign supreme after the end of the war, if the United Nations agree that the physical and mental health of Europe cannot afford to tolerate a festering boil in its very heart, then there can be no doubt that new democratic movements will arise in Germany and that men and women will be there to guide and lead such movements—men and women who were the pioneers (and many among them the first martyrs) of the anti-Hitler struggle long before the world at large declared war on Hitlerism.

INDEX

201

Young Plan, 134

Zetkin, Klara, 12, 14; struggle against the war, 1914, 27 *et seq.*; articles in *Die Internationale*, 28; International Socialist Women's Conference, 29; imprisonment of, 33

Zimmerwald: International Socialist Conference, 1915, 29

Zinoviev, at Halle Conference of U.S.P., 78

Zörgiebel-May-Day, 130 *et seq.*

Zörgiebel, Police President, 130 *et seq.*